TRAVEL GUIDE

BOSNIA
AND
HERZEGOVINA

in your hands

2014

BOSANSKA KRAJINA

EASTERN BOSNIA

CENTRAL BOSNIA

HERZEGOVINA

SARAJEVO

Author
Jörg Heeskens

Editor
Ivan Kovanović

Managing Editor
Branko Andrić

Research and Communication
Dimitrije Stamenković

Design
Ivan Grujić

Maps
Dušan Bročić

Guest Authors
Georg von Graefe
Michell Rohmann
Mateja Knežević

German Language Editors
Elke Meyer
Jan Sauer

Cover Photo
Ernst Röthlisberger

Photographs
Luka Esenko
Dragan Bosnić
Ernst Röthlisberger
Michell Rohmann
The Tourist Association of
Bosnia and Herzegovina
(www.bhtourism.ba)

Published by
KOMSHE d.o.o. Beograd

Acknowledgements:

We reserve special thanks for Georg von Graefe and
Michell Rohmann, for their scientific contributions and
invaluable assistance both as travel companions and
researchers, and Elke Meyer and Jan Sauer for tirelessly
reading, correcting and shortening the text. For her
support and research expertise, we also extend thanks to
Božidarka Došen.

We would also like to thank the Tourism Association of
Bosnia and Herzegovina and the Tourist Organisation
of East Sarajevo, whose help was invaluable in putting
together this guide.

About the Author:

Jörg Heeskens was born in Stuttgart in 1977 and has been
living and working in the former Yugoslavia for many years,
Bosnia and Herzegovina in Your Hands is the product of
his long-standing professional and academic engagement
with the country.

For information and distribution:

info@komshe.com

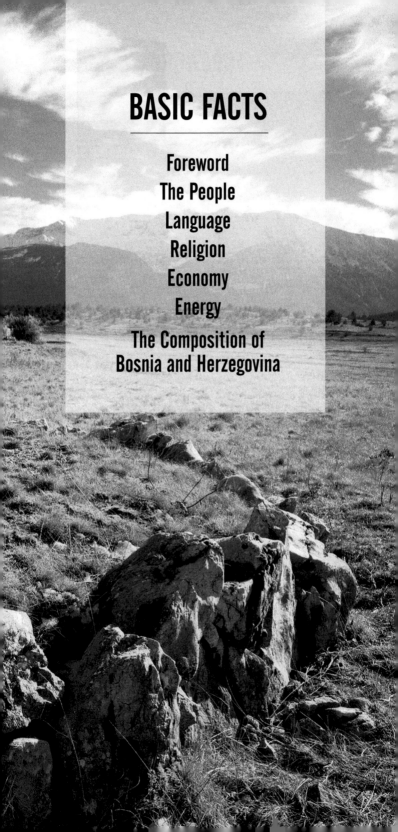

BASIC FACTS

FOREWORD

The Sebilj Fountain in Sarajevo's Baščaršija (see p. 107)

It is unlikely that you will find another European country as colourfully diverse in landscape and, as multi-layered and complex culturally and historically, as Bosnia and Herzegovina. While it shares a long border with the European Union (since Croatia's accession in July 2013) on maps of the EU Bosnia and Herzegovina appears as a greyed-out region and the country remains one of the last great mysteries of the European continent. Likewise, its enormous tourist potential goes unnoticed by established tour operators. What outsiders know about the country's 1990s war is vague and based largely on superficial accounts but, sadly, also tends to mirror the negative perception the inhabitants of Bosnia and Herzegovina often have of themselves. Although, the fact that the Bosnia and Herzegovina national football team has qualified for the World Cup Finals in Brazil in 2014 is bound to have an impact!

For both locals and the rest of Europe, Bosnia and Herzegovina has therefore, long been perceived as a failed and failing state in the heart of Europe so visiting and exploring this country or thinking of it as a holiday destination may, at first glance, seem a stretch too far. Those who do venture a closer look and leave their reservations aside, discover that the truth is more complex. Bosnia and Herzegovina, with its unique blend of cultures, its extremely diverse and often breathtaking landscape and with a population that is open, friendly

Oriental-style slippers on sale at a Sarajevo market

and offers genuine hospitality, simply invites you to leave your prejudices behind.

The religious social and cultural blend of Bosnia and Herzegovina is broad and multifaceted. Between the Adriatic and the Sava and Drina Rivers you can encounter a modern, European Islam as well as Catholic or Orthodox Christians; villages almost unchanged since medieval times and towns where you can pay for a parking space with a smartphone; humbling poverty and, probably just around the corner, gaudy, superficial wealth. These contradictions wind through Bosnia and Herzegovina like a thread and reflect the extremes of landscape and climate, from snow-capped mountains to just a few kilometres away, the distinctly Mediterranean feel of the Adriatic; from fertile farmsteads to barren rocky plateaus; from Europe's largest forest to the south-western reaches of the flat, wide Pannonian plain.

Visitors to Bosnia and Herzegovina have the golden opportunity to dive into a natural landscape that has barely been touched by tourism and which – thanks to the country's small (and declining) population density in rural areas and almost complete de-industrialization – is experiencing the re-emergence of wilderness; an exciting process and the polar opposite of the taming of nature underway throughout Europe. Wildlife, such as wild horses and brown bears, otherwise rare elsewhere are not threatened with extinction in Bosnia and Herzegovina and now are finding that their habitats are expanding.

Bosnia and Herzegovina is also a treasure trove of European history. Every age and every culture has left its mark, from the Romans and Byzantines through to the Christendom of the Middle Ages and the Ottoman occupation, the growth of a Jewish diaspora, the Austro-Hungarian administration, fascism, communism, capitalism, the American Dream, the civil war and now European integration – travellers can experience this distilled European cultural history as though in time lapse.

There is no denying that Bosnia and Herzegovina has, in the past, been an

Bosnia and Herzegovina is full of exotic and spectacular landscapes

Traditional mountain cabins on Prokoško Lake in Central Bosnia

attractive destination for visitors from Western Europe but it is now almost completely avoided by travellers. This fact, coupled with wartime de-industrialization, emigration and degradation of transport infrastructure has, however, proven to be a great blessing for flora and fauna. For nature lovers, Bosnia and Herzegovina can today be considered a dormant scenic gem, right on our doorstep.

The goal of this travel guide is an open-minded description of the country, its unique landscapes, its contrasting and varied regions and cities. Neither the recent history

of conflict nor the slowly evolving political and economic situation of the country, are the focus here. What is more, Bosnia and Herzegovina is an eager, young European country and it would be unflattering to rely on stereotypes without adopting a more nuanced and balanced approach.

We hope you have fun reading and browsing through this guide, that you will become as intrigued by this mysterious and captivating country as we have, and that you will become curious enough to embark on an exciting and enjoyable exploration of Bosnia and Herzegovina.

Bosnia and Herzegovina in a Nutshell

Name: Bosnia and Herzegovina
Population: 3,875,723
Land area: 51,197 km2
Capital: Sarajevo
Population: 392,000
Ethnic mix: Bosnian Muslims 48 %, Serbs 37.1 %, Croats 14.3 %, Other 0.6 %
Religion: Muslim 40 %, Orthodox 31 %, Roman Catholic 15 %, Other 14 %
Language: Bosnian, Serbian, Croatian
Currency: Konvertibilna Marka (KM) – Convertible Mark
GDP per capita: US$8,300
Unemployment: 43.3 %

THE PEOPLE

Bosnia-Herzegovina has a population of nearly **4 million people** and is two and a half times the size of Wales or nearly twice the size of Massachusetts but with a significantly lower population density than either of them. Bosnia and Herzegovina is not only very sparsely populated but is also experiencing a declining population. The birth rate is consistently below the death rate and large numbers of Bosnian citizens still choose to emigrate abroad. The population of Bosnia-Herzegovina is, therefore, expected to continue to decline in the future.

Half of the nearly 4 million inhabitants live in the cities and the other half in the country. This parity between rural and urban is currently shifting towards the city as younger people are leaving underdeveloped regions and rural areas and moving into the larger cities or, as is often the case, directly abroad.

Ordinary people enjoying refreshments outside a *kafana* in Sarajevo

The **average life expectancy** in Bosnia-Herzegovina is 78 years, with women (83) having a significantly longer life expectancy than men (75).

Town vs. Country

In Western Europe in recent decades some rural areas have increasingly blossomed as a preferred place of settlement for the affluent. As a result, parameters such as unemployment, education levels and life expectancy have improved in commuter belt areas around cities, unfortunately, in Bosnia and Herzegovina, there is no sign of this trend yet.

Quite the contrary, the gap between town and country in Bosnia and Herzegovina - as in the rest of South Eastern Europe - is extremely significant, and, sadly perhaps, in favour of urban life in every respect. Inadequate education, healthcare and transport make life in the country more difficult than in urban areas and, what's more, the country is experiencing a rural exodus causing the urban-rural gap to grow rather than to diminish.

The trend of working in the city and commuting in order to live in the countryside is essentially non-existent in Bosnia and Herzegovina. Additionally, a certain sense of superiority of the urban population towards the rural population still prevails, with villagers (singular: seljak, plural: seljaci) being regarded as backward and uneducated while the 'supposedly' educated urban elite is drawn to life in urban high-rise buildings rather than in natural surroundings.

Old Women and Young Men – Rural life in Bosnia and Herzegovina

In many villages and small provincial towns in Bosnia and Herzegovina an unbalanced composition of gender and generation is emerging. Perhaps it is a generalisation but in rural Bosnia and Herzegovina young men and old women seem to dominate.

For the younger generation the driving force behind this phenomenon is the more pronounced mobility of women who, unlike their male counterparts, tend to be more willing to migrate to urban centres, driven by the desire to achieve higher levels of education or experience new professional challenges. Many young men seemingly lack this motivation and are less ambitious or perhaps less 'adventurous', preferring, as they do, to remain in more familiar surroundings.

There is also a gender discrepancy in the older generation. The life expectancy for men is relatively low resulting in there being roughly three women over 65 for every two men who reach that age - at ages over 80 this imbalance is even more pronounced. The resulting image is of a rural population of young men in tracksuits and old women in headscarves - leaving the visitor with a somewhat bizarre impression of rural life.

Cafe culture is common and popular in the towns

Welcoming Hospitality

The people of Bosnia and Herzegovina are extremely hospitable. This is especially true in the rural areas – outside the tourist hubs of Sarajevo and Mostar – where locals are likely to spontaneously invite travellers for coffee or rakija. Such invitations are without ulterior motives and you can feel free to accept.

Should you be invited home by a family in Bosnia and Herzegovina, a rich and pleasing experience awaits you; the lady of the house will offer local dishes and delicacies and the host will likely open his best wine.

This generosity and openness to strangers is also noticeable when you stop someone to ask for directions. You will have your query answered in great detail and, if there is a language barrier, accompanied with a rich language of gestures.

LANGUAGE

Signs in Republika Srpska are often in Cyrillic script only

The official language of Bosnia and Herzegovina is Bosnian but Croatian and Serbian are also listed as official languages. Bosnian, Serbian and Croatian belong to the South Slavic group of languages and the three languages are very similar. Bosnian (*Bosanski*) was settled upon during the process of nation-building in the 1990s as an official language distinct from Serbo-Croatian and, though it is a catch-all term, is most commonly associated with the Bosnian Muslims.

Whether Bosnian should now actually be defined as a separate language or as a regional variant or dialect of Serbo-Croatian, is more a political than a linguistic question, but the fact remains that Bosnian, Croatian and Serbian, are comprehensible for almost all inhabitants of the former Yugoslavia. What each language is actually called we can safely leave to one side as this does not make a difference to people's everyday lives. People of all nationalities understand each other easily and still speak essentially the same language they spoke during Yugoslav times.

In Bosnia and Herzegovina you will find both the Cyrillic and Latin scripts, which visually denote the differences between the 'languages'. In Republika Srpska, with its majority Serbian population, virtually every road sign is in both Cyrillic and Latin while in the Federation of Bosnia-Herzegovina it is mostly only the Latin alphabet that is used.

RELIGION

Bosnia and Herzegovina has for centuries served as a crossroads between East and West – between the Eastern cultural area and the Western world – and the religions of Bosnia and Herzegovina reflect these intersecting cultural influences. Almost half of the population of Bosnia and Herzegovina are Muslims, while the remaining half are Christian. The Christians themselves are divided into the Eastern or Serbian Orthodox and Roman Catholic denominations, with there being approximately twice as many Orthodox Christians as there are Catholics.

The Muslims of Bosnia and Herzegovina, live predominantly in the cities Sarajevo, Tuzla and Zenica in central Bosnia, the Catholics are mostly settled on the Croatian border

The fact that Islam in Bosnia and Herzegovina is mostly practiced in a very liberal manner is also a factor in its popularity.

The religious expression of Muslims in Bosnia and Herzegovina ranges from the conscious and public demonstration of Islamic identity to rejection of religious precepts. The spectrum of religious adherence extends from the concealment of unmarried women to completely ignoring Islamic rules on alcohol, sexuality, etc.

Orthodox Christians in Bosnia and Herzegovina are almost exclusively members of the autonomous Serbian Orthodox Church. The approximately one million Orthodox Christians in Bosnia and Herzegovina are distributed among the five eparchies of Banja Luka, Tuzla, Sarajevo, Mostar and Bosanski Petrovac. Each eparchy is headed by

Minarets are a common sight throughout Bosnia and Herzegovina

in the north and in Herzegovina, while the Orthodox Christians live along the River Drina and in the cities of Banja Luka and Prijedor in the north of the country. This geographical distribution of the religions in Bosnia and Herzegovina has been exacerbated by the Dayton Agreement. Still, in many villages and towns and intermixed regions people of the three faiths coexist peacefully.

The **Muslims** in Bosnia and Herzegovina are organized into an Islamic community (*Islamska Zajednica*), which is led by a Grand Mufti (*Veliki Muftija*) who has his seat in Sarajevo. The large number of Muslims is primarily due to more than four centuries of Ottoman rule but also to the fact that before the arrival of the Ottomans, neither of the two Christian religions (Catholic and Orthodox) had established itself as the dominant religious force.

The Serbian Orthodox Church has its seat in Sarajevo

an Eparch while the head of the Serbian Orthodox Church is the Metropolitan of Belgrade and Karlovci in Serbia.

The **Catholic Church** in Bosnia and Herzegovina has about 500,000 members and is headed by the Archdiocese Vrhbosna in Sarajevo. The archbishopric, headed by an archbishop, was founded in 1881 after the Hapsburg occupation. Sarajevo Cathedral is the central building of Catholics in Bosnia and Herzegovina.

The Catholic and Orthodox populations of Bosnia and Herzegovina are defined by both their religious ancestry and their national identity.

The Kraljeva Sutjeska Catholic monastery

Consequently, Orthodox Bosnians identify mostly as Serbs and Catholics as Croats and often as residents of that country. This mixing of religion and nationality is one of the major hurdles preventing the creation of a joint Bosnian-Herzegovinian national identity, however, a slightly more relaxed approach to this issue has recently developed.

The Bogomils

Throughout Bosnia and Herzegovina one encounters Bogomil grave stones dating from the 12th to the 15th centuries. Some of the ornaments and dedications on the mostly square, grave stones from the Middle Ages are still in good condition. Around 60,000 such stones have been found on the territory of Bosnia and Herzegovina.

The Bogomils were a Christian religious movement in the Balkans during Ottoman rule, that are said to have originated from the teachings of a 10th century Bulgarian village priest named Bogomil. Their central belief was the view that the universe was created by a good God but a duality between him and the devil is important. After quarrels between the angels this universe broke apart and the angels were driven down to earth. God also sent a good angel in human form, Jesus.

This spiritual interpretation of the New Testament quickly spread throughout Bulgaria and lands in today's Bosnia and Herzegovina. Bogomilism demonized the material world and the hierarchical structure of the Church as well as its practices. Bogomilism was seen as a threat by the existing Church which sought to fight what they saw as a heretical movement. The political elements of the movement, however, led to its popularity in rural Bosnia and Herzegovina.

The era of the Bogomils in Bosnia and Herzegovina ended with the intensified encroachment of the Catholic Church from the West and Islam from the East. The large number of Bogomil grave stones remains as a clear sign of the movement's wide territorial spread across Bosnia and Herzegovina.

ECONOMY

Some traditional trades and crafts are still alive today

Until the outbreak of the civil war the economy of Bosnia and Herzegovina was mostly dominated by heavy industry, today however, the country can be described as quasi-de-industrialised. In terms of the environment and wildlife diversity, this can be viewed as beneficial, however, the human population of the country suffer from the high levels of unemployment. About 40 percent of the working population is unemployed and their job prospects – especially for young people – are disastrous. All over the country the landscape is scarred by abandoned, destroyed or run-down factories. The war and, later, corruption and a lack of political will to reform, have devastated the country's economic prospects.

Most employment in Bosnia and Herzegovina is in state-owned enterprises or in state administration. The private sector is small and often active mostly in the shadow economy. The process of privatisation of state-owned enterprises has made little progress while the partial privatisation completed thus far is due to be revised once again. Foreign investment is rare and mostly based on trade or sales. 47 percent of workers in Bosnia and Herzegovina are in the tertiary service sector (mostly in government administration), 32 percent in industry and 8 percent in agriculture and forestry. The average wage in Bosnia and Herzegovina is around €400. Value Added Tax (VAT) is set at 17 percent.

Much economic activity is still in agriculture

In 2011 Bosnia and Herzegovina exported goods worth €4.2 billion. Principal export customers, almost 60 percent, were the countries of the European Union. The main exports of Bosnia and Herzegovina are timber (or timber products), metals, food and textiles while the goods imported (worth €7.9 billion) were mostly machinery, chemicals and foodstuffs. The trade deficit, therefore, amounted to almost €4 billion.

Sarajevo, Mostar and Banja Luka are the economic centres of the country. Due to the high levels of unemployment, many people largely depend on family members who live abroad for existential and financial help. Remittances from the large diaspora community are by far the most important source of income – furthermore, Bosnia

Unsurprisingly, Sarajevo is the economic centre of the country

and Herzegovina would be insolvent without international donors and aid programmes.

ENERGY

Bosnia produces most of its power from hydroelectric plants like this one

One interesting and little known fact about Bosnia and Herzegovina is that it is a major energy exporter. Not only this but as much as half of generated electricity comes from a single renewable source: hydroelectricity.

The power generation capacity of Bosnia and Herzegovina's rivers already has a long tradition and dams on the Neretva, Vrbas and Drina have been generating electricity since Tito's time. These major hydroelectric plants have thankfully been constantly renewed and extended to help Bosnia and Herzegovina established itself as an energy exporter. Many new energy projects in the water sector have been planned and some are already underway.

In Bosnia and Herzegovina there are three utility companies that operate along ethnic lines. These are EP BiH, which caters mainly to Bosniak customers; *Elektroprivreda Republike Srpske* (RS EP), which supplies the Serb entity; and *Elektroprivreda Hrvatske Zajednice Herceg Bosne* (EP HZHB) for the Croatian part of the population. These are coordinated nationally, however, by the state transmission company (*Elektroprijenos BiH*) and the national network regulator (*Nezavisnioperator Sistema*).

THE COMPOSITION OF BOSNIA AND HERZEGOVINA

Bosnia and Herzegovina has existed as an independent, sovereign country since the 6th of April 1992. Previously it was the Republic of Bosnia and Herzegovina, one of six republics of the Socialist Federal Republic of Yugoslavia. The Declaration of Independence in April 1992 was preceded by a referendum and was followed by a brutal civil war, which officially ended in the autumn of 1995 with the signing of the US sponsored Dayton Peace Agreement by the warring factions. The Dayton Agreement laid out the political structure of Bosnia and Herzegovina, which has since cemented into the distribution of power between the political and administrative branches. The system established under Dayton, which is still in force, has seen the country divided into the two so-called Entities.

As its name suggests the country actually consists of two historical regions: **Bosnia** and **Herzegovina**. These historically separate cultural spaces are not to be confused with the administrative and political division (under Dayton) of territory into the Entities of the **Federation of Bosnia and Herzegovina** and **Republika Srpska**. The name Republika Srpska

is translated as "the Serbian Republic" and should not be confused with the neighbouring country, the Republic of Serbia. To avoid confusion, we will continue to use Republika Srpska to refer to this part of Bosnia and Herzegovina.

THE HISTORICAL LANDS OF BOSNIA AND HERZEGOVINA

Historically **Bosnia**, with Sarajevo as its capital, covers 42,000 square kilometres, about 80 percent of modern-day Bosnia and Herzegovina. The region owes its name to the river Bosna which emerges from a spring found in Ilidža near Sarajevo (see p. 121). The first written mention of Bosnia was in a 10th century Byzantine document. Until the Ottoman conquest in 1463, Bosnia, the land of many rivers, changed hands frequently. Up until the 12th century Bosnia was mostly ruled by outsiders but from then on sovereignty was held by the Bosnian kings. The Ottomans made Bosnia into an independent *Pashalik* in 1463, and until 1878 it remained one of the most important cornerstones in the Ottoman Empire. In 1878 the Habsburg Empire occupied the territory structured around the

Pashalik of Bosnia and turned it into Bosnia and Herzegovina.

The historical land of **Herzegovina** originated in the 13th and 14th centuries through the merger of several small principalities along the lower Neretva River, the mountains in the hinterland of Dubrovnik and the Adriatic coast. Its name comes from a local feudal lord, Stefan Vukčić-Kosača (1435-1466), who held the title of *Herceg* (derived from the German for duke, *Herzog*). The term "Duke's Land" was retained by the Ottomans who ruled Herzegovina from 1470. From 1580 Herzegovina became an independent Ottoman Pashalik before it was integrated into the larger *pashalik* of Bosnia. After its occupation of the Pashalik of Bosnia in 1878, the Hapsburg Empire retained the double name and ruled the two territories as Bosnia and Herzegovina.

Herzegovina covers an area of 9,800 square kilometres or about 20 percent of the total area of Bosnia and Herzegovina. The capital of Herzegovina is Mostar. In the western and northern part of Herzegovina the inhabitants are almost exclusively Catholics while the east and south of Herzegovina is mostly settled by Orthodox Christians and Muslims.

THE CONTEMPORARY COMPOSITION OF BOSNIA AND HERZEGOVINA

In addition to the historical distinction between Bosnia and Herzegovina, the country is now divided into two political Entities, the **Federation of Bosnia and Herzegovina**, on the one hand, and **Republika Srpska**, on the other – neither of which fits any geographical or historical boundaries. In the Dayton peace negotiations in 1995, the lines between the Entities were drawn largely according to the current front lines of the war. The military status quo was therefore cemented in peacetime. In many cases, this often meant that historically evolved lines of communication, geographical areas and cultural spaces were severed. A look at the political map of Bosnia-Herzegovina shows that it is purely political considerations rather than rivers, mountains or cultural areas that influence the country's territorial division.

The two Entities, the Federation of Bosnia and Herzegovina and Republika Srpska, are of almost equal size and together form the state of Bosnia and Herzegovina with its capital in Sarajevo.

The Federation of Bosnia and Herzegovina and Republika Srpska

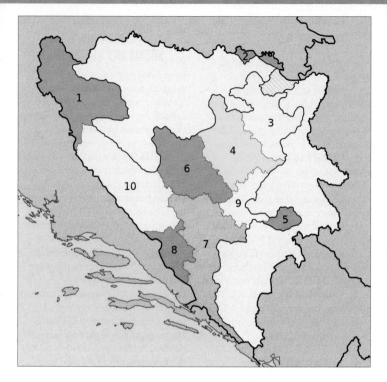

The Cantons of the Federation of Bosnia and Herzegovina

1. The Una-Sana Canton – capital: Bihać
2. The Posavina Canton – capital: Orašje
3. The Tuzla Canton – capital: Tuzla
4. The Zenica-Doboj Canton – capital: Zenica
5. The Bosnian Podrinje Canton – capital: Goražde
6. The Central Bosnia Canton – capital: Travnik
7. The Herzegovina-Neretva Canton – capital: Mostar
8. The West Herzegovina Canton – capital: Široki Brijeg
9. The Sarajevo Canton – capital: Sarajevo
10. Canton 10 – capital: Livno

The **Federation of Bosnia and Herzegovina** extends along the western border with Croatia and extends through central Bosnia and to Tuzla in the east of the country. The Federation is divided into ten Cantons, which are in turn divided into local municipalities. The Federation of Bosnia and Herzegovina covers 51 percent of the total area of Bosnia-Herzegovina and is thought to hold a population of about 2.2 million split between Bosnian Muslims (around 70 percent) and Catholic Croats (around 20 percent).

The Cantons are of different sizes and populations. The Sarajevo Canton has well over 400,000 inhabitants, whereas the Bosnian Podrinje Canton is just the area around Goražde and has only around 30,000 inhabitants while the Posavina Canton around Orašje has perhaps 40,000 inhabitants. The Cantons are also very different in terms of size, the largest cantons – Herzegovina-Neretva and Canton 10 – are 15 times the size of the Posavina Canton, which is the smallest.

Each Canton has its own political institutions and bodies such as parliaments (usually with 45 MPs) and governments, including a Prime Minister and President, with powers in the fields of security and justice. The idea behind the setting up of Cantons was to establish institutions free of nationalist tendencies and aspirations and create strong centralised federal structures in the Federation of Bosnia and Herzegovina. It has, however, ultimately resulted in a political apparatus that is much too large, inefficient and expensive.

Republika Srpska, in turn, does not have the intermediate administrative level of cantons. The Entity government rules from Banja Luka, is more centralised and acts directly in the 63 local municipalities and 7 regions. The 'missing' canton system in Republika Srpska leads to simpler and more efficient way of policy implementation than in the Federation of Bosnia and Herzegovina. Serbs form a majority of the population in Republika Srpska and the territory extends like a horseshoe around the Federation of Bosnia and Herzegovina. Virtually the entire northern border with Croatia and the south-eastern borders with Serbia and Montenegro are part of Republika Srpska. The Entity is home to a just under 2 million people and amounts to 49 percent of the territory of the state of Bosnia and Herzegovina.

SUMMARY

The two Entities have been in existence for almost 20 years but most often they block each other politically or administratively and go their own separate ways. In everyday life the effects of this are visible but only in a very limited sense, as the economic situation is disastrous in both the Federation of Bosnia and Herzegovina and Republika Srpska and the anger and disappointment of the population is directed at the whole political class regardless of ethnicity. Ordinary citizens of both the Federation and Republika Srpska are no longer interested in the nationality of the politicians who are ineptly running their country.

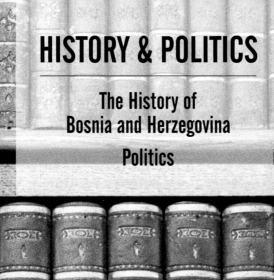

HISTORY & POLITICS

The History of
Bosnia and Herzegovina

Politics

HISTORY

As with any country, history in Bosnia and Herzegovina inevitably shapes the present. In Bosnia and Herzegovina, however, the influence historical events (both actual and imagined) have on political and social events in the present is far greater and more constant than in other countries. Politics and history are so closely linked and emotionally intertwined that differentiation between past and present is hardly possible. Frequently political and social discourse in Bosnia and Herzegovina – be it scientific, professional or private – does not lead to constructive problem-solving approaches, but to attributing historical blame.

Bosnia and Herzegovina's eventful history is dominated by the fact that the country has been at a meeting point of cultural influences and religious movements since time immemorial: Between East and West; between the Western and Eastern halves of the Roman Empire; between Rome and Constantinople; between the Hapsburgs, Ottomans and Russians; between Belgrade and Zagreb; between Catholic, Orthodox and Muslim, and so forth. The list of Bosnia's "betweens" seems endless.

All these historical trends and influences have left their mark on the country's architecture, food, music and painting, in language, religion and education, as well as on the day-to-day lives of the inhabitants. This bountiful treasure trove of cultural inheritance is, sadly, seldom perceived as such. In many ways the country is unfortunately still dominated by a way of thinking in which this interplay of differences is not seen as an asset, instead segregation and purity are often valued over diversity.

As the saying goes, history is written by the victors, and it is equally true that history is written mainly in the centres of power. However you look at it, Bosnia and Herzegovina has never been, and isn't now, a centre of power, but has always been peripheral. Throughout its history Bosnia and Herzegovina has always been viewed as provincial from some cultural centre, whether the view was from Istanbul, Vienna, Rome, St. Petersburg, Berlin, Belgrade or Zagreb. Consequently, it is not surprising that differing reports can be found throughout history as each centre defines its own vision and its own priorities. Consequently, a description emanating from the Vatican of the capture of a medieval fortress in central Bosnia by Ottoman troops is bound to differ from descriptions of the same event from Istanbul.

These external centres of power and opinion infiltrated Bosnia and Herzegovina with their own perceptions of events. These external perceptions have had a tendency not to value the rich diversity of cultures inside Bosnia and Herzegovina and have often seen it as a threat to their own interests. The result is that at times in the history of the country variety has been negated or is perceived as a disadvantage. These external points of view, emanating as they did, from outside the borders of the modern-day state, have not had the benefit of a local understanding of the situation – this is as true today as it has been throughout history.

The following chapter on the history of Bosnia and Herzegovina cannot possibly claim to resolve any of these problems, nor does it pretend to. We have tried hard to present a short historical overview as soberly, and as neutrally, as possible. For those interested in learning more about the complex but endlessly interesting subject of Bosnian history, there exists an abundance of English language sources.

ANCIENT BOSNIA AND HERZEGOVINA

The oldest source that mentions Bosnia by name, derived from the Byzantine historian Constantine VII Porphyrogenetos dates roughly from the year 1000 AD did not mean Bosnia, the current territory, but the region around the headwaters of the river Bosna. From 530 AD Byzantium had dominion over this land. Previously, Bosnia was part of the Roman Empire and was awarded to the Western Roman Empire after the schism of 395 AD.

However, the colonization of the territory of present-day Bosnia and Herzegovina extends significantly further. In antiquity, the areas along the rivers Bosna, Vrbas and Neretva were colonized by the Illyrians. Archaeological finds suggest that the Illyrians in the Bronze Age were concerned with agriculture and animal husbandry, and later with the first mining and processing of silver. Rome began from the third Century BC, and gradually absorbed the Illyrian territory, South Eastern Europe and the Adriatic Sea. Following the victory of Emperor Augustus in 9 BC, the Illyrians' territories were finally fully incorporated into the Roman Empire. The Roman provinces of Dalmatia and Pannonia were formed and encapsulated just about the whole area of present day Bosnia and Herzegovina. The province of Pannonia included the northern areas along the Sava, while Dalmatia covered part of today's central Bosnia as well as Herzegovina. The Romans built in the following centuries, a network of roads and defences and trade centres. Cities such as Tuzla and Vitez and many other still preserved forts date from this period.

Following the division of the Roman Empire in 395 AD, the territories of Bosnia and Herzegovina were awarded to the Western Roman Empire. The border between the two Roman empires was the river Drina, which today forms the border between Bosnia and Herzegovina and Serbia. The Western Roman Empire was in decline and its rule over this region lasted less than two hundred years. In 530 AD, the Eastern Roman, commonly known as the Byzantine Empire, took over control of this region and dominated it in the following centuries, but the Byzantines faced a whole new challenge: the arrival of the Slavic peoples.

Roman helmets at the museum in Trebinje

THE ARRIVAL OF THE SLAVS

When exactly the arrival and settlement of the Slavs to the territory of today's Bosnia and Herzegovina took place is unclear. It is known that the Slavic conquest of the Balkan Peninsula took place from about the middle of the 6th century. The Slavs first reached the lands of present-day Bulgaria and Serbia, then the Dalmatian coast and Bosnia and Herzegovina. The origin of the Slavic tribes has been proven beyond doubt. Their original homeland is the Carpathian Mountains and from the 2nd Century onward they have gradually moved westward. From the occasional forays at the beginning by the Slavs into Byzantine territories by the 7th Century when Bosnia and Herzegovina was occupied it was a veritable land grab. Large parts of Bosnia and Herzegovina were settled by Slavs quickly while Byzantium slowly but surely lost the upper hand over the Balkan Peninsula. Bosnia and Herzegovina became what it is today: Slavic.

THE BOSNIAN MEDIEVAL KINGDOM

Following the conquest and settlement of the Slavs the first regional Slavic principalities developed. These included, in some cases areas of Bosnia and Herzegovina. Some were part of the lands of the first Croatian king Tomislav (910-928), while eastern areas were under Bulgarian rule and then under Serb control. At the same time Byzantium was still hovering over all these regional principalities, and had not yet given up its claim of power over Bosnia and Herzegovina.

In 1102, after Croatia came under the rule of Hungary and Byzantium focused more on the defence of its capital, Constantinople, against the resurgent Ottomans the territory of Bosnia and Herzegovina inherited a power vacuum and it developed as the first independent Bosnian principality. Medieval Bosnia was not formally subordinate to Hungary and, because it virtually ruled itself it was perceived as an independent entity on the edge of Christian Europe.

Traces of medieval Bosnia can be found throughout the country

The Bosnian medieval rulers bore the noble title Ban, something approximate to an earl or duke. The first Ban, who founded the semi-autonomous Principality of Bosnia in 1154 was Ban Borić. Ban Borić did not stay in power long but his legacy is the foundation of the Kotromanić dynasty which lasted until the 14th century. The rulers who followed him, especially Ban Kulin (1180-1204) and Ban Stjepan II (1322-1353), succeeded in expanding Bosnian territory northwards to the Sava and southward to the Adriatic Sea. Thus, the mountainous lands of Bosnia were connected to important trade routes, which improved its economic situation and military power. The castles and fortifications that can still be seen today are remnants of those times.

A statue of King Tvrtko in Tuzla

In 1377, the Bosnian King **Stjepan Tvrtko I** of the Kotromanić family was crowned ruler of Bosnia and Serbia. At this time it had become possible to conquer large parts of the Balkan Peninsula and the kingdom of Tvrtko ranged from Dalmatia, Herzegovina and the Zeta (now Montenegro) in the south to parts of Croatia and Slavonia in the north and Serbia in the east. This period was the highlight of the independent Bosnian kingdom. Numerous military and stately buildings from the time of the Kotromanićs exist today or form the foundations for later buildings of the Ottomans and the Hapsburgs, such as the castle of Srebrenik or the Fortress of Travnik.

From the 1380s, Ottoman military incursions into Bosnia, and the whole Balkan peninsula increased rapidly. In 1386 the first Ottoman troops set foot on the territory of modern-day Bosnia and Herzegovina. Just a few years later (in 1389) Tvrtko's strategic ally, the Serbian Prince Lazar Hrebeljanović refused to recognize Ottoman sovereignty over parts of his territory and asked Slav and Christian kingdoms and principalities for military aid. In June of 1389, a large army sent by King Trvtko to join Lazar's armies, took part in the Battle of Kosovo Polje, a last ditch effort to halt the numerically superior Ottomans. The victory of the Ottoman forces at Kosovo Polje – to this day an event shrouded in legend – led to the final supremacy of the Ottomans in the Balkans, including Bosnia and Herzegovina.

Shortly after the defeat at Kosovo, King Tvrtko of Bosnia died and his death brought to an end the most stable and militarily successful independent Bosnian state. Tvrtko's successors were not able to withstand the increasing pressure from Hungary, in the north, and the Ottoman Turks, in the south. In addition to this external pressure, there was also pressure from the Bosnian nobility; internal intrigues, division and conflict saw to it that the decline of the independent kingdom of Bosnia and Herzegovina was inevitable. Nevertheless, it was not until the spring of 1463 before the last king of a now shrunken Bosnia was defeated. King Stjepan Tomašević was executed at the fortress in Ključ and, with his death, the rule over the medieval Bosnia of the Kotromanić family ended.

THE OTTOMANS IN BOSNIA AND HERZEGOVINA

There are contrary opinions and differing interpretations regarding the actions, performance, and actual effects of 400 years of Ottoman rule over the territory of Bosnia and Herzegovina. Indisputable is only the fact that the Ottoman period has contributed significantly to the emergence of Bosnia and Herzegovinian identity and there are clearly visible traces of this left. In addition to some words and phrases, architecture, infrastructure and cuisine the Ottomans also brought Islam, which continues to shape Bosnia and Herzegovina and makes it distinct from its Christian Slavic neighbours.

The 400 years of Ottoman rule over Bosnia and Herzegovina can be subdivided into three phases **rise, heyday** and **decline**. They each cover about 150 years. The 'small' history of the Ottomans in Bosnia and Herzegovina cannot be disconnected from the 'big' history of Ottomans in Europe. After the loss of its independence in the 15th century, Bosnia and Herzegovina's fate was no longer in its own hands, it was from then on in the hands of Constantinople (today Istanbul). Prior to the arrival of the Ottomans, Bosnia had known an independence of sorts, subsequent to their arrival the country would never again know anything other then foreign rule or, at the very least, foreign interference in its affairs.

The Ottomans conquered the area now known as Bosnia and Herzegovina in the period between 1386-1592. The eventual subjugation of this territory took around a century to complete but 1436, when Stjepan Tomašević, the last king of Bosnia was executed, can be used as a date to denote the Ottoman occupation of the whole of Bosnia. The Sanjak of Bosnia (*Sandžak*) was established in 1463 and the Sanjak of Herzegovina in 1470.

The Ottoman heritage of Bosnia and Herzegovina is more than evident today

Under Ottoman rule, medieval Bosnia and Herzegovina experienced a rapid **rise**. Cities, such as Sarajevo, were established; trade routes developed; and educational institutions and governing structures founded. The most significant and recognisable structures in Bosnia and Herzegovina were built during this period – for example, the Bridges of Mostar (see p. 134) and Višegrad (see p. 237) or the Baščaršija of Sarajevo (see p. 107).

Under Ottoman rule both Bosnia and Herzegovina became safer, wealthier and the population boomed. Farmers from Orthodox Christian lands, from Croatia, Hungary and Dalmatia, as well as Muslims and Jews, moved to the rapidly developing country – as did an army of Ottoman state officials and representatives.

The Islamization of the population of Bosnia and Herzegovina came mostly in the 16th Century. The immigrants, but also old established Christians of Bosnia and Herzegovina were attracted in large numbers by the legally and economically better-off Islamic community. The urbanization of the country contributed to the establishment and spread of Islam. The Slavic Bosnian Muslims retained their language and developed their own cultural and political identity within the Ottoman world.

The Ottoman Empire reached its **heyday** in the 16th century under Sultan Suleyman I (1520-1566). In addition to its far reaching territorial expansion, the Ottoman Empire had also expanded into areas such as urban development and the intricacy of its legal system to such an extent that it could be measured against any contemporary European rival. Of course, Bosnia and Herzegovina also benefited from the military and economic power of the Sublime Porte (the term often used to refer to official Istanbul). Sarajevo, Mostar, Tuzla, but also, Višegrad and Trebinje grew to become important pillars

in the Ottoman trade network and the geographical and linguistic proximity to Dubrovnik and the Hapsburgs contributed to the rise of Bosnia and Herzegovina's cities. The rural population of Bosnia and Herzegovina, however, benefited from this trend only partially and the gap between the mostly Muslim urban population and the Christian rural population increased.

Ottoman rule over Bosnia and Herzegovina at that time was influenced by the fact that it was the major European outpost of the empire. This brought Bosnia and Herzegovina both status and privilege; the Sultan's governor in Bosnia and Herzegovina was granted almost absolute power, and was one of the most powerful men of the Ottoman Empire.

With the conquest of southern Hungary and Slavonia by Prince Eugene at the end of the 17th century, Bosnia and Herzegovina, became the scene of regular fighting as Hapsburg troops made incursions into Bosnia in an attempt to wrest it from Ottoman control. Although the Hapsburgs failed to establish a beachhead in Bosnia and Herzegovina, Prince Eugene did manage to sack Sarajevo in a campaign in 1697.

Inevitably, the economic and political **decline** of the Ottoman Empire also affected Bosnia and Herzegovina. Attempts to reform the Ottoman Empire (known as the *Tanzimat*) in the 19th century could not resolve the problem, since they focused primarily on military and administrative matters. Muslim landowners opposed reforms that would improve the social and economic situation of the majority rural Christian population. A majority of the Bosnian Muslims had either extensive land holdings, farmed by tenant farmers, or found employment in the Ottoman civil service, from which avenues the Christians were largely excluded. The Christians and especially the Orthodox Serbs were mostly farmers who had to work as tenant farmers under very difficult terms set by the landowners.

An uprising of the Bosnian Serbs, which began in 1876, and was also supported by independent Serbia, marked the beginning of the end of Ottoman rule. In the same year Serbia and Montenegro started a war against the Ottoman Empire. The governments of the small Balkan countries, however, had underestimated the strength of the enemy and were soon on the defensive. The Serbs were saved from military disaster by the intervention of the Russians who were happy to pursue their own objectives in the Balkans.

"Herzegovinians Set an Ambush" depicts the uprising in Bosnia and Herzegovina

The Congress of Berlin

At the Berlin Congress in the summer of 1878, the major European powers tried to reach an agreement on the so-called 'Eastern Question'. The retreat of the Ottomans from Southeast Europe left a power vacuum and roused the territorial desires of the great powers and the Slavic peoples themselves. At the congress, Great Britain, France, Austria-Hungary, Russia and Germany finally agreed to the recognition of the following new states: Romania, Serbia and Montenegro. An enlarged Bulgaria (created by the Russians just two years earlier) was, however, divided into three provinces and Austria-Hungary was given a free hand to 'administer' Bosnia and Herzegovina. The Ottoman chapter of Balkan history was brought to a close by the Congress of Berlin, at which the relevant Southeast European nations participated only as observers.

Bosnia and Herzegovina, however, was neither recognized as an independent state nor as part of the newly independent Serbian state but was instead placed under the administration of Vienna. Additionally, the question of the ownership of Macedonia had not been solved, but was simply deferred. These were precisely the lines of conflict that ignited the first Balkan war in 1912, and ultimately the First World War.

THE HAPSBURGS IN BOSNIA AND HERZEGOVINA

Towards the end of the 19th century the Congress of Berlin ushered in a new era for South Eastern Europe. The Ottoman Empire was on the retreat and the resultant power vacuum was filled by the new Balkan states of Serbia and Bulgaria, the great powers of Austria-Hungary and Russia, and the new German Empire under Bismarck.

Austro-Hungarian rule over Bosnia and Herzegovina, declared at the Congress of Berlin, was met with opposition by both the Christian and Muslim populations of Bosnia and Herzegovina.

The Hapsburg monarchy, the rulers of Austria-Hungary, immediately began expanding and modernising infrastructure in Bosnia and Herzegovina. More than 10,000 Hapsburg officials arrived to oversee construction of schools, roads and government buildings. Vienna added Bosnia and Herzegovina to its existing rail network and thus connected it to the modern world. Several factories were built and contributed to an economic recovery. Numerous buildings from the period of Hapsburg rule are still around today and many are still in use. The economic success of the Hapsburgs in Bosnia and Herzegovina was tremendous but it didn't lead to a sense of multiculturalism or to the establishment of a common Bosnian identity. The assassination of the heir to the Hapsburg throne, Archduke Franz Ferdinand, on the 28th of June 1914 during a visit to Sarajevo (see p 113) led to the end of Austro-Hungarian rule, to the First World War and, ultimately, to the end of the Hapsburg monarchy.

BOSNIA AND HERZEGOVINA AS PART OF THE KINGDOM OF YUGOSLAVIA

Yugoslavia was founded at the end of World War II. The official name of the first Yugoslavia was initially the **Kingdom of Serbs, Croats and Slovenes**. The Serbian Karadjordjević dynasty served as the country's monarchs. The Bosnian state, politically autonomous under the Hapsburgs, suddenly found itself part of a new kingdom and lost its territorial integrity and political sense of self. Bosnia and Herzegovina was divided into 6 districts, all of which were directly subordinate to the central government in Belgrade and Sarajevo lost its status as the capital of Bosnia and Herzegovina.

Hapsburg troops in Bosnia and Herzegovina

The weak democracy of the young Yugoslav constitutional monarchy was not able to overcome the historical, social and religious divisions in the region and, in 1929, a royal dictatorship was proclaimed. King Alexander I of Yugoslavia tried to create a Yugoslav nation under the slogan: "One nation, one king, one state". The land was reorganized and divided into so-called Banats – which deliberately took no account of historical boundaries. Bosnia and Herzegovina was reshaped so that the Muslims were not in the majority in any Banovina. After the death of King Aleksandar – he was assassinated by Croatian nationalists in Marseilles in 1934 – his policy of ruthless centralism was pursued. The people of Bosnia and Herzegovina had little love for the Kingdom of Yugoslavia and, when in 1939 the territory was split between Serbia and Croatia, the resolve of the Muslims who opposed the kingdom strengthened.

The Second World War brought about the end of the Kingdom of Yugoslavia. After the occupation of Yugoslavia in April 1941, Bosnia and Herzegovina was ceded to the newly created fascist Independent State of Croatia. The tensions between the peoples of Bosnia and Herzegovina reached fever pitch and, in addition to a war of resistance against the German occupation, a bitter and bloody civil war between ethnic groups and political persuasions broke out. Royalist *Chetniks*, Tito's *Partisans* and the fascist *Ustasha* warred against each other violently and the chaos and conflict costs hundreds of thousands of lives throughout Bosnia and Herzegovina.

Crucial moments of the guerrilla struggle against the fascist occupation and for a new Yugoslav state happened on the territory of Bosnia and Herzegovina. The decisive battles of Neretva and Sutjeska and the constituent assemblies of Bihać and Jajce occurred in Bosnia and Herzegovina.

BOSNIA AND HERZEGOVINA AS PART OF SOCIALIST YUGOSLAVIA

The Socialist Federal Republic of Yugoslavia was founded after the Second World War and consisted of the six constituent republics of Slovenia, Croatia, Serbia, Montenegro, Macedonia and Bosnia and Herzegovina. Sarajevo became the capital of its own constitutional republic of Bosnia and Herzegovina.

The political transition from a centralised monarchy to a socialist federation went hand in hand with an economic transition with previously agricultural and rural Bosnia and Herzegovina becoming the heartland of the new state's industrial development. The

Josip Broz, aka Tito, the life-long president of socialist Yugoslavia

defence industry and other heavy industries were located in Bosnia and Herzegovina for strategic reasons; the mountainous territory was far from Yugoslavia's external borders. Just about every town of any size saw a new manufacturing plant spring up on its periphery. Industrial conglomerates emerged, especially around the towns of Zenica, Sarajevo and Tuzla. Near Mostar, a giant aluminium plant was built and the republic's rivers were dammed for hydroelectric power plants, such as those on the Neretva, Vrbas and Drina. Parallel to the state-planned industrialisation, the population of Bosnia and Herzegovina's towns boomed; the population of Sarajevo, for example, grew from less than 100,000 after the Second World War to half a million in the 1980s.

Despite massive industrialisation, it was not possible to compare the standard of

The coat of arms of the Socialist Federal Republic of Yugoslavia

living in Bosnia and Herzegovina with the average level of Yugoslavia. The republic was always in need of financial support. Away from the industrial centres life in the rural regions was far from easy and people emigrated to Western Europe in large numbers.

A Tito T-shirt on sale in Sarajevo

Tito

On a trip through Bosnia and Herzegovina, the former ruler of Yugoslavia is still omnipresent.

Josip Broz was born in 1892 in the Croatian village Kumrovac as the seventh child of a peasant family. He became a locksmith at the age of 15, when he left his home town. His travels took him to Austria and Germany and, during the First World War, the young craftsman joined the Hapsburg army and was captured by the Russians. When he returned to his home, he co-founded the socialist movement and gained a new nickname, "Tito". When World War Two came to Yugoslavia, Tito led the Partisans (*Partizani*) in a movement of active resistance to the fascist occupation forces. In the fall of 1943, Tito proclaimed a new socialist Yugoslavia, which was to be realised once the Partisans emerged victorious from the war in 1945.

From 1945 until his death in 1980, Tito was the life-long president of Yugoslavia. Although the ghosts of his governing methods and the lack of democracy and freedom of expression linger on, the success of uniting previously warring peoples and antagonistic ethnic and religious communities into one state for 40 years is truly monumental. Externally, Tito led Yugoslavia through the Cold War by balancing the superpowers against each other. He became one of the leaders of the Non Aligned Movement and a respected politician of international standing. Tito's Yugoslavia was also economically much better off than the countries of the Warsaw Pact and enjoyed much greater freedom in terms of travel, culture and participation in a Western-style consumer market.

Despite his undoubted successes, it was not possible for Tito to reconcile the destructive forces of the country permanently, and, after his death, much of what he achieved was dismantled. 10 years after his death, the republics he had created clashed bloodily and tore the country apart. These days in Bosnia and Herzegovina, Tito's name is associated with a more peaceful, prosperous age.

With the death of Tito in 1980, Yugoslavia gradualy embarked upon a process of economic stagnation, political instability and social disintegration. Bosnia and Herzegovina, with its diverse population and mix of religious denominations would prove vulnerable to the heady combination of nationalist sentiment and economic hardship. The military tensions between Croatia and Serbia first appeared on TV screens in Bosnia and Herzegovina in the early 1990s, and the Muslim politicians in Bosnia and Herzegovina saw a chance to strive for national independence. The referendum on the national sovereignty of Bosnia and Herzegovina was held in the spring of 1992 and was accompanied by armed confrontations.

THE WAR IN BOSNIA AND HERZEGOVINA IN THE 1990S

While in the rest of Europe the 1990s represented a new age ushered in by the end of the Cold War and the reunification of Germany, in Yugoslavia they represent the outbreak of a war that belonged to a previous age; a rebuke to the vision of a Europe, finally peaceful and democratic for the first time in its history. In multiethnic Yugoslavia the demise of socialism was accompanied by the awakening of radical nationalist tendencies. Nationalist movements, which fed ideologically on the historical wounds of the Second World War, managed to grasp the levers of political power and the tools of mass media. The religious and intellectual elites and the diaspora participated in the new discourse of hate and fear; the antithesis of the

Dayton

The 1995 Dayton Peace Agreement ended the war in Bosnia and Herzegovina. It was brokered by the United States, under the direction of former U.S. President Bill Clinton, and with the participation of the European Union. After lengthy negotiations the parties finally acquiesced and, on the 21st of November 1995, the agreement was signed by the Serbian President, Slobodan Milošević, Croatian President, Franjo Tudjman, and the President of Bosnia and Herzegovina, Alija Izetbegović.

Since then Bosnia and Herzegovina has been composed of two constituent republics (known as Entities): Republika Srpska (Serb Republic) and the (Bosniak-Croat) Federation of Bosnia and Herzegovina. The agreement calls for the complete freedom of movement of people and the granting of the right to return for refugees and displaced people. According to the agreement, Bosnia and Herzegovina would receive a new constitution that provides for democracy and a market economy based on five key institutions: the bicameral Parliament, the Presidency, the Council of Ministers, the Constitutional Court and the Central Bank. Even today, the Dayton Peace Agreement is the legal basis for the state of Bosnia and Herzegovina.

idea of a peaceful, democratic Europe. The declarations of independence of Slovenia and Croatia in the summer of 1991 broke the camel's back and brought war to Europe once more.

Multi-ethnic Bosnia and Herzegovina was particularly volatile and it was here that the fighting was at its most fierce. Between spring 1992 and autumn 1995 more than a hundred thousand people were killed and millions were displaced and fled the country forever. The country's economic infrastructure was utterly destroyed and Bosnia and Herzegovina still suffers from the consequences of the conflict to this day. The war in Bosnia and Herzegovina,

the shifting alliances, the treacherous massacres, land mines, prison camps and refugees, has been the subject of countless articles, books, reports, films and so forth. Furthermore, the war is still the subject of much controversy and is still hotly debated at every level from the village *kafana* to the highest academic circles. We have deliberately elected not to add to this debate and to leave out any detailed description of the war. Even a short account would likely cause offense to one side or another and would never be able to do justice to the tragedy of the conflict. Those interested in knowing more will likely find a wealth of published material and are free to form their own opinions.

TIMELINE OF KEY EVENTS

1200 BC	Illyrian settlements
9 BC	Roman provinces of Dalmatia and Pannonia created
395 AD	Breakup of the Roman Empire: The Balkans are initially part of the Western Empire
530	Byzantine rule over much of the Balkans
600 →	The Arrival of the Slavs
1102	Croatia and Bosnia fall under Hungarian control
1154	The Autonomous Principality of Bosnia under Ban Borić
1377	Stjepan Tvrtko I becomes King of Bosnia
1386	First Ottoman attack
1463	Ottomans defeat last Bosnian king and establish the Pashalik of Bosnia
1470	The Ottomans found the Pashalik of Herzegovina
1592	Bihać is the last city to fall to the Ottomans
1697	Prince Eugene of Savoy sacks Sarajevo
1878	The Congress of Berlin: Bosnia and Herzegovina is administered by the Habsburg Monarchy
1914	The assassination of Archduke Franz Ferdinand in Sarajevo, World War I begins
1918	The Kingdom of Serbs, Croats and Slovenes (The First Yugoslavia)
1941	Bosnia and Herzegovina becomes part of the fascist Croatian state (NDH)
1945	Bosnia and Herzegovina becomes part of the Socialist Federal Republic of Yugoslavia (SFRY – the Second Yugoslavia)
1980	Tito, the President of socialist Yugoslavia, dies
1984	The Winter Olympic Games in Sarajevo
1992	Bosnia and Herzegovina declares independence, civil war ensues
1995	The Dayton Peace Agreement

POLITICS

The Parliament building in Sarajevo

Bosnia and Herzegovina is a relatively young country, whose political system is not yet truly stable. In 1995 the country, once a federal republic in Socialist Federal Republic of Yugoslavia, had a constitution bestowed upon it by the Dayton Peace Agreement that ended the civil war. According to this constitution it is an independent, democratic, federal republic and consists of two largely autonomous Entities (regions): the Federation of Bosnia and Herzegovina and Republika Srpska.

Each of the two Entities has its own constitution, its own government and its own parliament – the central government also has a separate constitution. Due to the resulting number of mutually controlling, or more often mutually blocking, political institutions the political system of Bosnia and Herzegovina can be characterised as having **multiple, parallel centres of power**. No fewer than 126 ministries compete to devour some 70 percent of the country's budget.

The **Dayton Agreement** established a Constitution of Bosnia and Herzegovina under the motto "one state, two entities, three nations," with the aim of curbing the centrifugal forces threatening to pull the country apart – and so far it has worked. Although the Dayton Agreement was instituted with the consent of all of the warring parties, it has created a political system of such complexity and inefficiency that it outstrips almost all others. In a well-intentioned move aimed at improving minority rights and equal opportunities, a wide-ranging veto power was created for each ethnic group. The two Entities as well as the state as a whole are therefore often stonewalled, resulting in a resigned mood amongst the population towards the current political system.

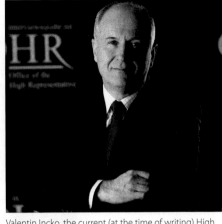

Valentin Incko, the current (at the time of writing) High Representative

Another criticism of the Dayton settlement is that the people of Bosnia and Herzegovina were not involved in the drafting of the constitution and to this day the functioning of the state infrastructure has never been democratically legitimated by a referendum. All attempts, both on part of the international authorities and by Bosnian politicians, to reform the constitution and ensure democratic legitimacy have failed entirely and thus the status quo, including the mutual blocking, is likely to remain in place for the foreseeable future.

This already complex political system was made more complex still by the establishment of the Office of the **High Representative**, which was put in place to coordinate and monitor the implementation of the Dayton Agreement. The High Representative is appointed by the international Peace Implementation Council and acts in union with the Special Representative of the European Union. The High Representative has *de facto* executive, legislative and judicial rights and can be replaced or dismissed at any time without the involvement

A meeting of the Council of Ministers

of local institutions or democratically elected representatives. This essentially means the High Representative – currently Austrian diplomat, Valentin Inzko – is above the law. On the one hand, this institution does inject some efficiency and vigour, but on the other, it contradicts every democratic principle and compromises the country's process of democratisation. Bosnia and Herzegovina can, therefore, be said to only have limited sovereignty and is in a sense a protectorate of the international community.

The main government building of Republika Srpska is in Banja Luka

The central government is administered not by a single president but by a three-member committee or **Presidency** (*Predsjedni*štvo). This committee consists of one representative from each of the three ethnic groups who rotate every eight months as Chairperson of the Presidency. The term of office of the Presidency collectively lasts 4 years and there can be no revocation of their mandate by the people, only the international High Representative is authorised to dismiss one or more members of the Presidency. The powers of the Presidency are largely symbolic in nature but do include some real powers such as articulation of the country's foreign policy. Because of the constant rotation of the Chairperson and the institution's very limited political capacity, most Bosnian citizens are relatively indifferent to who heads the Presidency at any one time.

The legislative branch consists of two parliamentary chambers: the House of Representatives (*Zastupnički Dom*) and the House of Peoples (*Dom Naroda*). Two thirds of the 42-member House of Representatives is composed of representatives of the Bosnian-Croat Federation, with representatives of the Republika Srpska making up the remaining third. Each ethnic group sends five representatives to the House of Peoples. Together the two chambers make up the **Parliamentary Assembly** of Bosnia and Herzegovina, which is responsible for drafting legislation and the budget, the ratification of international treaties and to keep in check or confirm the appointment of ministers to the central government.

The central government is officially known as the **Council of Ministers** or the Cabinet. The head of Cabinet is proposed by the Chairman of the Presidency and elected by the House of Representatives for 4 years. The head of the Cabinet is responsible for his ministers and, as in all institutions in Bosnia and Herzegovina, the Cabinet is based on the principle of equal representation of the three ethnic groups. For example, each minister is obliged to have two deputies from the other ethnic groups and a consensus is required for decisions to be made. Even within the Cabinet itself every ethnic group has a *de facto* power of veto, so that decisions between ethnic groups that still tend to treat each other with distrust are very difficult to reach.

Political decision-making and practical implementation at the level of the two Entities is slightly more efficient. The Entities were guaranteed relative autonomy by the Dayton Agreement and pledged far-reaching powers. **Republika Srpska**, with Banja Luka as its capital, is significantly more organized and more centralized in comparison to the Bosnian-Croat Federation. The bicameral legislative branch of Republika Srpska is selected for mandates of four years and elects a cabinet. According to the constitution the cabinet of Republika Srpska should include eight Serbian, five Bosniak and three Croatian ministers. Between the entity government and local municipalities there is no other form government in Republika Srpska.

In contrast, the **Bosnian-Croat Federation** has, in addition to the cabinet and the two chambers of parliament in Sarajevo, another federal administrative unit: the Cantons. These ten Cantons each have their own parliaments and governments. Given this range of competencies and responsibilities as well as the power of veto held by all three ethnic groups across all political levels, it can come as no surprise that the political landscape in Bosnia-Herzegovina does not seem to evolve.

This is also clear when you take a closer look at the parties and other actors. Even without going into the intricacies of party politics and regional differences, it is still obvious that to a large extent the same parties and people have been in the corridors of power for the last 20 years. Almost all parties are reduced to representing the interests of their ethnic group and fail to pursue other interests.

SUMMARY

The political system was a good idea at conception, but ethnic group veto rights plus the Office of the High Representative (installed from the outside and in no way an organic part of the political system in Bosnia and Herzegovina) can be regarded as a failures and need urgent and thorough alteration and simplification. The Office of the High Representative should be abolished if Bosnia and Herzegovina is to become a serious country standing on its own two feet.

Frequent protests are a sign of the discontent

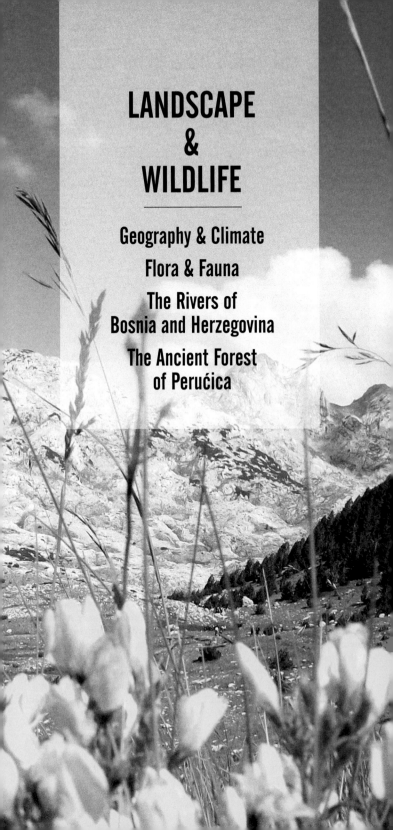

LANDSCAPE & WILDLIFE

Geography & Climate

Flora & Fauna

The Rivers of
Bosnia and Herzegovina

The Ancient Forest
of Perućica

GEOGRAPHY & CLIMATE

Kotleničko Jezero, a lake in southern Bosnia

Bosnia and Herzegovina has a total land area of 51,197km² with just 20km of coastline along the Adriatic. Bosnia and Herzegovina is about two and a half times the size of Wales or nearly twice the size of the US state of Massachusetts. The country straddles the western part of the Balkan Peninsula, and has a 1,500km long external border. In the west and in the north it is bordered by Croatia while to the east, its borders follow the course of the Sava and Drina rivers. In the mountainous south it borders Montenegro and Serbia.

Typical throughout Bosnia and Herzegovina are numerous rivers, canyons, several glacial lakes, around 70 thermal springs as well as large deciduous and mixed forests (about 45% of the total area of the country is forested). Large areas of Bosnia and Herzegovina's forests are relatively unaffected by human interference and are rich in wildlife. Perućica, in the southeast of the country, one of the last and largest primeval forests in Europe stretches across the landscape.

The mountains of Bosnia and Herzegovina often reach over 2,000 meters. The highest peak in the country, Maglić at 2,386 metres above sea level, is located in the border region with Montenegro in the Sutjeska National Park. The Perućica primeval forest extends out from below Maglić's snow-capped summit. Central Bosnia and the Sarajevo region also have peaks over 2,000m with Prenj at 2,103m, Lelija at 2,032m and Bjelasnica at 2,076m.

Bosnia and Herzegovina is as diverse in terms of its geography and climate as it is in terms of history and culture and can be divided into two main parts (see p. 16). On one hand, **Bosnia**, encompassing the northern part of the country, including the Sava river basin, known as Posavina, is open and spacious. The region is bounded in the south by a high, arid karst region but much of Central Bosnia is mountainous and heavily forested. The climate here is continental, with snowy, harsh winters and hot, dry summers. Vegetation in Bosnia is, therefore, comparable to that in

The Bjelasnica mountains wreathed in winter snow

Central Europe, including dense forest cover. In the lowlands to the north, the typical deciduous and mixed forests are dominated by beech, oak and alder. Forests in the mountainous south of Bosnia are, however, predominantly spruce, pine and fir.

Herzegovina, the other half of the country's climactic and geographical split, has a more Mediterranean climate. In the summer months temperatures peak along the Neretva delta and can maintain a constant 40° Celsius. Herzegovina also experiences relatively cold, frosty winters and snow is not unusual - supporting a few small ski centres. The major river in Herzegovina, the Neretva, carves its way through the Dinaric Alps and flows into the Mediterranean. Vegetation in the higher karst landscapes of Herzegovina struggles through the harsh winters and scorching, dry summer temperatures. On the other hand, due to a favourable climate and its proximity to the Adriatic, the Neretva basin is ideal for the cultivation of fruit and vegetables.

The rolling hills of Central Bosnia

The Neretva river in Herzegovina

Karst

Guest Post: Michell Rohmann, hydrologist, Subotica (Serbia)

Karst (Slovenian: Kras) was originally the name of a limestone plateau in western Slovenia. There the phenomenon was first described by Slovenian Renaissance man, Janez Vajkard Valvasor, in the 17th century. In the late 19th century, Valvasor's initial work was expanded on by Serbian geologist, Jovan Cvijić, who initiated scientific study of karst and karst fields such as those in Bosnia and Herzegovina. Karst is a geological formation in which soluble rock such as limestone is shaped by dissolution and weathering. The two most important factors for the development of karst are sufficient solubility of the rock and the presence of liquid water – the best karst formations are developed in limestone.

The Dinaric Mountains are a limestone mountain range, which extends south into Bosnia and Herzegovina from the Julian Alps in northeast Italy, Slovenia and Croatia. The Dinaric Alps number amongst Europe's most rugged and mountainous regions. The outer Dinaric Alps are characterized by its strong karstification, which is formed from limestone formations four kilometres thick. In geology these formations are known as karst landforms. In the late 19th Century the phenomena of Dinaric karst made these mountains the traditional location to study karst landscapes.

Karst Fields

Karst fields are formed on the valley floors of karst mountain formations and provide very fertile soil. Karst fields can occupy areas of just a few square kilometres to hundreds of square kilometres (for example Livanjsko Polje – see p. 145), making them the largest karst forms. Karst fields are usually flat and covered by sediment that have gathered after they have been eroded from the slopes of the surrounding mountains. In the Dinaric Alps these slopes are often bare and rocky, so that only the Valley floor can be used for arable farming. The Bosnian word polje (literally field, pronounced 'polyeh') is so commonly used to denote karst fields that it has become the international geological term for this phenomenon and is regularly used even in English.

FLORA & FAUNA

FLORA

Bosnia and Herzegovina provides a habitat for numerous endangered and protected plant species. The Perućica forest in the Sutjeska National Park (see p. 243) is an ideal environment for many species including the endangered white trees and the rare, endemic black pine. In the lower altitudes (500 - 1,000 meters) of Bosnia and Herzegovina, oak and beech are the dominant tree populations while in higher regions spruce, fir and pine. Classic alpine flora such as anemones, thyme and catmint can be found in the meadows of virtually every mountain in the country.

Wild flowers prosper in Bosnia and Herzegovina's mountain meadows

In the spring there is a wide range of wildflowers to discover: violets, gentians, narcissus, chamomile, cowslip, snake heads and pansies litter the mountainsides. Many varieties of orchids and lilies benefit from the calcareous soils found throughout the country. Endangered flowers like the Red Helleborine Orchid or the Wild Hyacinth grow in Bosnia and Herzegovina as well as rare species of the tulip, such as the *Tulipa Tulipa Bifloraoder Orphanidea*. The country also has a significant number of endemic species.

Alpine flora is common throughout Bosnia and Herzegovina's mountainous regions

Wild horses on the Livanjsko Polje karst field

FAUNA

Many animal species that are extinct in other parts of Europe have survived and thrived in Bosnia and Herzegovina. The richness of aquatic life in the numerous mountain lakes and rivers is pronounced. Trout, carp, eel and perch are the most common types of fish and rare river crustaceans have found a home in the country's rivers. Snakes, especially vipers and adders, are common in the drier areas of Herzegovina.

The Hutovo Blato reserve (see p. 134) offers sanctuary to over 240 species of birds, an ideal breeding and nesting ground. Herons, Wine and coot, pheasant and wild ducks have settled here and many species of migratory birds from Northern Europe inhabit the lakes temporarily. Birds of prey such as eagles, falcons and hawks are also common throughout Bosnia and Herzegovina.

The largest animal in Bosnia and Herzegovina is the brown bear, around 2,800 of which are thought to be scattered around the country. The bears are most common in the Sutjeska National Park, but also in Herzegovina and the mountains around Sarajevo. Deer and wild boar are so abundant as to be popular with hunters throughout the country. The wolf is also widespread and wild horses have a habitat in Livanjsko Polje (see p. 145).

There are around 2,800 bears in Bosnia and Herzegovina

THE RIVERS OF BOSNIA AND HERZEGOVINA

The rivers of Bosnia and Herzegovina are an essential component of the country's landscape, geography and topography. The numerous waterways – some small, some large, some low and meandering, others fast-flowing and wild – carve through the landscape and shape the countryside. The rivers flow out past the borders of the country, connecting its interior with other parts of the country and with its neighbours but also divide the land into distinct regions. Bosnia-Herzegovina has benefited enormously from its rivers, from the fertility they provide to the development of an emerging river tourism. Furthermore, the country's energy supply is primarily generated from its rivers.

Here is a selection of the country's most beautiful rivers which provide a perfect introduction to the landscape of Bosnia and Herzegovina.

THE DRINA

The Drina is Bosnia and Herzegovina's longest waterway and also its most celebrated river. The novel, "The Bridge on the Drina", by a Nobel Prize winning author Ivo Andrić is set on the river's banks at Višegrad, making this river literally world famous.

The Drina originates with its source rivers the Tara and Piva, in the high karst of the central Dinaric Alps in Montenegro and flows 350km to Bijeljina and into the Sava, the Danube and eventually into the Black Sea. With a catchment area of 19,926 km², the Drina is the largest river of the Dinaric Alps and represents an enormous hydrological system for the cities it passes through, and additionally to the eastern Bosnian towns Višegrad, Foča, Goražde, Zvornik and Bijeljina. The Drina River, with its numerous hydroelectric power plants is also a major electricity producer in Bosnia and Herzegovina.

The 92km long upper reaches of the Drina meander through deep ravines and canyons. This part of the river, due to the high lime content of its waters which leave a distinct greenish trail, is often called the "Green Drina". You can also find fantastic locations for swimming in the upper reaches of

The green Drina as it passes under the famous bridge at Višegrad

The limestone karst gives the Drina its unusual colour

the Drina, for example in Medjedja, between Višegrad and Ustiprača.

The 163 kilometre middle section of the Drina begins just before Višegrad, where the River Lim flows into the Drina. This section is characterised by strong currents and is difficult to access for visitors. This part of the river also contains the 93 metre high Perućačko dam, which forms the 50 kilometre long Perućačko reservoir. On the Serbian side of the Drina, along the Perućačko reservoir, lies the Tara National Park.

The the 91 kilometre long lower section begins from Zvornik: This section has all the characteristics of a lowland river (a meandering flow, oxbow lakes, natural damming). The confluence of the Drina into the Sava is just north of Bijelijina.

In the autumn of 1914, as the First World War was in its early stages, the Drina was witness to bloody battles between Serbian and Austro-Hungarian troops. Nearly 40,000 soldiers died or were injured in the battles along the middle reaches of the Drina and as a reminder of this battle, the Serbian composer Stanislav Binički composed the famous Serbian song "March on the Drina".

Kayaking and other water sports are increasingly popular on the Drina

THE NERETVA

The Neretva is the main river in Herzegovina and the only river in Bosnia and Herzegovina, which doesn't flow, ultimately, into the Black Sea. Instead it flows into the Adriatic near the Croatian town of Ploče. The Neretva, whose source is in the highlands of Bosnia and Herzegovina, travels just 200km on its way to Croatia. The Neretva is special and unique not only because of its deep emerald colour but also for the canyons and ravines it carves through the landscape.

The source of the Neretva is at an altitude of 1,000 metres close to the Montenegrin border, in Držirep, in the Gacko district, south of the Zelengora mountains. On its way to Konjic it flows first in a northwesterly direction through the sparsely populated valley between the Lelija, Visočica and Bjelašnica mountains in the northeast and the Crvanj and Prenj in the southwest. The Neretva is dammed at Jablanica near Konjic. The imposing Neretva Gorge begins beyond Jablanica and continues on to Mostar. The best way to explore the

The Neretva carves its way through the landscape

canyon is by train. The tracks of the Sarajevo-Mostar line, built in 1886, follow the flow of the river (see p. 72).

Mostar, the largest city in Herzegovina, is halfway down the Neretva's course. During the civil war, the river was the front line and Mostar's famous Ottoman era bridge was destroyed in the fighting (see p. 135). Beyond Mostar, the narrow canyon opens out

Mount Prenj, along the Neretva valley

The Neretva as it enters Mostar

onto a broad plain, which closes again at the confluence with the Buna, after which the Neretva flows for another 20km before reaching a narrow valley. In Počitelj, whose fortress once dominated the river (see p. 132), the canyon finally opens towards the Adriatic Sea.

The lower reaches of the river are used for agriculture. The actual delta of the Neretva begins only after Metković and is thus in Croatia.

The Neretva basin, whose catchment area is 5581km², includes most of Herzegovina. At its entrance into the sea the Neretva's average flow is 378 cubic metres per second. It is, therefore, the second largest river in Bosnia and Herzegovina, after the Sava, and the only river in Herzegovina that runs entirely above ground.

THE MILJACKA

The 36 kilometre long Miljacka flows through Sarajevo and, due to its high red soil content, is often known as the Red River. The source of the Miljacka is in the mountains looming over Sarajevo at the Romanija, near Pale

A view of Sarajevo down the Miljacka river

The Una as it rushes through the Una National Park

(see p. 230). A few kilometres west of Sarajevo the Miljacka flows into the Bosna.

In Sarajevo, the river runs parallel to Obala Kulina Bana and the Zmaja od Bosne boulevard, the two main thoroughfares through the city. The most famous of the many bridges over the Miljacka is the Latin Bridge where Hapsburg heir to the throne Archduke Franz Ferdinand was assassinated on the 28th of June 1914 (see p. 113). The assassination is widely perceived as the event that triggered the First World War. During the period of socialist Yugoslavia the bridge was named in honour of the assassin, Gavrilo Princip, however, in 1993 the bridge was renamed, receiving again its original name, the Latin Bridge.

The Bosnian singer Halid Bešlić published in 2008 a love song called Miljacka, which was a big hit in the states of the former Yugoslavia.

THE UNA

The Una is a tributary of the Sava and rises near Donja Suvaja in Croatia, on the border with Bosnia and Herzegovina. After 212 km

The upstream reaches of the Una are intersected by falls and rapids

it flows into the Sava at Kozarska Dubica. Between Novi Grad and its confluence with the Sava, it follows the border with Croatia. The Una is one of the defining characteristics of the Bosanska Krajina region and its namesake, the Una National Park.

The two most important tributaries of the Una are the similarly named Unac, which flows into the Una at Martin Brod, and the Sana, which joins the Una near Novi Grad. Larger towns along the Una are Bihać, Bosanska Krupa, Bosanska Novi Grad and Dubica. Between Bihać and Bosanska Krupa the Una flows through miles of canyons, while numerous rapids and waterfalls make the river's upstream reaches great for canoeing and rafting.

The high average discharge rate of 202 cubic metres per second at its source, the Una is just behind the Sava, the Drina and the Neretva as one of the major rivers of Bosnia and Herzegovina. Its catchment area covers an area of 9,368km². A special feature are its limestone formations (*Sedra*), which are caused by the high calcium content of the water.

THE BOSNA

The Bosna rises 10km west of Sarajevo at the foot of Mount Igman and, after 271km, ends at Bosanski Šamac where it flows into the Sava.

The source of the Bosna (*Vrelo Bosne*) at Ilidža is a hydrological attraction, as this large river pours directly from the mountain and is not formed by the union of several streams. The park at the source is a popular tourist destination (see p. 122). The main tributaries of the Bosna are the Miljacka, the Krivaja, the Spreča and the Lašva. Important cities along the Bosna are: Visoko, Kakanj, Zenica, Doboj, Modriča and Bosanski Šamac.

THE SAVA

The Sava forms the natural border between Bosnia and Herzegovina and Croatia. It rises from the territory of Triglav in Slovenia's Julian Alps and ends in Belgrade after 940km, where it flows into the Danube. The main tributaries of the Sava are the Una, the Vrbas, the Bosna and the Drina. With a mean flow of 1,513 cubic meters per second, the Sava is the largest river that feeds into the Danube. Its catchment area extends over 95,000 square kilometres; and the river is 940km long.

In Bosnia and Herzegovina, the largest towns on the banks of the Sava are Bosanski Šamac, Brčko and Srpski Brod.

Just after its source, the Bosna flows through Ilidža in Sarajevo

The gentle flow of the Sava

The Sava is navigable from the point where the Krupa flows into it at Sisak in Croatia. The lowlands that flank the Sava through its eastern marches are called Posavina (see p. 212).

At one point the Sava runs more or less parallel to the north-flowing Drava for 30 kilometres before performing a series of huge meanders from Šamac to Brčko and finally, after another 100 km, flowing into the Danube in Belgrade. The course of the Sava before it meets the Danube is, in geographical terms, part of the demarcation of the Balkan Peninsula.

THE KRIJAVA

The Krijava, whose name means "curvy river" or "crooked creek", is not a rich nor particularly long, deep or even famous river, however, it is ideal for being explored by bicycle and along its length there are numerous picnic spots, bathing areas and hiking trails. It is an ideal location for a day trip from Sarajevo. It flows through the town of Olovo and down to Zavidovići where it flows into the Bosna. The Krijava winds its way artistically through the mountains of eastern Bosnian through Zvijezda Smolin and flowing into a small tributary of the Bosna. It is very easy to reach as the small country road to the north of Olovo is fully paved but rarely visited. What's more, the Krijava does not have a particularly strong current so you can share its beauty only with other river lovers.

Fly Fishing

Fly fishing is very popular in Bosnia and Herzegovina. Fly fishing is a kind of angling that uses artificial bait, most often a 'fly', that is cast onto the surface of the water using a different kind of rod and tackle from other kinds of fishing. Fly fishing baits are made of all sorts of material, such as fur, plastic or bird feathers.

As a sport, fly fishing doesn't aim to bring as many fish as possible to the grill, instead, fish are caught, weighed, measured, categorized, and thrown back again. Fly fishing competitions are held on almost every river in Bosnia and Herzegovina.

THE ANCIENT FOREST OF PERUĆICA

A view of Maglić through the trees of the Perućica Forest

Guest writer: Georg von Graefe, forestry expert, Zurich

Occasionally, the great forests of the world have survived thanks to an almost inadvertent protection from man. This happened with Bosnia and Herzegovina's oldest national park, the Sutjeska National Park. During World War Two, Tito's Partisans hid from the Nazi occupiers in the rugged mountains hugging the northern slopes of Maglić, a mountain on the Montenegrin border. It was from this secluded camp that in 1943 the Partisans managed to rout a force of German, Croatian and Italian occupying troops in a battle that came to be seen as a turning point in the war. In memory of the battle and of the river now rich with legends of the socialist proto-state, the Sutjeska National Park – covering a respectable area of 175km^2 – was established in

The Perućica Forest can be a magical place

1962. Today, visitors to the National Park Centre in Tjentište will find what is a still spacious, if crumbling, visitor centre, that in its heyday welcomed hordes of schoolchildren from all over Yugoslavia. Any hike around the park is sure to lead visitors to innumerable war memorials commemorating the battle of Sutjeska and other achievements from WWII.

As well as war memorials, the park also contains one of the most impressive virgin forests in Europe. Hugging the northern slopes of Bosnia and Herzegovina's highest mountain, the 2,386 meter high Maglić, is the ancient forest of Perućica. Nestled in its craggy mountain home, the Perućica forest has been spared the ravages of human settlement mostly thanks to its inaccessibility. The boughs of beech, silver fir and black pine (a species found only here, which grows up to 50 metres high), create halls of rare beauty throughout the forest.

The primeval feel of the forest is accentuated by the 75 meter high Skakavac waterfall, formed by the Sutjeska river as it gouges out a canyon through the park. The source of another powerful river, the Neretva, the main river in Herzegovina, is just south of the park.

Virgin forests or ancient forests, such as Perućica, are those whose development has not been significantly disrupted by people, and are quite rare in Europe. During the long colonisation of the continent by people returning as the ice-age glaciers retreated, much of Europe's forested land ended up being used as arable or pastoral land and few European forests have remained as absolutely untouched as the ancient forest of Perućica. For botanists the Perućica forest is an important place of study and research, especially with regards to the processes of natural growth and decay in forested areas. For wildlife zoologists the perfect natural balance of the eco-system can be seen in the continuous settlement of large indigenous predators, such as bears and wolves. The fact that silver birch saplings thrive here is evidence that or the forest's neatly balanced eco-system and of its powers of rejuvenation. Hikers and other visitors often report being able to feel the natural eco-balance of this pristine and magical woodland environment.

A major motion picture, "The Battle of Sutjeska", was made about the battle in 1972 and featured Hollywood greats such as Richard Burton and Orson Welles.

The Skakavac Waterfall does nothing to detract from the magical forest environment

EXPERIENCE
BOSNIA
AND
HERZEGOVINA

Winter Sports
Rafting
Caving
The Neretva Gorge by Train
Scenic Drives
Hiking the Karst Rivers

The Una National Park
A Taste of Bosnia and Herzegovina

FOREWORD

Paragliders of the "Bjelasnica" extreme sports club from Sarajevo

Bosnia and Herzegovina offers visitors a wide and extensive range of activities and destinations. These range from classic walking or cycling holidays to rafting and climbing, skiing and any number of adventure sports. For those less interested in adrenaline-seeking, the country offers opportunities to immerse oneself in its Oriental atmosphere, discover its Hapsburg past, explore its varied townscapes, taste the many gastronomic delights or just enjoy the slower pace of traditional rural life.

On the following pages of "Bosnia and Herzegovina in Your Hands" we aim to show how there is no such thing as a typical tourist visit to Bosnia and Herzegovina and how the range of activities and experiences is limitless and will entice you to return again and again to this diverse and welcoming country.

There is no such thing as a typical visit to Bosnia and Herzegovina

WINTER SPORTS

Skiing at one of Bosnia and Herzegovina's resorts

Sarajevo and its surrounding local mountains Jahorina, Bjelasnica, Trebevic and Igman were the venue for the Olympic Winter Games in 1984. Bosnia and Herzegovina's capital was presented to sports fans in February 1984 as a tolerant and energetic city, passionate about winter sports. Winter sports giants such as Katarina Witt, Matti Nykänen and Jens Weißflog were 'discovered' in Sarajevo and many of them still have fond memories of the 1984 Olympics, the great atmosphere at the venues and the welcoming city itself. The infrastructure and sports facilities – from the biathlon and the ski jump to the bobsled and the ice-skating rink at Zetra – were the most advanced at the time. Sarajevo and its surroundings were to become an attractive, European winter sports destination after the Olympics. The mascot of the games, Vučko (the Little Wolf, see box on p. 62), was a

Snowboarding on Bjelasnica

The pleasure of European alpine skiing, without the crowds... or the cost!

symbol of the beginning of a new era of winter sport tourism in Bosnia and Herzegovina.

The Olympics are now three decades in the past and instead Sarajevo has tragically become known as a war zone rather than a winter sports paradise. The sports facilities were bombed in the fighting and the Olympic Village has now become an orphanage. Sadly, Sarajevo could not rely on the optimism and hope of the Winter Games to create a more positive future.

Over the last few years, albeit slowly, new winter sports infrastructure has been redeveloped. At the beginning of the new millennium only a few adventurous skiers and Olympics nostalgics ventured onto the partially mined slopes of Bjelasnica and Jahorina, however the number of winter visitors has since grown steadily. Today, visitors flock from all over the former Yugoslavia and increasing numbers of guests from the classic Alpine countries such as Austria, Italy, Switzerland and Germany spend their winter holidays in Bosnia and Herzegovina. The Olympic city of Sarajevo however has still not returned to its past glory. The development is a step in

the right direction and Bosnia and Herzegovina is today well worth visiting in winter.

The climatic conditions around Sarajevo, as well as the geographical and topographical conditions, mean that the city is well placed to compete with traditional winter sports resorts in Central Europe and the Alps – but with unbeatable value for money. The Jahorina and Bjelašnica ski resorts have plenty to offer off piste too. Bosnian ski resorts don't have traditional *après-ski* entertainments, however, they more than make up for this with *ćevapčići* grills, plenty of Balkan folk music and a great atmosphere.

In addition to the skiing areas close to Sarajevo, there is also the Vlašić Mountain near Travnik with functioning skiing facilities. Although Vlašić has only two ski-lifts, it is an ideal location for beginners, but may be a little unadventurous for advanced skiers. Also noteworthy are the magnificent scenic surroundings around Vlašić and the impressively appointed resort: the reserve ski-jump built for the Winter Olympics was destroyed during the war and its ruins stand as a reminder of those sad days.

More ski resorts can be found on the Kozara mountain near Prijedor, in Rostovo by Bugojno and on Bledinje in Herzegovina. These three mountains do not, however, guarantee snow but the facilities are still satisfactory and they afford local skiers and foreign visitors great locations to learn the ropes. More experienced skiers are, however, more likely to enjoy the Jahorina resort. This ski resort, at 1300 meters above sea level, in the immediate vicinity of Sarajevo, is worth a visit even for non-skiers and we are more than happy to include it in our guide!

JAHORINA

The Jahorina ski area is located 20km east of Sarajevo. It you do not have a car you can use one of the many ski-transfers and shuttle buses from Sarajevo. A number of hotels in Sarajevo can provide transport to the Jahorina Olympic Centre, for day-trippers from the capital, this is an interesting opportunity. However, to ski and snow enthusiasts we recommend a longer stay on Jahorina. The ski area offers excellent downhill and slalom slopes and its very own winter charm.

In 1984, Jahorina was reserved for the women's ski competitions. Tragically, the infrastructure built for this occasion – the hotels, holiday houses, roads, etc. – suffered tremendous damage during the war in the 1990s. The majority of the facilities built for the Olympics were bombed, destroyed or dismantled, while numerous sections of the pistes were mined and traces of the war are still visible in several places on Jahorina. In between the new hotels and modern lifts are burnt-out houses and ruined buildings. The war-ravaged buildings contrasted with new facilities make for a bizarre and novel skiing experience. Ultimately, however, you get used to the contrast and the pristine white slopes and the lively, cheerful bustle of the winter tourists will quickly wash away the sorrow of past events.

Jahorina has nine ski-lifts and three modern six-seater lifts were installed in recent years in addition to the old-school double chairlift from the time of the Winter Olympics, which takes skiers to the starting point of the women's slalom. Three drag lifts and lifts for children and beginners also mean that one is spoilt for choice with ways to get up the mountain. Jahorina covers just over 20km of slopes and extends from 1300 meters to 1889 meters above sea level, at its highest point, Ogorjelica. The lifts can transport 12,500 skiers per hour to the summit. The levels of difficulty of slopes range from beginner (blue) to the black slalom run, so there is

The winter wonderland that is Jahorina in winter

The snow-covered woods on Jahorina

something for every type of skier. Furthermore, the slopes are, for the most part, well operated by the state-owned corporation *Olimpijski Centar Jahorina*.

On average over recent years there has been approximately 175 days of snow on Jahorina during ski season, which usually lasts from October to early May. The February snow levels over the last ten years have averaged well over 1m, ensuring the ski resort has very good levels of snow and a long ski season. The prices for the daily ski pass are between €10 in low season and €16 in high season and weekly tickets cost €90 in high season and in low season €60.

Jahorina, which has served as a ski resort since 1952, has about 5,000 places to stay. Half of these are the many private pensions, apartments, condos, and small mountain cottages (*vikendica*). The other half of the beds on Jahorina are in hotels. The hotels range from the small, private and new (the Nebojša Hotel) to the large, government-owned and old (the Bistrica Hotel) while the rates for stays range from €5 in private

One of the hotels of the Jahorina ski resort

Jahorina is a resort on the rise with new cable cars planned for 2015

accommodation in the preseason up to €100 in high season and in newer hotels. In general, however, Jahorina primarily offers simple, and therefore affordable, accommodation. These days it's easy enough to book accommodation on Jahorina online, as well as travel agencies in Sarajevo. Numerous arrangements on Jahorina include half board and a lift ticket. Renting ski equipment on Jahorina is possible in all hotels as well as in the numerous shops on site. The cost of renting skiing equipment can be between €5 and €10 per day. For longer stays it is easy to negotiate a lower price. Ski schools – including for snowboarding – are also numerous on Jahorina.

The resort is made up of three different districts. Coming from Sarajevo and Pale you first reach Jahorina Poljice. This is the central point and essentially the heart of Jahorina. From Poljice, two ski lifts transport skiers to the summit. Numerous restaurants, steaming barbecue stalls and loud speakers surround the ski schools and create a sociable atmosphere. Below the hotel Rajska Dolina (which translates

Enjoy frequently perfect skiing conditions

Jahorina – The Professional's Point of View

Guest Writer: Mateja Knežević – Ski instructor

Although it is smaller and less well developed than the largest, most popular European resorts, Jahorina still has much to recommend it.

Until a few years ago the resort hadn't been renovated or upgraded since the 1984 Olympics but recently new lifts have been installed and the centre is clearly improving again – though it is still, sadly, far from being in any condition to host another Winter Olympics.

When compared to other European resorts, skiing on Jahorina is extremely affordable – even in comparison to other resorts in the region. This extends beyond the price of ski passes and equipment to the cost of off-piste spending such as accommodation, food & drink and entertainment – all of these are significantly cheaper than just about any other resort in Europe.

In recent years, several new, modern, well appointed hotels have sprung up – they offer all the mod-cons any visitor can expect and their appearance has definitely improved the Jahorina experience. The quality of apartments and other private accommodation is a bit more varied – often it includes large dormitories that aren't as private or as comfortable as hotel rooms. On the other hand, there are several well-appointed mountain cabins offering accommodation for groups of four to fifteen, that make for a unique and wonderful Jahorina experience.

Jahorina, like many resorts in South East Europe, doesn't offer much in the way of traditional *après ski* available at other European resorts but that isn't to say there is a lack of entertainment! Much of the entertainment occurs in a more 'Bosnian' setting, in other words in a *kafana*. Indeed, you often see kafanas full of people still fully kitted out for the slopes partying late into the night. That said, the larger hotels are beginning to lay on quite extensive entertainment programmes during the ski season.

Of course, Jahorina still has a way to go to becoming a fully-fledged member of the club of top European resorts. It needs to improve its facilities for beginners – the current beginners' slope is still quite hard to get to – and the resort could offer more off-piste activities for non-skiers and those still learning. However, serious skiers will not notice any of these shortcomings and will easily lose themselves in exploring the exciting slopes and enjoying the breathtaking views. In short, though it is still up and coming, Jahorina is a fantastic place to go skiing!

COMPLETE EQUIPMENT – ADULTS	Per day for three days or less	25 KM	12.90 EUR
COMPLETE EQUIPMENT – ADULTS	Per day for more than three days	20 KM	10.30 EUR
COMPLETE EQUIPMENT – CHILDREN	Per day for three days or less	20 KM	10.30 EUR
COMPLETE EQUIPMENT – CHILDREN	Per day for more than three days	15 KM	7.70 EUR
SNOW BOARDING EQUIPMENT	Per day for three days or less	25 KM	12.90 EUR
SNOW BOARDING EQUIPMENT	Per day for more than three days	20 KM	10.30 EUR
SKIING COURSE – 1 PERSON	1 Lesson	25 KM	12.90 EUR
SKIING COURSE – 2 PEOPLE	1 Lesson	40 KM	20.60 EUR
SKIING COURSE – 3 PEOPLE	1 Lesson	55 KM	28.30 EUR
SKIING COURSE – 4-5 PEOPLE	1 Lesson	70 KM	36 EUR

Vučko

Vučko is prevalent throughout Bosnia and Herzegovina, but especially in Sarajevo and on Jahorina. Vučko will greet you from restaurant menus and T-shirts and is still a regular in TV commercials and in toy stores. The Little Wolf (*vučko* is the Serbo-Croatian diminutive of wolf, *vuk*) was designed by the Slovenian designer Jože Trobec as the official mascot for the 1984 Winter Olympic Games. With its joyful appearance, it not only inspired the Olympic audience in the 80s, but is still the (unofficial) symbol of the city. In recent years especially Vučko has increasingly been making something of a comeback. The Little Wolf with his red skis and red scarf exemplifies a positive attitude and a bit of a departure from the constant visual reminders of the war of the 90s. Vučko is fast becoming a cult symbol for Yugonostalgics.

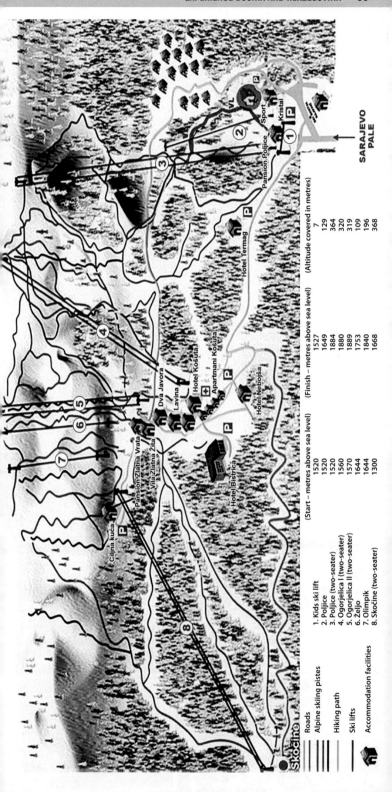

	(Start – metres above sea level)	(Finish – metres above sea level)	(Altitude covered in metres)
Roads			
Alpine skiing pistes			
1. Kids ski lift	1520	1527	7
2. Poljice	1520	1649	129
3. Poljice (two-seater)	1520	1884	364
4. Ogorjelica I (two-seater)	1560	1880	320
5. Ogorjelica II (two-seater)	1570	1889	319
Hiking path			
6. Željo	1644	1753	109
7. Olimpik	1644	1840	196
Ski lifts			
8. Skočine (two-seater)	1300	1668	368
Accommodation facilities			

SARAJEVO
PALE

as Valley of Heaven) is a large car park which is usually the start and end point of stays on Jahorina. From Poljice you can reach the Šalor Weekend settlement (*Vikend Naselje Šalor*) by following the road to the right of the car park. There is the majority of accommodation is of a small private hotels and lodges type. If you follow the street on your left after some 800 meters you will reach the valley of the Ogorjelica lifts and hotels Bistrica (clear water), Rajska Vrata (Heaven's Gate) and Lavina (avalanche). This rear part of Jahorina is slightly higher than Poljica and quieter and less frequented. All lifts and runs on Jahorina are connected and allow you to directly reach a slope from almost every hotel.

The special thing about skiing on Jahorina, besides the excellent and varied pistes, is the easygoing coexistence and cooperation of a modern, professional ski resort and charming, laid back Balkan chaos. On Jahorina one finds the high-tech lift chair with upholstery and windshields as well as the open metal lifts from the 70s. While the lift ticket on Jahorina is a modern smart card and together with the hotels offers wellness and spa packages to the modern customer, while local merchants grill ćevapčići and sell "rakija to go" for 1 Convertible Mark directly on the ski slopes. While a bombed-out building serves as an impromptu overnight and illegal *kafana*, which serves the best bean stew in the world by a roaring open fire. Just across the road is a new five star French restaurant, a perfect metaphor for the contrasts of Jahorina and Bosnia and Herzegovina as a whole – as are the cars parked out front, clapped out old Yugos right next to flash modern cars.

This mix between modernity and tradition is, in many places, underpinned by a significant Yugo-nostalgia. The visitors who flock to Jahorina come from all the republics of the former Yugoslavia and they have a common motivation for coming: a shared nostalgia for the good old days of the Winter Olympics and a love of winter sports, Balkan style.

RAFTING

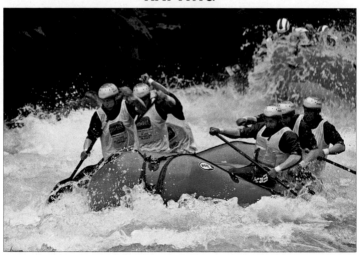

Rafting along the Vrbas, near Banja Luka

There is a growing trend of exploring the unique river landscapes of Bosnia and Herzegovina through rafting, a trend that is not only popular with young adventure sports enthusiasts, indeed there is something for everyone. With so many rivers offering such various degrees of difficulty, you do not have to be an extreme athlete to enjoy a rafting holiday. The watercourses are very different and the local tourism industry has adapted to this growing market and the specific needs of its visitors. A trip to one of the rafting centres is therefore recommended for everyone and anyone. There is no better way to access the canyons, to see the spectacular views of the rivers and waterfalls, or to experience Bosnia and Herzegovina in all its intensity – the only thing you need to be ready for is to get a bit wet. In Bosnia and Herzegovina the rivers are usually clear and clean and are wonderful for a quick dip whether you meant it or not.

Since it is not possible to list all the rivers of Bosnia and Herzegovina and the constantly increasing rafting excursions on offer, we have decided to single out rafting on the Tara. Of course, this does not mean that it may be less exciting or less beautiful on any of the other rivers. The Lim in Eastern Bosnia and Herzegovina near Višegrad should be mentioned here as an insider tip which offers experienced water sports enthusiasts a bit more of a challenge. Next to the Una river, the Tara is the most famous rafting destination in Bosnia and Herzegovina. The necessary facilities are in place and the various packages are flexible enough to offer a number of different rafting adventures.

RAFTING ON THE RIVER TARA

The 78km long Tara Canyon harbours depths up to 1300 meters, making it Europe's longest and deepest canyon. The majestic mountains and the perennial power of the river that has carved over millennia into the solid are impressive in their sheer power and size. The Tara forms a natural border with Montenegro, before it unites with the Pliva and the Drina. The course of the Tara is ideal for rafting due to its smooth descent and gentle curves, as well as the water's tempered pace.

Rafting along the cool canyon of the Tara is an ideal opportunity to take a break from Sarajevo during the searing

Rafting on the Tara

heat of the summer. An organized 1 day tour of Sarajevo starts early in the morning, at 6 or 7 o'clock, depending on the provider, and the departure is usually directly from your hotel or a central meeting place in the city centre. Usually a minibus will take you past Sarajevo airport in the direction of Foča.

As you leave the city, on the left you will see the Jahorina mountains and on the right the Treskavica mountains – offering a taste of the mountainous landscape to come. After about an

hour of driving the bus arrives to the area around Foča and thus the Drina. Now you are on Highway 5, which runs from Višegrad to Trebinje, and continues along the Montenegrin border. The road here is narrow but well developed. On its side you can see the deep canyon of the Drina and on the other side of up to 1,500 metres high mountain sides.

For most agencies base camp is usually the first stop of the tour. It serves as a starting point for the subsequent rafting destinations. In the base camp you will

The Treskavica mountains near Sarajevo

The green Tara carves a canyon through the landscape

usually be served a traditional breakfast menu – burek, yogurt, and Bosnian-style coffee. Then the organisational preparation begins, the organisers provide professional equipment, including wet shoes, helmets and life jackets. Once you are ready and geared up, minibuses take the groups to the starting point, which is actually in Montenegro. The border is initially crossed by land – a procedure that can often be quite drawn out, especially on the weekends and during the summer tourist season. The best way to get through the long wait – sometimes more than two hours – is to enjoy the views of the mighty mountains and the merry rounds made by the obligatory *rakija* bottle – something of a tradition when setting off on a rafting trip in these parts.

About 5km after crossing the border and a bit of bouncing around on dirt roads, you reach the starting point of the rafting tour. The local skippers wait with the rafts which can accommodate 6-10 people while you quickly test how cold the Tara really can be and become resolved to reduce any chance of an involuntary swim.

Following a brief instruction to rowing techniques by the skipper and what to do in the event that the raft capsizes – i.e. don't panic – the tour begins. It is usual for several boats to start in a row. So there is an opportunity for a boat race or some friendly splashing. The speed of the rafts can depend on the season, the water level and how adventurous the group is feeling – but most of the time you move pretty fast. There is one thing which is guaranteed; no matter where you position yourself in the boat and regardless of whether one belongs to a rather quiet or a dynamic steering group – you will definitely get wet. The valuables that you don't want to leave behind at the base camp can be deposited with the skipper in a

A traditional breakfast menu – burek, yogurt

waterproof swimming bag.

How much actual rowing you do depends on the water level (which changes depending on the time of year): at times the raft will simply flow down the river, propelled by the current, but at other times the rapids, the rocks and water resistance mean you will have to be more active to stay on course. As each boat is commandeered by an experienced local skipper, who can in theory do all the work on his own, it is ultimately up to you how much you want to help out – alternatively, you can just sit back and enjoy the ride.

The journey is usually interrupted two or three times for a rest and it is possible to take a quick swim or look for unique photo opportunities. The more energetic adventurers like to climb the rocks to plunge into the clear waters of the Tara. At the halfway point, drinks are served at a makeshift resting place and usually this is the point even the most resolute lose their fear of the cold water.

Finally, you will pass under the bridge which crosses the Bosnia and Herzegovina-Montenegro border. During the first leg of the trip you are flanked on either side by two countries, Montenegro on the left and Bosnia and Herzegovina on the right but once you pass the confluence with the Pliva, you are back on the territory of Herzegovina. The Pliva and Tara come together to make the Drina and the scenery and character of the river is different from this point on. The shore becomes more sandy and light and the river assumes the characteristic green colour the Drina is famous for.

After the final, quieter section you return to the base camp and once there you can take a relaxing swim again in the Tara. After a hearty feast on an open fire the bus takes you back to Sarajevo.

For those interested in a longer stay on the river there are many camps along the Tara and the upper reaches of the Drina with suitable accommodation. Most campsites also offer simple accommodation in rustic wood cabins. Thanks to the growing popularity of rafting the facilities of these campsites have greatly improved in recent times. A longer stay in this peaceful, natural environment, far from the stress and noise of the cities, offers many opportunities for relaxing hikes, climbing and swimming. Also, if you do decide to stay longer, there are many possible excursions from the canyon, including the nearby Sutjeska National Park and Bosnia and Herzegovina's highest peak, Mount Maglić (see p. 244).

Base camp is usually the first stop of the tour

CAVING

Cave drawings in the Vjetrenica Cave

Bosnia and Herzegovina is downright full of caves thanks to its karst landscape – due to its water permeability karst is the ideal terrain for cave formation. Amongst cavers around the world Bosnia and Herzegovina has gained a reputation as a bit of a cave paradise, this is also because its numerous caves have only been partially explored, if at all!

The particularly spectacular Hrustovačka cave was discovered in the vicinity of Ključ, and we are keen to present some of the lesser known caves, besides the better known Vjetrenica, Bijambare and Orolovača. In addition to these four caves there are thousands of other caves in Bosnia and Herzegovina and new caves are still being discovered all the time.

HRUSTOVAČKA - THE FORGOTTEN STALACTITE CAVE

The most interesting from the caver's perspective is the Hrustovačka cave. It is located about halfway between the

Dabarska Cave, just one of the many more to discover in Bosnia and Herzegovina

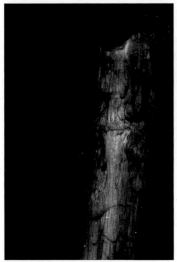

Rock formations in the Hrustovača Cave

cities of Ključ and Sanski Most, near the village of Hrustovo, the namesake of the cave. The relatively large entrance of the cave is located in a slightly elevated little forest behind the village exit. Shortly after the entrance into the Hrustovačka cave one comes upon stalagmite and stalactite formations millions of years old.

After about 400 meters, the cave splits off in two directions, the right section is huge and is probably the older of the two. In quite a few places the cave ceiling is five or even ten metres above the visitor's heads. After about 800 metres the two sections rejoin in a long, high chamber.

The section that leads off to the left is longer but this part of the cave also contains fewer stalagmite and stalactite formations. While the right arm can be explored easily and up to a short narrowing without much physical exertion, you do however have to overcome a number of bodies of water, negotiate boulders and pass through narrow gaps in the left section. According to local guides, no other exit from the cave has ever been discovered. Please do not attempt to negotiate the caves without sturdy footwear, warm clothing and other appropriate equipment.

About two and a half hours into the cave's left arm you will come across the first of its lakes, a second lake is after some 4 hours of walking further in. Only legends have made it further than the second lake. One of these says that, during the First World War, a group of farmers managed to find their way all the way to Jajce (about 70km away) through the cave. No one has so far been able to confirm whether this legend is anything more than a tall story conjured up by local peasants. So far, there is very

The entrance to the Hrustovača Cave

little "scientific" information about the cave and the relevant Bosnian ministries and university research centres seem to have no detailed information regarding the cave. An exploratory venture initiated by Swiss cave exploration experts came to the conclusion that the cave air is completely harmless for humans and that in fact there is a continuous flow of air to be found in the cave. This air movement is easily noticeable in the narrow cave passages and therefore suggests that there must be another entrance to the cave somewhere.

VJETRENICA

Vjetrenica is the longest known cave in Bosnia and Herzegovina. It extends below the Ravno karst field in the town of Popovo Polje, the southwestern-most town in Herzegovina. The cave is about 6,500 meters long and characterized by its numerous pools and small waterfalls. The largest lake in the cave – and the cave's most well known landmark – is 180 meters long. The name of the cave derives from the Bosnian term for wind (*vjetar*) and points out that a particularly strong wind blows through the cave. The cave is home to rare plant and animal species and is one of the few European caves with an abundance of flora and fauna.

Stalactites descend from the ceiling of Hrustovača Cave

BIJAMBARE

Due to their easy accessibility the five Bijambare Caves – just off the M18 highway between Sarajevo and Tuzla – are the most visited and developed caves in Bosnia and Herzegovina. Bijambare caves are located in the 400 acre Bijambare nature reserve. The caves and the reserve are a well-known recreational and health resort. The largest and longest of the Bijambare caves is 420 meters

The Vjetrenica Cave, the longest cave in Bosnia and Herzegovina

An impressive cavern in the Bijambare Caves

long and has an imposing main cavern, which is 60 meters wide and 30 meters high. It is nicknamed the concert hall because of its dimensions and acoustics. There are numerous stalagmite and stalactite formations to be discovered in the Bijambare caves.

ORLOVAČA

The Orlovača cave is located in the Romanija above Sarajevo and can be reached from the capital in about 30 minutes. The Orlovača cave offers a wealth of magnificent stalagmites and stalactites. The cave is accessible and well lit, making the stalactites in the cave look particularly colourful. Near the entrance to the cave there is a spring, the source of the River Sinjevo.

The Orlovača Cave

THE NERETVA GORGE BY TRAIN

It is possible to experience a truly unique day in Bosnia and Herzegovina by riding a train along the River Neretva from, Sarajevo to Mostar (and back again). This may not be the most glamorous and luxurious travel option, but it's certainly the prettiest and is sure to leave you with lasting memories.

Before setting off on the railway journey, you should be aware of two things. First, a train ride in Bosnia and Herzegovina is a journey into the history of the Hapsburgs and second: the fact that Bosnia and Herzegovina has three railway companies split along ethnic lines means that, as is the case with so many projects in Bosnia and Herzegovina, any attempted improvements to the rail infrastructure may be difficult to discern.

Construction of the narrow gauge line (760mm) from Mostar to Sarajevo began in 1886 and was completed in an impressive five years – the completion date was in August 1891. Particularly impressive considering the total length of the line is some 135 kilometres. The construction work was carried out in three sections:

The Swedish carriages of the Sarajevo-Mostar line

Mostar to Ostrožac (66km), Ostrožac to Konjić (13km), Konjic to Sarajevo (55km). The last section of line, from Konjic to Sarajevo, and the sections along the Neretva gorge itself, were an engineering masterpiece in their day and still remain impressive today. The line had to be dynamited through the rock massif along the Neretva river and is supported by stone pillars along much of the route. Also, to successfully negotiate Mount Ivan, the line had to employ an innovative cog and pinion system in order to cope with the hairpin bends and the astounding 60% gradient!

The carriages used on the Neretva line are of Swedish design and exude a nostalgic, old world charm. The lounge car, in particular, with its roomy chairs and ample leg room, is pleasant for all travellers but exciting for railway enthusiasts. The cars were donated during the 1990s by the Swedish state railway company and to this day still carry Swedish labels and signs.

The journey along the Neretva begins in Sarajevo train station at around 7am in the morning and ends there again in the evening at 10pm. As is often the case with vintage railways, the exact time of departure and return time may depend on the 'mood' of the train. In general, train delays are not uncommon in Bosnia and Herzegovina but as you are on holiday there is no reason not to take these small setbacks in your stride.

For the first hour of the two and a half hour train ride the train rumbles

An impressive cavern in the Bijambare Caves

Mountain huts on Bjelasnica

through the Sarajevo suburbs which may be devoid of beautiful scenery but are nonetheless interesting for the abandoned industrial landscape and communist-era housing blocks. You will also pass a large number of decrepit freight cars and kilometres and kilometres of overgrown track, a reminder that in days now long gone, the railway was an important part of the country's transportation infrastructure.

Beyond Sarajevo the train will climb to its highest point, 877m above sea level, between the peaks of Bjelasnica and Vučevo, before embarking on a journey of S-bends down and through the valley of the Neretva River.

Beyond Konjic, the first station along the Neretva Valley, the river transforms into the 31km long man-made Jablanica Lake (*Jablaničko Jezero*), a result of the dam at Jablanica.

Take the time to explore Mostar

On this section the line crosses bridges across the river frequently, to the delight of the passengers. After Jablanica, the Neretva valley narrows steadily and the river and the railway line sailing along its banks become surrounded by almost vertical rock faces 1,000 metres high. The emerald green waters of the Neretva paired with the blue sky and gray rock of the gorge are an unforgettable sight. A few kilometers before Mostar, the Neretva valley opens out onto the orchard covered plains of Herzegovina. You will reach Mostar in two and a half hours (and change) and

Lake Jablanica

it will be time to take your leave from the comfort of the Swedish wagons. Exploring the town of Mostar (see p. 134) is best done on foot and, for those who enjoyed the train ride, the return journey to Sarajevo is at 7pm.

The Battle of the Neretva

The part of the Neretva close to the Jablanica dam was the scene of an epic battle in World War II. In the spring of 1943 a large joint force of German, Italian and Croatian units sought to wipe out Tito's Partisans once and for all. Their aim was to complete the destruction of their foes in three phases, the first of which were successful and the Partisans found themselves surrounded with their backs to the Neretva. The crucial third phase was planned for March of that year, with the occupiers feeling confident of victory. However, a strategic masterstroke by Tito changed the situation completely. Tito ordered the destruction of the only bridge across the Neretva that could serve as an escape route to the mountainous hinterland to the south. As a result, the Germans and their allies expected the Partisans to attempt to break out of the encirclement in a northerly direction and positioned their troops to prevent this. Tito anticipated this and in one foggy night his engineers laid down a temporary bridge across the Neretva, enabling them to escape the encirclement. When the Germans realised that their prey was escaping, they gave chase but the Partisans blew the bridge up again.

The destroyed bridge can still be seen in Jablanica and a museum devoted to the battle gives visitors more information. In 1969 Tito ordered the filming of a Hollywood-style movie devoted to the battle, "The Battle of the Neretva", starring Yul Brunner and Hardy Kruger and which was nominated for an Oscar for Best Foreign Film in 1970.

SCENIC DRIVES

The Pionirski Put offers views of the Drina Canyon

To experience landscape and nature of Bosnia and Herzegovina and enjoy the visit we recommend it is approached either on foot or by bicycle. However, not all the land can be traveled easily and if going by bicycle it is a good idea to get more information and prepare in advance. We provide you here with four suggestions on the routes that you can enjoy and where you will find a wide range of experiences with fascinating landscapes if traversed by car or motorbike.

VIŠEGRAD - USTIPRAČA (M5)

The M5 highway runs parallel to the River Drina and has numerous places with great views of the shimmering green river. The so-called 'Pioneer Road' (*Pionirski Put*) was built in 1988 and has more than 30 tunnels through the mountainous karst landscape. During the summer months, motorcyclists particularly enjoy this road with its many twists and turns but good road surface all the way to the Drina Canyon.

Hutovo Blato

The canyon of the Vrbas between Banja Luka and Jajce

Tip: take the bridge crossing onto the southern side of the river, halfway between Višegrad and Ustipraca in the village of Meremišlje and follow the course of the River Lim. The landscapes will take your breath away and with not a soul in sight.

THE COUNTRY ROAD FROM HUTOVO TO NEUM

Neum is the only town in Bosnia and Herzegovina that is on the Adriatic coast. It is usually approached via Croatia and the M8 highway but there is also an old through road over the mountain Zaba. Hutovo is in the Neretva Valley where countless serpentines along the narrow uphill road lead to the abandoned hamlet of Gradac and down to the Adriatic Coast. The scenery along the 35 km long route transforms before your eyes from lush and fertile to arid and barren. The woods are well known for annual forest fires so please take care. Along the route you come across a Marian shrine and numerous stone villages, which still exist in these parts. After about an hour you will be treated to glorious views of the Adriatic Sea.

BANJA LUKA - JAJCE (M16)

The canyon of the Vrbas is without a doubt one of the scenic highlights of Bosnia and Herzegovina. Thanks to the M16 highway the canyon can easily be reached and explored giving it its international reputation as a venue for numerous kayak and rafting competitions. The M16 highway partly follows the flow of the Vrbas, but also at certain points the road is some one hundred meters above the river. It is possible to park and take pictures at numerous points along the route or even to pause and take a refreshing dip in the cool waters of the Vrbas along the way. The 68 kilometre route from Banja Luka to Jajce crosses the Vrbas 3 times.

ŠIPOVO – KUPREŠ

The road from Šipovo on the Pliva to Kupreš along the Herzegovina Plateau is well made and blissfully traffic-free. From Šipovo, follow the River Janj and then wind up the mountain road to the karst field (see p. 42) at 1,000 metres above sea level. Along the road you will notice numerous karst sinkholes. This route is very much suitable for motorcyclists.

A waterfall on the Janj river near Šipovo

HIKING THE KARST RIVERS: THE SANA, SANICA AND RIBNIK

The stunning clear waters of the Sana close to its source

Karst springs are known for their crystal clear, turquoise shimmering water and numerous such springs can be found throughout Bosnia and Herzegovina. Three such springs, easily reachable by one-day hikes can be found in Bosanska Krajina (see p. 149). And don't worry: there are definitely no mines along these walks.

The River **Sana** is nearly 150 kilometres long and is one of the longest rivers in Bosnia and Herzegovina. Her clean spring water certainly impressed the Romans, who gave the river her name (*Sanus* is Latin for "health"). The six mile walk to the source of the Sana begins where civilization ends: in Donji Vrbljani. Donji Vrbljani is a sleepy little village in the municipality of Ribnik, near the town of Ključ (see p. 173), where the paved road ends and a winding two-hour trail through the green hills of Bosanska Krajina begins. Following maps or marked routes is unlikely to be of much use, which is why we recommend organising a local guide for this hike. Along the way there are many abandoned houses and dilapidated, overgrown mountain

cemeteries whose graves mark the way. Locals, usually old men and women, often appear spooked by the sight of foreign travellers, hunched over under their hiking packs but are always happy to point the way to the *izvor* (source).

From the valley the trail leads up a small hill to three abandoned farmhouses that were once a cheerful homestead. Following the trail that goes around the face of the mountain, through lush green meadows, the view of the valley is like a glimpse into a long forgotten past of almost alpine meadows, picturesque wooden mountain huts, ancient stone walls overgrown with lichen and moss.

The rocky trail begins to descend slowly and brings us into the valley from which the Sana springs. A dilapidated, but still usable wooden bridge leads over the first glimpse of clear water, only a few hundred metres from the source. Even during the hot Balkan summers, the temperature of the water is never much more than 10° Celsius. No good for swimming – unless you are feeling particularly hardy – but just right for drinking.

The valley of the Sana river

Following the river, the trail meanders along through scrubby woods – quite a challenging hike. After about 500 meters, there is another river crossing, a simple wooden bridge, about seven meters wide, that has seen better times and consists only of loose boards which are held together by wires. But despite its apparent structural deficiencies the bridge is sound enough for the crossing to be effortless.

The last two hundred metres to the spring lead you through lush deciduous woods. The spring itself is like a big, rocky cave entrance leading into the karst massif and resonating

with the roar of the clear water of the source. The forces of nature are palpable and the cooling effect of the water and the mountain lend the immediate area an almost autumnal feel even in the midsummer heat.

The spring is not easy to find. There are no signs and following the path is an adventure in itself, but well worth the effort! The river and the area around it are almost completely unspoilt by tourists – something that is evidently good for the natural environment.

Finding and reaching the source of the **Ribnik** is comparatively much

The stunning landscape around Gornji Ribnik

The emerald green waters of the Sanica near its source

easier. The source lies just south of the village of Gornji Ribnik, which is itself just to the north of Donji Vrbljani. It is possible to get within around 500 meters of it by car and the trail to the source is clearly signposted and not particularly demanding. Locals have built a small dam near the source in order to divert some of the water to a nearby trout farm and the resulting lake offers crystal clear, turquoise waters ideal for a swim in warm weather. Please be aware, however, that the water temperature is unlikely to be much above 10° Celsius.

The source of the **Sanica** worth visiting and easy to reach, being as it is just 17km north-west of Ključ, near the village of the same name. It's possible to get within a mile of the source by car. To get to the source, cross the bridge that is just behind the old sawmill in the centre of Sanica and follow the river upstream. You can also park your car just by the bridge. Reaching the source is well worth the short hike. The powerful flow of the Sanica squeezes through a narrow gorge of karst rocks and emerges as a fully formed river several metres wide.

The source of the Sanica has yet another gem to offer visitors. About 100 metres downstream from the bridge is the famous trout restaurant Pajo's "Ribnjak" (fish pond). The fish soup and freshly grilled trout are of exceptional quality and in terms of taste and presentation, without rival in Bosnia and Herzegovina. Pajo's cooking is well known and well regarded locally but people also come from as far away as Sarajevo and Zagreb to enjoy grilled trout by the Sanica.

The spring of the Sanica

THE UNA NATIONAL PARK

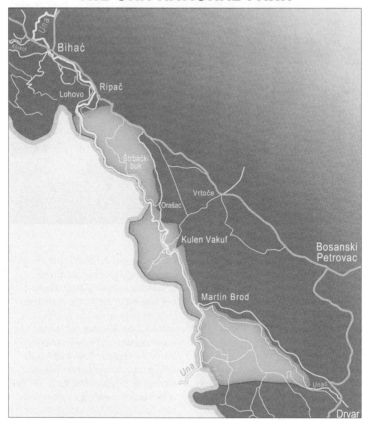

The Una National Park is a scenic unspoiled nature reserve and one of the most interesting and beautiful landscapes in Southeast Europe. The canyon of the Una is ideal for hiking, biking, boating, rafting, fishing, diving and swimming. Because of its remoteness and the simple tourist offer it makes it possible to meet Bosnia and Herzegovina unadorned and in an authentic way.

Along the Una, where the two rivers Krka and Unac flow within the National Park, numerous natural wonders can be discovered and admired: smaller and larger waterfalls, natural stowage locations and rapids, cascade-like limestone formations (*Sedra*) and numerous exchanges between calm waters and torrential flow. The bed of the river Una has dug deep into the Dinaric Alps and is surrounded by the 1,000 meters high peaks of the mountains Osječenica, Grmeč and Pelješevica. This contrast between the green, fertile river valley and the rugged peaks is one of the main features of the Una National Park.

The Una National Park was founded in 2008 by the Government of the Federation. The aim is on the one hand protecting and preserving the flora and fauna of the upper reaches of the Una and the promotion of sustainable, nature-based tourism in the region. The total area of the protected Una National Park is 19,800ha with two-thirds of this area (13500 ha) defined as untouchable and completely free from human influence. The idea to develop the Una National Park for sustainable tourism is still in

Waterfalls of the Una

its infancy. Biking and hiking trails are in the making and newly-appointed ranchers monitor compliance with the rules for visitors, which also apply to the few people living within the park in the settlements Orašac, Kulen Vakuf and Martin Brod.

It is located in close proximity to the Croatian Plitvice Lakes National Park which is visited annually by millions of tourists and is fully commercially exploited. Environmental protection is a priority of the Croatian Plitvice Lakes National Park but is not always implemented properly. Suffice to say, the Una National Park should not necessarily follow the model of its sister park across the border. A unique individual day out instead of mass-tourism, and relaxed walking instead of organized bus tours, is the long-term goal and the development concept of Una National Park. The first steps towards building a sustainable high quality holiday destination are completed. Now we can only hope that both the nature park management

The Una National Park

The rapids of the Una

and the local tourism organization and especially the private owners of pubs, rafting agencies, campsites and hostels abide by the rules imposed and do not succumb to the temptation of easy money at the expense of nature. The badly war-torn region around Bihać could become one of the most valuable natural landscapes in Bosnia and Herzegovina and the Una National Park could earn a place among the country's most prized tourist attractions.

The source of the Una is on the Croatian side of the border, below the Čemernica mountains at Donja Suvaja. The underground karst spring that gives life to the Una also gives it its deep turquoise colour. The Krka, one of the Una's tributaries, flows into the Una precisely on the Bosnia and Herzegovina-Croatia border, 5km above the village of Cvjetnić. The short flow of the Krka forms the boundary lines between Bosnia and Herzegovina and Croatia. Beyond the town of Martin Brod and its spectacular waterfall, another tributary, the Unac, also joins the Una. The source of the Unac is located 66km away in the Šator mountains and, on its way to meet the Una, the Unac has ten tributaries of its own.

From the Una-Unac confluence, the Una flows for about 50km before it reaches Bihać. From there it continues through Bosanska Krupa and Novi Grad to its confluence with the Sava. With a descent averaging 3 meters per kilometre within the National Park, the Una is characterised by its many waterfalls and rapids. The most spectacular waterfalls plunge into Martin Brod and down onto Strbački Bug. Shortly before Lohovo there also double and triple waterfalls (*dvoslap* and *troslap*), which form the climax and conclusion of most rafting trips on the Una. While a boat (with a skilled skipper) can mostly cope with the double rapids without its passengers getting wet, this is not possible with the infamous Strbački Bug. This 20m high waterfall has to be bypassed on foot, while the boats are manhandled down the sides of the waterfall.

The starting point for trips to the Una National Park is Bihać, opposite the hotel where you can find the Park's official information centre. There, both current information on events, tours and activities can be obtained, and also the information on available rooms and campsites. The information centre is still in the development phase and this

The Una passes through Lahovo

also applies to the development and expansion of the rest of the infrastructure within the park. Bike paths and a hiking park are still to be created while the signs for these are already set up and they are already present on the maps and in brochures. Therefore you should seek local advice before taking these trips to check whether they are ready for tourists. A second, smaller information centre is operated by the National Park in Martin Brod, inside the national park.

In addition to offering rafting the Una National Park can be enjoyed mainly

for hiking and cycling. For a nice walk, for example, begin at **Lahovo**, the northernmost point of the park. Here you will also find a number of base stations and camps of the rafting agencies. From there you can reach in about 30 easy minutes the *dvoslap* and *troslap* rapids. Along the shore there are a number of small restaurants which have settled there and offer fresh grilled fish straight from the river Una.

The 20m high waterfall **Strubački Bug** is easily reached by a boat during a rafting tour, or – easier and

A view of Kulen Vakuf from the Ostrovica fortress

The falls at Martin Brod

less adrenaline-pumping – by car or bicycle via Orašac. From Orašac, via a dirt track through the middle of the National Park, you can reach the park gatehouse where you will be asked to pay 5 Convertible Marks as an entrance fee before you can cover the last 1.5 kilometres to the waterfall. Don't miss the view of the waterfall from the wooden bridge!

The town of **Kulen Vakuf** has a small private campground, which is located right on the river Una and is an ideal base and starting point. The camp site belongs to the "Discover"

rafting agency and also offers rooms with breakfast. The covered terrace above the Una offers sublime views of the river. From the camp, you get to walk to the fortress Ostrovica. This is located above the village of Kulen Vakuf and dates from the early 15th Century. The fort is now in ruins, however the structure of the old building is recognizable.

The road from Kulen Vakuf to Martin Brod runs along the left bank of the Una and the rest facilities offer great spots for picnics and fishing. On the right bank of the Una a

Fishing on the Una

trail from Kulen Vakuf leads to the **waterfall of Martin Brod**, 7 km away. One of the first decisions of the national park administration was the establishment of a new ridge below the waterfalls. Just as at Strubački Bug, an entrance fee is payable here (this was 2 Convertible Marks at the time of writing). In Martin Brod there is the Serbian Orthodox monastery Rmanj from the 14th century. The beginning of the canyon, just beyond the Unac, is not accessible to visitors. A gastronomic tip in Martin Brod: the unassuming seafood restaurant by Zora can be found just before the entrance to the waterfall. In Martin Brod there is an information office where you can hire mountain bikes at the rate of 3 Convertible Marks per hour. With these one can easily ride to the waterfall and the small town Očigrije on the opposite bank.

The climatic conditions within the Una National Park provide a wide variety of species and a colourful flora. Numerous rare plant species such as gentian, edelweiss and juniper are native to the National Park, as well as the Una Bellflower, which owes its name to the river and the Bosnian iris. More than **1,900** different **plant species** and over **60 species of mammals** are native along the Una.

Including the three largest European predators: wolves, lynx and brown bear. It is unlikely that you will meet them in the flesh as they live primarily in the non-accessible parts of the National Park. The National Park is a rich habitat for over 120 species of birds, including the rare Black Grouse but also Common Grouse, Corn Rake and numerous varieties of Snaps, Hawks, Owls and Woodpeckers. For ornithologists and birdwatchers the National Park offers bird-watching tours and excursions. The park is also home to a broad range of reptiles such as lizards, snakes and terrapins. The European viper is the largest snake in the National Park and can grow up to one meter long.

Anglers must also pay to use the National Park. The fishing season extends from spring to late September. Information about terms and conditions for fishing can be obtained from the management of the National Park, and if you are into fly fishing it is widespread in Bosnia and Herzegovina and possible in the Una National Park. The Una and Unac have some 28 species of fish with the largest being the salmon, which can be up to 30 kg. Trout, grayling, whitefish and minnows are also widespread.

The Rmanj Serbian Orthodox Monastery near Martin Brod

A TASTE OF BOSNIA AND HERZEGOV...

A very traditional tea service

The cuisine of Bosnia and Herzegovina is rich and varied in a way that reflects the cultural and climatic diversity of the country. One can expect to encounter light, Mediterranean-style cuisine just as readily as rustic home cooking. Desserts range from Austrian-style apple strudel to baklava just as mouth-watering as you might encounter in Istanbul. Similarly, the drinks menu varies from Oriental chai (*čaj*) to white wine spritzer (*špricer*). One thing no visitor can fail to notice; in Bosnia and Herzegovina, food and drink are both plentiful and satisfyingly abundant.

Meat plays an important part and features frequently in the country's traditional cooking. Although, it can be said that, as a rule, Bosnian cooking is less dependent on meat

The cuisine of Bosnia and Herzegovina is hearty and satisfying

A plate of *ćevapčići* and a skewer

that that of neighbouring countries, such as Serbia and seasonal vegetables are just as important a component. Most fresh produce is purchased directly from the farmers at the many local markets or grown in vegetable patches. The main result of this is that the quality of ingredients, sourced locally, is generally very high. Global trends such as ready meals and flavour enhancers have, however, also begun to get a foothold in Bosnia and Herzegovina. Alas, the often traditional cuisine is beset on all sides by the seemingly unstoppable advance of frozen pizza and fast food.

A traditional meal in Bosnia and Herzegovina begins with a soup course, as a local saying has it: at least one dish a day should be 'taken with a spoon'. During the week this part of the meal is traditionally a stew but family lunches on the weekend usually include a soup (**supa**) – most often homemade veal soup. Easily the most famous main dish in Bosnia and Herzegovina is a serving of *ćevapčići*; small, mincemeat kebabs which are rarely prepared

at home, but eaten in one of the numerous ćevapčinićas (ćevapčići houses). Fat red peppers stuffed with minced meat and rice (**punjene paprike**) and similarly filled sour kraut rolls (**sarma**) are the most common main dishes prepared in traditional home cooking.

Grilled or, more commonly, slowly roasted meat – lamb (**jagnjetina**) or pork (**prasetina**) – are so popular

Stuffed peppers (*punjene paprike*) are a popular dish

Bosnian cuisine is rich with a wide and varied range of filled pastries

as to almost be mandatory at every major family event or every special occasion. While cooking in Bosnia and Herzegovina largely remains a female-dominated activity, the ceremonial spit-roasting of lamb and pork is traditionally a task for the men. A common side dish for roast meat are potatoes braised under the *sač* – this refers to a local technique of stewing vegetables or meat deep in a charcoal fired stone oven.

Bread (*hleb* or *kruh*) is an obligatory accompaniment to any meal, whether soup, stew or main course and pasta is also an integral part of everyday cuisine. More intricate baked goods include widely popular puff pastry dishes such as *burek* and *pita*.

The impact of Oriental cuisine is inescapable in Bosnia and Herzegovina and this is especially evident in the most popular desserts.

Turkish-style desserts like baklava are popular and usually extremely well made

Baklava, rich with walnuts almonds and pistachio and sweetened with a sugary syrup is originally from the Middle East. **Halva**, another equally popular Turkish sweet, is made with sesame paste and honey and is locally garnished with nuts, almonds or dried fruit.

In terms of non-alcoholic drinks, the range of options in Bosnia and Herzegovina is not so widely different to the rest of Europe, however, the oriental influence is also to be recognized here. Bosnian-style coffee is served everywhere and a drinking yoghurt is a common accompaniment to every breakfast. In spite of the strong Islamic influence, alcoholic drinks are widely consumed but generally in moderate quantities.

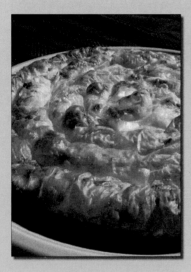

Burek

Pastry dishes in Bosnia and Herzegovina come in many shapes and sizes. The most ubiquitous and the dish that the country is most famous for is *burek*. *Burek* is a meat stuffed pastry, which is best eaten fresh from a baking dish that is buried in hot coals. Burek is sometimes a catch-all term for similar pastries but is more properly a term for just the meat variety. Similar dishes with fillings as varied as cheese, greens (such as spinach) or sweet jams or fruit fillings are more properly called pita (pie). Don't miss a chance to try as many of these filling, hearty pastries – either as a late night snack or a filling breakfast.

Kajmak

Kajmak is a typical dairy product as popular in Bosnia and Herzegovina as elsewhere in the former Yugoslavia. It resembles a thick cream but has a unique flavour and texture. It is prepared by slowly heating cow's milk, fresh from the cow. The resulting crème de la crème is gradually siphoned off and then allowed to cool. Kajmak, like many varieties of cream is not only a popular spread but is also served as an accompaniment to main dishes and stews. If you ask a Bosnian living abroad which food he misses most, the response will almost certainly be kajmak.

Fildžan and Džezva

Bosnian Turkish-style coffee is served in a *fildžan*, a small cup without a handle. The coffee is brewed in a small copper vessel with an extended handle, called a *džezva*. For best results water is heated in the džezva almost to boiling point, then a very large heaped teaspoon of freshly ground coffee is added. Bosnian coffee is traditionally sweetened with lots of sugar. Traditional handmade copper fildžan and džezva sets are on sale throughout Baščaršija (see p. 109).

Rakija

Fruit-based spirits or brandies (*rakija*) are a specialty with local varieties all over the former Yugoslavia. In Bosnia, the most common of these is plum brandy (*šljivovica*), which is made and consumed with equal enthusiasm. This spirit, often with an alcohol content of around 40%, is often made at home and for personal use or for sale to friends and acquaintances. Šljivovica made by registered producers is in the shops but is not necessarily recommended. The best way to get your plum brandy is straight from the farmer, you can then be sure it is free of any additives. This local liquor is sometimes sold at the roadside or at farmers' markets, often in re-used Coca-Cola bottles.

Ćevapčići

Ćevapčići are Bosnia and Herzegovina's most famous fast food. Ćevapčići (the diminutive of ćevapi) are rolled mincemeat kebabs popular throughout the Balkans but with regional differences. In Bosnia and Herzegovina ćevapčići are smaller and less likely to be made with pork. Minced beef is mixed with salt, pepper, paprika and a little garlic. The ćevapčići are usually grilled and served with pita bread (lepinja), Ajvar and diced onions.

The ideal place to enjoy authentic ćevapčići is Sarajevo's Baščaršija.

THE REGIONS OF BOSNIA AND HERZEGOVINA

Sarajevo
Herzegovina
Bosanska Krajina
Central Bosnia
Eastern Bosnia

THE REGIONS OF BOSNIA AND HERZEGOVINA

A panoramic view of Sarajevo

✦ The geographical breakdown of Bosnia and Herzegovina is complex, natural landscape boundaries and transitions are often in contradiction to the political division of the country (see p. 16). In order to make our guide more manageable and to make it easier for the reader to find the information they need, we have divided the country up into five regions, taking into account historical, cultural and topographical considerations. The five regions are: Herzegovina, Bosanska Krajina, Central Bosnia and Eastern Bosnia with a special chapter devoted to the capital, Sarajevo.

✦ **Sarajevo** draws in visitors, business travellers and tourists from around the world all year long. This, combined with the fact that most visitors to Bosnia and Herzegovina start their stay in Sarajevo, makes the country's capital the most frequently visited destination. Sarajevo's history is inseparable from the history of Bosnia and Herzegovina and its influence on the country as a centre of culture, learning and politics, is undeniable.

✦ **Herzegovina** is the country's second most visited region, and for

Mostar is the capital of Herzegovina and the region's most popular tourist attraction

The waterfall at Jajce

good reason: it is rich in history and culture, from Mostar, with its Ottoman bridge, to the wine-rich Neretva valley and the breathtaking karst plateaus. The region also has a distinct Mediterranean feel thanks to its proximity to the coast. In short, more than enough to entice visitors to come back again and again.

✦ **Bosanska Krajina**, in the northwest of the country, primarily attracts nature lovers who are drawn to the rivers Una, Vrbas and Sana. The capital of Banja Luka, the country's second city, is fast becoming a mini-metropolis in its own right, with the corresponding culture and nightlife.

✦ **Central Bosnia** is the heartland of Islam in Bosnia and Herzegovina, especially in Zenica and Travnik. In Jajce, you can explore the capital of the Bosnian kingdom in the 13th and 14th centuries. The region is rich with the legacy of the Ottoman Empire and of medieval Bosnia and is something of an undiscovered country for most foreign visitors.

✦ **Eastern Bosnia** is the least well explored region of Bosnia and Herzegovina and is far from the bustle of the better known tourist attractions but full of interesting destinations to discover, not least the River Drina, the little-known gem of the country, and the Sutjeska National Park.

The breathtaking landscape of the Sutjeska Canyon

SARAJEVO

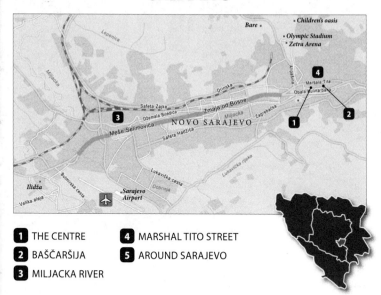

1 THE CENTRE

2 BAŠČARŠIJA

3 MILJACKA RIVER

4 MARSHAL TITO STREET

5 AROUND SARAJEVO

✛ Sarajevo is the capital of Bosnia and Herzegovina and is both literally and figuratively the country's heart. The city on the Miljacka reflects so much of what makes this country unique: the coexistence of different religions and cultures in a confined space, the interplay of influences of East and West on architecture, lifestyles and cuisine.

✛ The Ottoman old town, Baščaršija, and the up-market shopping street, Ferhadija, reflect the history of the country as a whole, giving the visitor a good overview of its multi-faceted nature. In a relatively small space, Sarajevo presents the visitor with important buildings which are the heritage of the Ottoman and Hapsburg Empires, of socialist

A panoramic view of Sarajevo

Sarajevo today is a blend of the modern and the traditional

Yugoslavia and of an emerging modern Bosnia and Herzegovina; including a mix of Islamic, Catholic, Serbian Orthodox and Jewish places of worship. In short, much of Europe's history and culture are distilled and captured in one city.

✦ With a population of over 300,000 inhabitants, Sarajevo is Bosnia and Herzegovina's largest city and is home to the country's most important cultural and political institutions. The city is also the transport and economic centre of Bosnia and Herzegovina, with the country's only international airport and with train and bus connections with neighbouring countries and to cities across Europe. Since the 1995 Dayton Peace Agreement, the international staff of various NGOs and multi-national organisations such as the UN, OSCE, EU, etc. have lived and worked in Sarajevo in their thousands, giving the city a worldly flair. A mixture of many European languages can be heard in the city centre's restaurants and cafes.

Sarajevo's Baščaršija quarter where the Ottoman legacy is evident

+ The two events for which the city is most famous are the 1984 Winter Olympic Games and the war of the 1990s. Both have shaped the city, leaving their mark in the form of the traces and memories to be found wherever one wanders in Sarajevo. Reminiscence and remorse are inextricably linked in the city's everyday life. But Sarajevo has so much more to offer that reducing this vibrant and varied city only to the Winter Olympics and the civil war would not be entirely fair.

+ Beyond its colourful and historic city centre, the outskirts of Sarajevo are also worth discovering. The city's mountain, Trebević, rises above the Grbavica district and provides opportunities for hiking and other types of recreation. The 'Olympic mountains' Igman, Jahorina and Bjelasnica are easily and quickly accessible. The suburb of Ilidža has been a health resort since Roman times and has one of the most beautiful parks in the country, containing the source of the Bosna river.

+ Sarajevo has overcome the war and its murky past, and this rebirth is visible across the city; shopping centres have sprung up, destroyed houses are being renovated, new churches and mosques are completed almost weekly. In other words, the events of the 1990s are no longer

Traditional huts on Mount Bjelasnica near Sarajevo

the overriding theme. However, the picture is not entirely rosy. High unemployment, the overall situation of political and economic stagnation in the city and the country and the cumbersome transition from a state-run economy to a free market system have become the dominant public discourse in Sarajevo.

+ Most visitors, however, are unlikely to encounter these problems. Sarajevo's open and positive atmosphere, its treasures and special features so numerous that only a few of them can be covered in this book: if you approach Sarajevo warmheartedly and with an open mind the city will always return the favour.

The Tram – a Sarajevo tradition

Sarajevo was one of the first cities in the world to get streetcars! The first tram embarked on its scheduled route on New Year's Day 1885. Drawn by horses, the trams used rails of the so-called 'Bosnian gauge' of 760 millimetres. The trams were electrified in May of 1895, and the final conversion to the European gauge of 1435 mm was made in 1960. Today Sarajevo has six tram lines. Lines 3, 4 and 6 connect the city centre with the suburb of Ilidža. Lines 1 and 4 take passengers to the main train station, while to reach Baščaršija you take lines 1, 2, 3 and 5. A single ride on the tram in Sarajevo costs 1.60 Marks.

The History of Sarajevo

The history of Sarajevo reflects the history of the country as a whole. Bosnia and Herzegovina's location between Orient and Occident is particularly well reflected in the capital, with the two helping to shape many dimensions of everyday life and history.

The city's oldest archaeological remains date from the **Neolithic** period, around 2600 – 2400 BC. The remains of an entire village from this period were excavated in Butmir, today located near the airport. In particular it was the ceramics found here which caused a stir among archaeologists, giving a name to a prehistoric society, the Butmir culture. It would be possible to go and see these figurines and pottery in the National Museum of Bosnia and Herzegovina in Sarajevo – if it was not closed.

The **Illyrians** left their mark on Trebević (a mountain near Sarajevo) and excavations on Debelo Brdo, another mountain near Sarajevo, have turned up Bronze Age artifacts, mostly tools, weapons, and jewellery.

The **Romans** also left a legacy behind them, some traces of which can be seen in Ilidža. There you will find the remains of a sulphur bath and a bridge over the Bosna. Evidence of Roman settlements on Trebević mountain and in the area of today's Marindvor have also been unearthed. The sulphur waters of the Aquae Sulpharae initiated the tradition of Ilidža as a health resort. The baths had under-floor heating and mosaics which are partially preserved even today, providing evidence of detailed and meticulous construction.

Little is known about the early **Middle Ages** and the arrival of Slavic tribes to the territory of modern-day Sarajevo. Apart from some Bogomil grave stones (see p. 13), there are few remains from this period. The settlement of Vrhbosna was probably founded around the year 1270 and is likely to have been a merger of several smaller market towns. The political and military events of medieval Bosnia took place far away from the present-day capital.

Traces of Sarajevo's Roman heritage live on: The Roman Bridge at Ilidža

It was only with the arrival of the **Ottomans** that Sarajevo became the focus of attention. Isa-beg Ishaković, the first Ottoman administrator of Bosnia and Herzegovina, founded the city on the Miljacka river in 1462. Its name comes from the Ottoman name for the city, *Ovasi Saray*, a term describing a lawn in front of a home or residence. It

Sarajevo's Ottoman heritage lives on in its architecture

was Isa-beg Ishaković who built the first urban infrastructure, including a mosque; a marketplace; a public bath; an inn for travellers; as well, of course, as a residence for the Ottoman governor himself! Thus, Sarajevo became the official capital and trading centre of the Bosnia Pashalik.

An important step in the development of Bosnia and Herzegovina's principal urban centre came under the rule of Gazi Husrev-beg in the first half of the 16th century. His reign left many Islamic buildings and administrative facilities in the Baščaršija district, most notably the mosque that still carries his name, the Gazi Husrev-Begova Džamija. Sarajevo became a truly Islamic city during this time and by the middle of the 16th century there were around 100 mosques in the city. By 1660, the city, now with a population of over 60,000 inhabitants, became the second most important Islamic city in Europe after Istanbul. However, in addition to its strong Islamic roots, the Jewish and Christian communities were also an important element of Sarajevo's cityscape.

In 1697, the Hapsburgs under Prince Eugene managed to wrest control of Sarajevo from the Ottomans. The invasion was initially far from benign and led to the violent destruction of the city and the end of the golden era of its urban development. Prince Eugene's forces, however, could not hold the capital, and in the ensuing conflict the city was almost completely razed to the ground. It would be a

long time before the city could recover from the devastation. The population decreased abruptly and the Ottoman heyday turned to decline. In the middle of the 19th century, Bosnian nobles, under the leadership of Husein Gradaščević (see p. 221) – also known as the Dragon of Bosnia – rebelled against Ottoman rule, and though the uprising was ultimately unsuccessful it signalled the end of Ottoman rule over Sarajevo and Bosnia and Herzegovina as a whole.

In the end, it took until the 1878 Congress of Berlin to formally end the 400-year history of Sarajevo within the Ottoman Empire. Now the **Hapsburg** flag flew over the hills of Sarajevo. The Hapsburg Monarchy embarked with gusto upon the task of transforming the city into a European capital. Large administrative and cultural buildings such as the City Hall, the Theatre, the National Museum and the City Library were constructed. But it was ultimately the new tramway and railway which brought the greatest changes to people's everyday lives. Even the Latin script entered the lives of the people. Although these technological and economic developments did lead to a limited identification of the city's 50,000 residents with their new ruler in Vienna, the fact that neighbouring Serbia had been an independent state since 1860 led to a growing resentment of the occupation. The Orthodox population of the city in particular longed for greater links with independent Serbia, and on 28th June 1914 this longing led to the assassination of the heir to the Austrian throne. The shots that killed Archduke Franz Ferdinand initiated the First World War and subsequently led to the end of Hapsburg rule in Sarajevo.

Although the First World War was triggered by the assassination in Sarajevo, the capital of Bosnia and Herzegovina was largely spared the fighting. The capitulation of Austria-Hungary, thus far the 'protector' of Sarajevo, in the autumn of 1918, caused a reorganization of Southeast Europe along national lines. Sarajevo became part of the newly established Kingdom of Serbs, Croats and Slovenes (later known as the **Kingdom of Yugoslavia**) not as a capital city, but politically and administratively demoted to the status of provincial capital. In the interwar period, Sarajevo stagnated economically and in terms of architecture. The centres of the new Yugoslav kingdom were Belgrade and Zagreb, with Sarajevo relegated to the sidelines. By the early 1940s the population of Sarajevo had grown to around 80,000. This broke down as roughly 34 percent Muslims, 29 percent Croats and 25 percent Serbs with the remaining 12 percent representing Jews and other ethnic minorities.

Unlike its experience of WWI, multicultural Sarajevo was unfortunately not spared the fighting during the **Second World War**.

On the 15th of April, the German *Wehrmacht* marched into Sarajevo largely unopposed, annexing Bosnia and Herzegovina to the fascist puppet-state, the Independent State of Croatia. Tens of thousands of the city's Jews and Serbs were killed or deported and the Muslim inhabitants were degraded to second class citizens. The fascist reign of terror in Sarajevo ended on the 6th of April 1945 with the liberation of the city by Tito's communist partisans.

In the new **socialist Yugoslavia**, the multi-ethnic city of Sarajevo blossomed. The new Sarajevo came to epitomise the economic and social changes in the country. New neighbourhoods emerged as schools were built, factories sprang up around the city, and the city's infrastructure was modernised and adapted to the needs of the rapidly growing population. As the city's population represented the cultural and ethnic diversity of Yugoslavia, Sarajevo became a model city for Tito's Yugoslavia and one of the cultural and intellectual hubs (if not the actual centre) of socialist Yugoslavia. In the mid-1980s, when athletes from all over the world came to Sarajevo for the Winter Olympic Games, the city's growth had peaked, with the population approaching 500,000. Just four years

Sarajevo's Latin Bridge, where Archduke Franz Ferdinand was assassinated

The Opening Ceremony of the Winter Olympics in 1984

after Tito's death, with the whole world marvelling at the emergence of this multicultural city in the middle of Europe, Sarajevo's future seemed assured.

The **Civil War of the 1990s** hit Sarajevo very badly. From April 1992 to February 1996 Sarajevo was besieged and almost entirely cut off the outside world. Bosnian Serb units surrounded Sarajevo and bombarded it for almost four years from the surrounding mountains from. The population of Sarajevo – which was made up of members of all three ethnic groups – defied the attacks. Support from the international community was little more than hot air and the citizens of Sarajevo were left to defend themselves. Violent skirmishes and artillery fire destroyed thousands of buildings, and cost several thousands of civilian casualties. A mass exodus of refugees left the city.

After the signing of the Dayton Peace Agreement in November 1995, the

Parts of Sarajevo still bear the scars of war

situation improved rapidly and on 29 February 1996 the siege of Sarajevo ended after 1425 days.

The Cellist of Sarajevo

Among the most famous images from the time of the siege of Sarajevo is one of the Cellist of Sarajevo. Vedran Smajlović refused to allow the war to dishearten him and continued to play solo concerts at various public places around Sarajevo. His concerts were not only a sign of resistance but also a commemoration of the victims of the siege. In 1992 a photograph of the proud, bearded cello player amidst the ruins of the National Library became world famous and symbolised spirit of the people of Sarajevo in the face of hardship.

The Sarajevo Film Festival

The Sarajevo Film Festival (SFF) is held every August and brings the capital to life with a number of cultural events and is a showcase and meeting point for South East European film. The first SFF took place in the summer of 1995, during the siege of Sarajevo. The wartime beginnings of the festival continue to factor strongly as theme for this alternative festival. Social issues, war, persecution and the rights of minorities and marginalised groups very much remain part of the thematic focus. Also, by focusing on the South Eastern European film, Sarajevo is very different from the big, glamorous European Film Festival such as Locarno, Cannes or Venice. But for fans of alternative cinema, the SFF is certainly one of the most exciting festivals in Europe.

1 The Centre

The rooftops and minarets of central Sarajevo

The following description of Sarajevo's historic centre follows a suggested three hour walking tour starting from Ferhadija and covering Baščaršija, Miljacka and finally on to New Sarajevo. The different parts of the city appear in order of this tour and no other value should be attached to the order of their appearance.

FERHADIJA

▶ We start the tour at the **Eternal Flame** (*Vječna Vatra*) at the fork in the road between Ferhadija and Ulica Maršala Tita, behind the main post office. The Eternal Flame commemorates the city's liberation from Nazi and Ustaša occupation on

The Eternal Flame commemorates the city's liberation from the Nazis

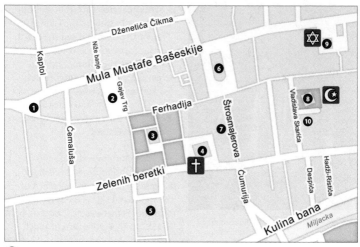

1. Vječna Vatra (Ethernal flame)
2. Gradska Tržnica
3. Trg Oslobođenja (Liberation Square)
4. New Orthodox Church (Saborna crkva)
5. Dom Armije (Army house)
6. Sacred Hearth Cathedral
7. Štrosmajerova street
8. Ferhat-Pašina Džamija
9. Old Synagogue
10. "Evropa" Hotel

6th April 1945. Even today wreaths are regularly laid by WWII veterans and locals. The flame is part of the city's culture of remembrance and is also a popular meeting place.

▶ **Ferhadija**, the capital's longest pedestrian street, begins at the flame. This end of the street mostly features buildings from the 1950s and 1960s, while halfway along Hapsburg-era architecture becomes evident. The far end of Ferhadija is already part of the pedestrian zone of Ottoman Baščaršija. A walk along Ferhadija is a journey through the historical periods which have formed Sarajevo.

The entrance to the covered market, Gradska Tržnica

▶ **Gradska Tržnica**, the old municipal covered market, is located on Galev Square (*Galev Trg*). This Renaissance Revival building, dating from 1894, was designed by Austrian architect August Butcha. The market, where local farmers come to sell their goods, is nicknamed Markale (from the German for market) and houses a simple restaurant on the upper floor.

▶ Opposite the covered market is **Freedom Square** (*Trg Oslobodjenja*), partly occupied by a park. Here old men play chess among sculptures of local literary greats such as Ivo Andrić and Meša Selimović, as well as a new bust in honour of the first president of Bosnia and Herzegovina, Alija Izetbegović.

▶ On the eastern side of the square are the Economics Faculty of Sarajevo University and the **New Orthodox Church** (*Saborna Crkva*). The church was built in 1868 and is one of the largest Serbian Orthodox churches in the world. Interestingly, its construction was substantially supported by funds

The Orthodox church elegantly lit at night

from the Ottoman authorities, in an attempt by the Sublime Porte to win the loyalty of the Orthodox population of Bosnia and Herzegovina.

▶ Opposite the church is **Army House** (*Dom Armije*), an impressive building from 1881 which once served as an officers' club during Hapsburg rule but today hosts cultural and social events. The socialist department store *Svjetlost* (Light) is found at the western end of the square.

▶ Continuing along Ferhadija you will find the **Sacred Heart Cathedral** on the left hand side. Built between 1884 and 1889, it serves as the seat of Vrhbosanska diocese, the only Catholic diocese in Bosnia and Herzegovina. The Cathedral's construction was led by then Archbishop Josef Stadler, whose grave is to be found inside. This three-nave neo-Gothic basilica is decorated in white marble and has a rounded choir on its northern side. Its entrance is flanked by two bell towers.

One of the towers of the New Synagogue

▶ **Strossmayerova** street begins on the square in front of the Cathedral. This small pedestrianised street is a hub for Sarajevo's colourful nightlife, especially in the summer months when cafes spill out onto this and the surrounding streets. Because of this, Hotel Evropa and Ulica Zelenih Beretki are barely accessible by car on weekend evenings.

▶ As we return to Ferhadija and head east, the atmosphere changes, becoming increasingly oriental. On the right hand side is the **Ferhadija Mosque** (Ferhat-Pašina Džamija), built in 1562, with a grave yard in which many Janissaries are buried.

The seat of the Catholic diocese in Sarajevo

▶ Opposite the mosque, and somewhat hidden, is the old Jewish synagogue, built at the end of the 16th century. The synagogue has been devastated several times during the turbulent history of the city –most recently in World War II. The **Old Synagogue** is no longer used as a place of worship, nor is the New Synagogue (*Novi Hram*), built directly opposite in 1921, and which now houses a museum. Sarajevo's Jewish community, once one of the richest and most active in Southeastern Europe, today numbers very few. Besides these two synagogues, Sarajevo has a number of other Jewish institutions, including the Ashkenazi synagogue on the banks of the river Miljacka.

2 Baščaršija – The Ottoman Old Town

Map of Baščaršija showing streets: Mula Mustafe Bašeskije, Đulagina, Prote Bakovića, Kračule, Telali, Luledžina, Gazi Husrev-begova, Čizmedžiluk, Sarači, Čulhan, Baščaršija, Kazandžiluk, Oprkanj, Brodac, Ćurčiluk veliki, Ćurčiluk mali, Kundurdžiluk, Bazardžani, Abadžiluk, Bravadžiluk, Ašćiluk, Obala Kulina bana, Miljacka, Pariske komune

1 Bezistan Gazi Husrev-beg
2 Gazi Husrev-beg Mosque
3 Sahat Kula (Clock Tower)
4 Kuršumlija Medresa
5 Kolobara Han
6 Sebilj Fountain
7 Kazandžiluk
8 Bravadžiluk
9 Old Serbian Orthodox Church

The Baščaršija is the Ottoman core of Sarajevo

▶ **Baščaršija**, Sarajevo's well known Ottoman quarter, dates from the middle of the 16th century. Although the original buildings have for the most part sadly not survived, the Ottoman architectural style has been strictly adhered to during the numerous reconstructions of the subsequent centuries. The paved alley known as Sarači is surrounded by craft stalls, and the aroma of grilled *ćevapčići* hangs in the air around the small stone town houses. Baščaršija was badly damaged during the war in the 1990s. Images of Sarajevo's cultural heritage ablaze went around the world and many valuable buildings and historical documents were utterly destroyed. Tragically, many of these testimonies to history were lost forever. But much of the architecture has not been lost forever since many buildings have been rebuilt in the original style. Baščaršija remains a proud bastion of oriental culture which is unique in continental Europe.

▶ At the entrance to Baščaršija, on the right hand side, is the covered market **Bezistan Gazi Husrev-beg**. The building, built between 1537 and 1555 and over 100 metres long, is home to numerous small jewellery and leather boutiques. The rectangular hall has four entrances and is reminiscent of the Egyptian Bazaar in Istanbul on which it was modelled.

The covered market, Bezistan
Gazi Husrev-beg

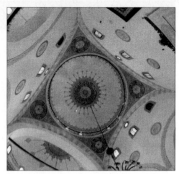

The interior of the Gazi Husrev-beg Mosque
in Baščaršija

▶ Perhaps the most important mosque in Bosnia and Herzegovina, the **Gazi Husrev-beg Mosque** (*Gazi Husrev-begova Džamija*) is located immediately behind the covered market which bears the same name. The mosque's 45 metre-high minaret, built in 1531, was at the time one of the tallest and most architecturally ambitious structures in the Ottoman world. As well as the actual place of worship, the historic mosque complex also contains a fountain with a wooden roof located in the atrium and a separate stone laundry room for ritual cleansing of the body before prayer. The traditional Ottoman tomb (*turbe*) of Gazi Husrev-Beg is also located on the premises. The mosque is used by worshippers, but outside of prayer times it is also open for visits by non-Muslims. Women may visit the mosque but must ensure their hair is covered and that they are modestly dressed – the separate entrance for women can be found on the left hand side of the building.

▶ Near the Gazi Husrev-Beg Mosque is the 17th century **Clock Tower** (*Sahat Kula*), informing devout Muslims of the time of the five daily prayers.

The covered fountain in front of the Gazi Husrev-beg Mosque

Gazi Husrev-beg – the benefactor of the city

The name of Gazi Husrev-Beg can be found in various places around the city. A number of buildings in the Old Town – primarily educational and charitable buildings which he supported, as well as mosques – are named after him. Gazi Husrev-beg was born in 1480 in Serres in modern-day Greece. His father was originally from the Herzegovinian city of Trebinje, while his mother was a daughter of the Ottoman Sultan Bayezid II. His career began as a commander in the Ottoman army and, after military successes in the name of the Sublime Porte in 1521, he was awarded the governorship of the Bosnian Sanjak, a title he held until his death in 1541. In addition to his military successes, which led to an extension of the possessions of the Sanjak, Gazi Husrev-beg devoted much of his energy to developing and expanding Sarajevo. The mosque in Baščaršija which bears his name is also where he was interred.

The Sahat Kula rises above the surrounding buildings

▶ The **Kuršumlija Madresa** is the oldest educational institution in Sarajevo; it has been in existence since 1537 and today it is an Islamic education centre. Surrounding a courtyard with a small fountain is a rectangular portico, from which one can reach the teaching rooms. Each of the 12 small stone classrooms has its own dome, made of lead.

▶ **Kolobara Han**, the first Ottoman style inn (*han*) in Sarajevo, was built at the end of the 16th century in the Sarači alley and has served travellers and traders alike ever since. Together with the guesthouse opposite, the Morićan Han, the inn is one of Sarajevo's main focal points and can serve several hundred travellers. Sarajevo's economic rise in the 16th and 17th centuries was closely connected with these two merchant-friendly facilities. The Kolobara Han (on

The Kuršumlija Madresa, an Islamic educational institution

the right hand side) has changed greatly since it was established but the Morićan Han (on the left) has maintained the feel of the original. Both *hans* are still working restaurants and cafes. All travellers should enjoy a Bosnian coffee under the impressive linden tree in the courtyard of Morićan Han.

▶ The Sarači alley leads to Baščaršija square, one of the most recognizable symbols of the city. **The Sebilj Fountain** on the north side of the square was built in 1753, but did not take its present form until the end of the 19th century. The four steps at the

The Sebilj Fountain is lit for nighttime visitors

base of the rounded, wooden fountain with a copper roof serve as a meeting place. The Sebilj fountain is probably the most photographed object in Sarajevo.

▶ Traditional craftwork is to be found in **Kazandžiluk** and **Bravadžiluk** streets. Bravadžiluk is the home of locksmiths, while Kazandžiluk specialises in coppersmiths and boilermakers. Look for the typical souvenir of Baščaršija in these narrow streets: the Bosnian coffee set of *fildžan* and *džezva* (see p. 91).

Traditional tea and coffee sets on sale at Kazandžiluk

centuries, meaning that its interior has become a kind of cellar. The square church is full of golden icons and a large round chandelier hangs in this narrow but welcoming building. Upstairs, a child's coffin is laid out. This is a space devoted to young women who have been unable to have children yet.

▶ Across from the two synagogues, on the other side of Mula Mustafe Bašeskije street is the **Old Serbian Orthodox Church** (*Stara Pravoslavna Crkva*). Behind its high walls is a small two-story church and a museum (admission 2 KM). The church building dates from 1539 and is one of the oldest surviving buildings in Sarajevo. The church has sunk over the

The unassuming exterior of the Old Orthodox Church

3 Along the Miljacka

Sarajevo developed and expanded along the banks of the Miljacka river, which has its source in the Romanija – the mountains above Sarajevo – and flows west into the city. The Miljacka is a tributary of the Bosna, with which it converges on the edge of the city. Though it is rather a small river, the beauty of its historic bridges as it flows through the capital has inspired many songs and poems.

▶ The easternmost of the city's bridges over the Miljacka, Šeherćehajina Ćuprija, connects the Ottoman Old Town of Baščaršija with the Bistrik

The Latin Bridge crossing the Miljacka as it flows through Sarajevo

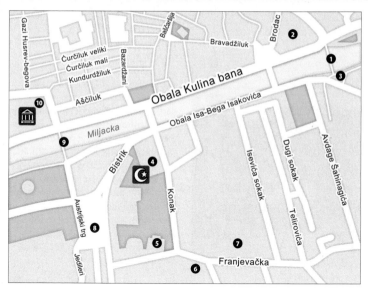

1. Šeherćehajina Ćuprija
2. Vijećnica (Town Hall)
3. Inat Kuća (House of spite)
4. Careva Džamija (Emperor's Mosque)
5. Konak
6. Franciscan Monastery of St Anthony
7. Sarajevska Pivara (Brewery)
8. Austrian Square
9. Latinska Ćuprija (Latin Bridge)
10. Museum of Sarajevo

The Vijećnica looking resplendent lit by floodlights at dusk

The pseudo-Moorish façade of the *Vijećnica*

district. The stone bridge dates from 1540, with its three columns and four arches and with the **Town Hall** (*Vijećnica*) in the background it is a popular spot for tourist photos. The Town Hall was built in 1894 and is the most imposing building of Hapsburg-era Sarajevo. Austrian architect Alexander Wittek adapted an otherwise oriental building with a Western-style façade and roof. The pseudo-Moorish elements of the design are found in numerous representative buildings of this period.

In this case the mix of occidental and oriental seems particularly apt, since the town hall represents the transition between the old Ottoman and Hapsburg districts along the Miljacka. Under socialist Yugoslavia the building was used as a library, but tragically it was one of the first tangible victims of the 1990s war. It was burned down and many historic documents and books were lost forever. Although renovation began immediately after the war ended in 1995, it is yet to be completed.

The House of Spite (*Inat Kuća*)

▶ The **House of Spite** (*Inat Kuća*) is a typical Bosnian restaurant. The building owes its name to the fact that the former owner refused to allow his house to be demolished in order for a new road to be built by the Hapsburgs – then settled on the opposite bank. The stubborn owner eventually relented when he was promised a house across the river.

▶ On the south side of the Miljacka is the **Emperor's Mosque** (*Careva Džamija*). The mosque, with an octagonal minaret, in its present form was built in the mid-16th century, at exactly the point where there was an Islamic place of worship since 1460. Furthermore, the mosque also has a library and a cemetery. The highest Muslim cleric (Reis-ul Ulma) also once resided in the Emperor's Mosque.

▶ Directly behind the Emperor's Mosque sits the magnificent **Konak**, the palatial official residence of high Turkish officials. It was built in the last days of Ottoman rule in 1868 to serve as the residence for the Vizier. The rulers who followed also took advantage of this elegant building and, once they left, it was converted to a luxury residence. Archduke Franz Ferdinand and his wife Sofia spent their last night here before they were assassinated. The Konak today is the official residence of the president of Bosnia and Herzegovina and is used for formal events such as state visits.

▶ Just a few meters south of the Konak and the Emperor's Mosque rises the dark imposing **Franciscan Monastery of St. Anthony** (*Franjevački Samostan Svetog Ante*). The close proximity of the Muslim mosque and the Catholic monastery is typical of the peaceful and tolerant coexistence between religions in the city. Built to the design of Czech architect Ivan Holz, the monastery was constructed in 1893. The associated church, designed by Josip Vancaš, was built in 1912 in the neo-Gothic style.

▶ Diagonally opposite the monastery is another dark looming structure, which might appear at first glance to be part of the monastery. However, on closer inspection it turns out to be the **Sarajevo Brewery** (*Sarajevska Pivara*). The building in its present form was erected in 1893 under Hapsburg rule. Beer has been brewed here since 1864 and its restaurant also offers hearty dishes alongside draught beer – in an atmosphere reminiscent of an Austrian beer hall. Unusually for a brewery in Bosnia and Herzegovina or

The neo-Gothic church of the Franciscan Monastery

The Old Brewery in Sarajevo looks almost like a cathedral to beer

for former-Yugoslavia as a whole, the Sarajevo Brewery is an independent corporation with local management and is not yet part of an international brewery chain.

▶ Heading east from the brewery via Franjevačka Ulica, one reaches **Austrian Square** (*Austrijski Trg*). This square is a central hub for the Miljacka quarter. Located on the square is the City Barracks; built in 1882, the barracks of the Hapsburg army was the most important military institution in the city. In the forecourt of the barracks stand a pavilion and a cafe, which host outdoor concerts of classical and orchestral music in the summer.

▶ After Austrian Square comes the most famous of Sarajevo's bridges over the Miljacka, the **Latin Bridge** (*Latinska Ćuprija*). Built in 1565, this bridge consists of five stone columns and four supporting arches, with a railing of sturdy white stone and arcs gently over the river. Its name comes from the fact that the bridge once connected the city with the Sarajevo's Latinluk suburb, where Catholic merchants from Ragusa (modern day Dubrovnik) traditionally resided. During the period of Bosnia and Herzegovina's inclusion in Yugoslavia, the bridge was named after Gavrilo Princip, assassin of the heir to the Hapsburg throne.

▶ The **Museum of Sarajevo** (*Muzej Sarajeva*) just north of the Latin Bridge is open weekdays from 10am-3pm and on Saturdays from 10am-4pm. For just 2 marks, visitors can learn about the era of Hapsburg rule in Sarajevo from 1878 to 1918. A list

The Latin Bridge with the Museum of Sarajevo in the background

The shot that was heard around the world

One sunny June day in Sarajevo the heir to the throne of the Hapsburg Monarchy, Archduke Franz Ferdinand, was gunned down along with his wife Sophie by an inexperienced assassin as they drove through the town in an open-topped car. The shots were fired just as they had crossed the Latin Bridge, by a member of the organization "Mlada Bosna" (Young Bosnia), a group campaigning for an independent Bosnia and Herzegovina and perhaps union with Serbia. The death of the Austrian aristocrat and his wife was the final straw for the Austro-Hungarian Empire, which was at the time already straining at the leash to go to war with the Kingdom of Serbia. Exactly one month later, on July the 28th 1914, the First World War began.

The Main Post Office (*Glavna Pošta*), part of Sarajevo's Hapsburg legacy

language barrier – is nonetheless recommended for the theatre's special atmosphere. Only the back of the theatre is visible from the banks of the Miljacka, the main entrance being on the other side.

of Sarajevo's Hapsburg-era buildings can be found in the museum – most of these are along the north bank of the Miljacka.

▶ Other attractions along the Miljacka include the **National Theatre of Bosnia and Herzegovina** (*Narodno Pozorište Bosne i Hercegovine*). Originally built as a gentlemens' club in 1899, the building was converted into a national theatre in the early 1920s. The building was designed by prolific Czech born architect Karel Pařík, who designed more than 160 buildings in Sarajevo. After the Second World War, the dramatic focus of the National Theatre was expanded to include ballet and opera. These three divisions keep the theatre active even today. Attending a performance at the National Theatre of Sarajevo – challanging perhaps due to the

The National Theatre was a grand gentlemens' club at the turn of the century

▶ Returning to the south side of the Miljacka, the former **Evangelical Church** (*Evangelistička Crkva*) is now visible. This was built in 1899, also by Karel Pařík, in a romantic-Byzantine style. The dome inside the main entrance is crowned by a small steeple. Sarajevo's Evangelical Church was used as such for only a short time. Since 1972, the former church has housed the Academy of Fine Arts. The white building is brightly illuminated at night, and a futuristic looping bridge crosses the Miljacka nearby.

The building that once housed the Evangelical Church is now the Academy of Fine Arts

A closer view of the former Evangelical Church

4 Marshal Tito Street

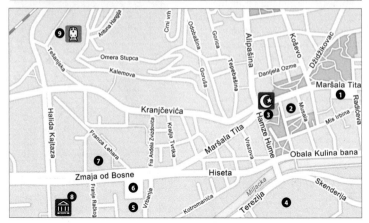

1. Children Square
2. The Presidency
3. Ali Pasha's Mosque
4. Skenderija
5. Parliamentary Assembly
6. Bosnia and Herzegovina Square
7. The Holiday Inn
8. The National Museum
9. The Main Train Station

▶ Continuing the tour, join **Marshal Tito Street** (*Ulica Maršala Tita*) by heading northwards from the Miljacka along Radićeva Street. Marshal Tito Street connects the centre of Sarajevo with its suburbs and along its length are many of the city's important institutions and landmarks, including the National Bank and the offices of the national government and the city and regional administration. The fact that this prestigious central thoroughfare still bears Tito's name indicates the importance which he still has for Sarajevo.

▶ The first sight encountered is **Children Square** (*Trg Djece*), notable for the BBI Centre, one of the many new shopping malls in Sarajevo which symbolise its recovery and development. The square serves as a memorial to the children who died during the civil war in the 1990s. Just opposite, in the City Park, are the graves of fallen Green Berets (*Zelene Beretke*), a Muslim paramilitary unit active from 1992 to 1995, which defended the city during its long seige. In May 2010, a memorial to young people killed in the war was built.

▶ On the left side of Tito Street, behind the City Park, is Sarajevo's government district. Established here in 1884-1886, the government district contains the **Presidency** (*Predsjedništvo*), which today is the seat of the government and the president of the country and

A monument on Children's Square (*Trg Djece*)

the Federation of Bosnia and Herzegovina. Two other representative administrative buildings from the Hapsburg era close to the Presidential Palace now house the Foreign Ministry of Bosnia and Herzegovina and administrative institutions of the City and the Canton of Sarajevo.

▶ **Ali Pasha's Mosque** (*Alipašina Džamija*), dating from 1560, forms a nice contrast to the ostentatious government buildings. In line with

The Presidency, just of Marshal Tito Street

The 16th century *Alipašina džamija* seen through cherry blossom

architectural styles eminating from Istanbul, Ali Pasha, the Ottoman governor of Bosnia, built a mosque with a square base. Three smaller domes dominate the entrance hall and a larger dome encompasses the prayer room. The mosque was tragically destroyed during the civil war in the 1990s, but it has since been restored. Victims of the civil war are buried in the old cemetery outside the mosque.

▶ Looking across the Miljacka from the mosque,

Skenderija, a large sports and leisure centre built in the 1960s, is visible. Formerly a venue for ice hockey games and the media centre for the Winter Olympics, Skenderija now hosts major events and also contains an underground shopping centre, restaurants and nightclubs within its 70,000m² of floor space. Skenderija is still in fairly good condition, but the city will sooner or later need to come up with an investment plan for renovating the centre.

▶ Towards the end of Tito Street is the **Parliamentary Assembly** (*Parlamentarna Skupština*) of Bosnia and Herzegovina. Designed in 1954, but only completed in 1982, the 107 metre high-rise building houses the

The Brutalist lines of the socialist-era Skenderija Centre

country's two parliamentary chambers. The 40 storey building was heavily damaged during the civil war in the 1990s, but was rebuilt in the mid-2000s. **Bosnia and Herzegovina Square** (*Trg Bosne i Hercegovine*) in front of the Parliament is popular with protesters with some kind of protest or political action taking place almost every day.

The Parliament building – one of the tallest buildings in Sarajevo

THE DRAGON OF BOSNIA BOULEVARD

▶ Marshal Tito Street comes to an end after the Parliament and the Court of Bosnia and Herzegovina, and from here on, moving into New Sarajevo, the architecture is of a more recent vintage. **Zmaj od Bosne** (*Dragon of Bosnia*, see p. 221) Boulevard

The iconic Holiday Inn has seen better days

continues on from Tito Street, forming the main road between the old town and the suburbs of Sarajevo. Located along this multi-lane thoroughfare leading to Ilidža are numerous shopping centres, hotels and academic and scientific institutions, including Sarajevo University's Faculty of Philosophy and the Technical High School. The new, spacious and fortress-like U.S. embassy is also located here.

▶ The legendary yellow **Holiday Inn** is also located on Zmaj od Bosne Boulevard. Once the best hotel in town, it has unfortunately been seriously neglected in recent decades, and with no serious renovation on the horizon, it is recommended mainly as a novelty these days. During the civil war of the 90s, the hotel was home to the foreign press corps covering the conflict and so it has become something of a cult location in the minds of a generation of Western war correspondents.

▶ Opposite the Holiday Inn is the **National Museum of Bosnia and Herzegovina** (*Zemaljski Muzej Bosne i Hercegovine*). Designed by architect Karl Parzik, a follower of the Italian Renaissance, and constructed in 1888, the building was then expanded significantly just before the beginning of the First World War. The four buildings of the National Museum form a courtyard containing a botanical

The National Museum of Bosnia and Herzegovina

Sarajevo's main train station was expanded for the Winter Olympics in 1984

Herzegovina, has served as the headquarters of the Avaz newspaper since its completion in 2009. Take a trip to the 35th floor, where there is a café and a viewing platform offering breathtaking views of Sarajevo – on clear days you can see across to Igman and Jahorina mountains.

garden. Damage from the civil war has largely been repaired, but the most recent attempt to re-open the museum failed and it has been closed since autumn 2012.

▶ Sarajevo's **main train station** (Željeznička *Stanica*) lies behind the new American Embassy. The impressive station building was built in 1947 and was extended for the Winter Olympic Games in 1984. The over-sized station also serves as the municipal tram and coach station. Many coaches connect Sarajevo daily with all the major towns and cities in Bosnia and Herzegovina and numerous destinations in Western Europe. The hustle and bustle of the bus station is in complete contrast to the atmosphere of the railway station, from which only a few trains depart daily. In the summer months the station is mostly used by backpackers and Inter Rail travellers.

▶ The **Avaz Tower**, at 142 metres high the tallest building in Bosnia and

▶ Another way to get a bird's eye view of Sarajevo is to visit **Kibe**, a restaurant located in the steep hills above Baščaršija in the Hrsatovi district (address: 164 Vrbanjuša). This two-story restaurant offers local dishes and a fantastic view over Sarajevo's old town. The meals in Kibe are rich and the reasonably sized portions are not overpriced.

The Avaz Tower, a symbol of Sarajevo's recovery

Mirza Delibašić led Bosna to victory in the 1979 European Championships

Bosna Basketball Club

The Bosna Basketball Club (*Košarkaški Klub Bosna*) is Sarajevo's most successful and longest established sports club. The club, which plays its home games at Skenderija, won the 1979 European Champions' Cup when it boasted stars such as Mirza Delibašić and Svetislav Pašić. Today's Bosnian national team still looks back to those glorious days.

5 Around Sarajevo

The concrete highrises of New Sarajevo

▶ Sarajevo has plenty to offer outside the city centre. This is a city of impressive contradictions: on the one hand there is the old historic city centre with its own constellation of suburbs Ciglane, Koševo, Breka and Hrastovi. On the other hand there is **New Sarajevo** (*Novo Sarajevo*), the westward extension of the city which is home to the majority of residents. Passing through the neighbourhoods of Grbavica, home of Sarajevo's most famous football club, Hrasno and Otoka you reach the airport and the historical suburb of Ilidža, where the source of the Bosna River is located.

▶ The Sarajevo Olympic Centre, including the stadium where the opening ceremony of the 1984 Winter Olympics was held as well as the venue where all the ice events took place, is located in the northern part of the city, just a fifteen minute walk from Marshal Tito Street along the Koševo road. The **Olympic Stadium** was purpose built for the games in1984 but there had been a stadium on the site since 1948, home to local football club Fudbalski Klub Sarajevo (*Sarajevo Football Club*). The Olympic opening ceremony on

7 February 1984 was attended by 50,000 spectators. Today, the Asim Ferhatović–Hare stadium (named after a former FK Sarajevo player), has a capacity of nearly 40,000. In addition to FK Sarajevo games, the stadium also hosts the home games of the Bosnia and Herzegovina national football team as well as concerts. U2's concert here in 1997, when Sarajevo was still largely destroyed from the war, was seen around the world.

▶ Right next to the stadium is the **Zetra Olympic Arena**, which hosted ice hockey and figure skating competitions in 1984. This sports complex, with a capacity of nearly 12,000, was built in 1983 in an unusual architectural style which at the time made it one of the most modern buildings in the world. The arena

The Olympic Stadium

was almost completely destroyed during the war but a comprehensive reconstruction was completed in 1999 which also included the addition of a small museum. Today this multi-purpose hall hosts concerts and fairs. Besides the Olympic Stadium and the Zetra Arena, the Olympic Centre has a number of tennis and basketball courts, a skating rink and several smaller football fields.

▶ Following the Koševo road northwards, the name of the road changes to Patriotske Lige. This leads to the **Children's Oasis** (*Dječija Oaza*) with a small zoo. The entire complex, in communist times a park dedicated to Tito's youth movement, the Pioneers, is now a family-friendly destination close to the centre of Sarajevo. The zoo covers a wide area and houses more than 40 different species as well as a botanical garden. A small amusement park is also sure to attract kids and force parents or grandparents to dig deep. The urban Children's Oasis is open all year round.

▶ Directly west from the zoo, through the Betanja Park, is the largest and most interesting cemetery in Sarajevo. The cemetery, known as **Bare**, can be reached from the centre by the number 16 bus. By 1966 over 60,000 people had already found their final resting place in this huge landscaped cemetery. Bare is divided into several sectors, with each religious denomination having its own area. Five identical chapels serve Muslim, Christian (Catholic and Serbian Orthodox), Jewish and atheist communities. The numerous white grave stones of the Muslims and Christians alongside the black marble stones of atheists, often decorated with a communist star, form an image of conciliation.

▶ **New Sarajevo** (*Novo Sarajevo*) begins in earnest west of the Skenderija leisure centre. Most of the buildings of New Sarajevo were built in the period after the Second World War in communist-style 'blocks'. Forced into a narrow strip by the mountains, New Sarajevo extends for several kilometres along the banks of the Miljacka river. Thanks to the beautiful mountainous surroundings, even the communist-era tower blocks don't look so bad. Traces of the war are still occasionally visible, but they no longer dominate visitors' impressions in the way that they have done for so long. Almost all of New Sarajevo's many neighbourhoods have their own infrastructure, including a market (*pijaca*), a health centre (*dom zdravlja*) and a primary school (*osnovna škola*).

A view of the Bare cemetary

▶ After about 10 kilometers along the Miljacka from New Sarajevo you will reach a district called **East Sarajevo** (*Istočno Sarajevo*). This is also where Sarajevo International airport is located. Curiously, East Sarajevo is not to the East, but to the south and west of the city centre. Until 2004, this area was known as Serbian Sarajevo (*Srpsko Sarajevo*), due to its location on the other side of the border with the Republika Srpska. The largest districts in East Sarajevo are Dobrinja and

The seemingly endless residential blocks of East Sarajevo

During the siege a tunnel was dug from the city centre to the airport

Lukavica, the latter forms the centre of East Sarajevo. The bus station in Dobrinja connects Sarajevo with other cities in the Republika Srpska and Serbia and Montenegro. East Sarajevo also has its own university. The distinction between Sarajevo proper and Serbian East Sarajevo has been greatly reduced in recent years. The two areas use the same public transport system and the population is no longer divided. In fact it is almost impossible to see where the border between the two urban areas is.

▶ **Sarajevo Airport** (international abbreviarion: SJJ) was opened in 1969 and connects Sarajevo with major European cities. Because of its valley location, the airport is prone to fog, meaning that delays are common. During the war, a tunnel to the airport was built, under the control of UN peacekeepers, supplying the besieged city with food. The former tunnel is now a small museum and is located south of the airport.

▶ **Ilidža** is an independent community below Mount Igman, on the western edge of the capital. From the centre of Sarajevo Ilidža can be easily reached by tram. Ilidža boasts the source of the Bosna river as well as the hot springs which for centuries have given it the status of a spa resort. Ilidža is situated at an altitude of 499 meters above sea level and is surrounded by forested mountains. Its name comes from *iladž*, an Old Turkic word for medicine, showing that even the Ottomans used the waters for healing purposes. But Ilidža's historical roots go much further back. Neolithic

The Roman Bridge at Ilidža

people settled here as early as 4,000 years ago, and the Romans built the first baths.

▶ Ilidža's heyday came under the Hapsburgs. Although they were here for only a short time, they built much of the resort's infrastructure, including hotels, spas, parks and villas for upper class Sarajevans. The hotels 'Bosna', 'Herzegovina', 'Austria' and 'Hungary' were the first in the region. Ilidža is now trying to market itself as a modern spa resort. The hotels and the spa have been renovated and a new water park, Termalna Riviera, has already been completed, while the Hollywood Hotel offers a large outdoor pool.

▶ The **Grand Avenue** (*Velika Aleja*) leads from Ilidža to the source of Bosna. The 3.5 kilometre-long avenue, popularly called the green tunnel, was built in 1892 and consists of 726 plane trees and numerous chestnuts.

▶ The extensive park at **the source of the Bosna** (*Vrelo Bosne*) is a popular

The Grand Avenue (*Velika Aleja*)

tourist destination with its numerous benches, picnic areas and barbecue areas. The source is like a miniature lake district, with small ponds and lakes, walkways and bridges through the miniature underwater world. The Labud (*Swan*) restaurant, with its terrace overlooking the water, offers grilled trout, freshly caught from the source.

A bridge close to the source of the Bosna river

AUTHOR'S PICK: HOTELS & RESTAURANTS

Due to the abundance of hotels and restaurants on offer it would be impossible to list them all and to keep the list current. Instead, please find below a selection of hotels and restaurants recommended by the author:

HOTELS

Sarajevo	**Hotel Evropa**	Probably the best hotel in Sarajevo, centrally located with views of Baščaršija and all the amenities including a car park, pool, restaurant etc.	Vladislava Skarića 5 +387 33 580 400
Sarajevo	**Hotel Old Town**	A small, simple and very clean hotel in the middle of Baščaršija, buffet breakfast, Wi-Fi and help with finding a parking space on request	Mali Čurčiluk 11a +387 33 574 200
Sarajevo	**Hotel Bristol**	This large hotel (186 rooms) has a swimming pool, spa, parking, Wi-Fi and is just 2km from the centre – alcohol is not served	Fra Filipa Lastrica 2 +387 33 705 000
Sarajevo	**Hotel Central**	This newly renovated boutique hotel right in the centre, near the Miljacka, boasts 15 rooms, a swimming pool, spa and Wi-Fi	Čumurija 8 +387 33 561 800
Ilidža	**Hotel Hollywood**	With over 400 rooms this is the largest hotel in the country and boasts several pools , sports courts, restaurants and nightclubs	Dr. Pintola 23 +387 33 773 100
Sarajevo	**Hotel Sarajevo**	The best hotel in New Sarajevo, with 69 air conditioned rooms, Wi-Fi, parking, restaurant, swimming pool, gym and roof terrace	Džemala Bijedića 169 +387 33 777 900
Ilidža	**Spa Hotel Terme**	This hotel and spa has 180 recently renovated rooms, Wi-Fi, parking, restaurant and ample parking	Hrasnička cesta 14 +387 33 772 000

RESTAURANTS

Sarajevo	**Restaurant Kibe**	Great views of Sarajevo from the terrace. Traditional Bosnian cuisine and an authentic interior with a welcoming fireplace	Vrbanjuša 164 +387 33 441 936
Ilidža	**Restaurant Labud**	With its large terrace right by the source of the Bosna and serving fresh trout, this restaurant is a popular addition to family excursions to Vrelo Bosne	Vrela Bosna +387 33 772 000
Sarajevo	**Restaurant Sarajevska pivara**	Quaint yet somehow chic, this restaurant serves fresh beer and hearty Bosnian and Hapsburg style cuisine	Franjevačka 15 +387 33 239 740

HERZEGOVINA

CENTRAL BOSNIA

CROATIA

6

4

5

3

2

1

ADRIATIC SEA

1 TREBINJE   **3** ČAPLJINA   **5** MEDJUGORJE

2 NEUM   **4** MOSTAR   **6** LIVNO

✛ Herzegovina is the most varied of the regions of Bosnia and Herzegovina. It extends from the Adriatic coast, via the hot but fertile Mediterranean landscape of the Neretva Valley to the white snow-capped mountains of southern Bosnia. It ranges from the sea to about 2,000 meters above sea-level; from luscious green forests to scorched arid terrain; in short, from the Mediterranean to the Alpine. Herzegovina has a broad range of climatic, geological and cultural characteristics and the population of this sparsely populated region has developed a certain penchant for extremes. In such a small region one can encounter a mix of conservative Catholic, Muslim and Serbian Orthodox institutions, places of pilgrimage and political parties. The patriotism of the ethnic groups seems to play a greater role here than elsewhere in the country, or so it seems if you go by the number of Croatian, Serbian or Bosnian flags on display.

The Žitomislići monastery, half way between Čapljina and Mostar

The Glamočko Polje karst field is one of Herzegovina's highland plateaus

✦ In the far north, on the border with Bosanska Krajina, are the largest high-level plateaus in the country, the karst fields of Kupreško Polje, Livansko Polje and Glamočko Polje. These three karst fields are some of the most unusual in the world and are also one of the last nature reserves in Europe where wild horses roam free – fittingly they were also once a location for the filming of the western, "Winnetou 2: Last of the Renegades". Lake Busko, between Livno, Tomislavgrad and the Croatian border is fed by rivers from the karst fields and serves the arid plateau as a water reservoir.

✦ Below the karst plateaus of central Herzegovina, the Neretva River and its tributaries shape the landscape. The Karvica waterfalls near Čapljina, the Hutovo Lake District with its many bird species, the impressive source of the Buna and the Old Bridge across the Neretva in Mostar itself combined with the Mediterranean climate mean Herzegovina cannot hide its obvious appeal. Bosnia and Herzegovina's only city by the sea, Neum, is a popular destination with local holidaymakers. The Dervish Monastery in Mostar and the Catholic pilgrimage in

Lake Busko, near Livno, is fed by karst rivers

The Dervish monastery at the source of the Buna

Medjugorje are markers of the strong religious tradition of the region.

✦ The southern part of the region, far from tourist hotspots, is quieter. On the Montenegrin border, Gacko and Nevesinje sit against the backdrop of the snow-capped Maglić and Zelengora mountains. Another characteristic of southern Herzegovina is a sporadic sprinkling of lakes and karst fields. Last, but certainly not least, the town of Trebinje, with its plane-

lined central market is perhaps the most beautiful town in the region.

Trnovačko lake from Maglić

The Wines of Herzegovina

Herzegovina's climate supports a rich viticulture. The fertile valley of the Neretva, for example, has fostered wine culture since ancient times. Local grape varieties such as Žilavka and Blatina are the most widespread. Žilavka, giving a white wine, is primarily grown in the area around Mostar and is characterized by a low acidity and a fruity flavour that melts in the mouth. The red Blatina is a simple country wine, robust and rustic.

There are many vineyards (*vinarija*) that offer wine tasting: "Vukoje", in Trebinje, an emerging wine producer, offers tours of its vineyards, as does "Čitluk", near Čapljina, the country's largest and most professional wine producer.

1 Trebinje

The Trebišnjica flows through Trebinje

▶ The city on the **Trebišnjica river** has got to be one of the most beautiful cities in the heart of the country. The marketplace, lined with plane trees, is particularly special and on its own makes Trebinje worth visiting. Trebinje, the southernmost city in Bosnia and Herzegovina, lies at an altitude of 274 meters above sea level and is just half an hour drive from the Croatian Adriatic Sea. Trebinje is in the territory of the Republika Srpska and, with its 35,000 inhabitants, is the second largest city in Herzegovina, after Mostar.

▶ **Freedom Square** (*Trg Slobode*) is lined with well-preserved buildings representative of the era of Hapsburg rule. Of particular interest is the late-19th century Catholic Cathedral amidst the plane trees for which Trebinje is famous. The plane trees make this market square almost reminiscent of Aix en Provence in the South of France. The daily farmer's market (*Zelena Pijaca*) on this square offers a touch of colour and fresh local produce. Numerous cafes and restaurants invite you to take a load off and enjoy the Mediterranean bustle of the market.

A view of Trebinje from the river

▶ The Ottoman **Old Town** (*Stari Grad*) follows the semicircular curve of the Trebišnjica. To reach the Old Town you pass the Western Gate, a huge tunnel through the city walls. In the square behind the tunnel is the Osman Pasha Mosque (*Osman Pašina Džamija*) built in 1726. As is so often the case, the mosque was sadly destroyed during the war in the 1990s but was rebuilt in 2005. Along the streets of the old town, artisans, cafes and restaurants set up their businesses.

The 18ᵗʰ century mosque, *Osman Pašina Džamija*

▶ The **City Park** of Trebinje is dedicated to the locally born poet, Jovan Dučić. A memorial to Dučić, born in Trebinje in 1871 forms the entrance to the park. Dučić who, in its prominent position, is the Serbian Orthodox Church on **Mount Crkvina**. The church, an identical copy of the Gračanica Monastery in Kosovo, was built in 2000 and now houses the remains of Jovan Dučić. The complex around the church contains a museum of Serbian Orthodox icons and an open-air theatre. Views from the churchyard over Trebinje and the Valley of Trebišnjica are, to say the least, impressive.

The impressive Orthodox church on Crkvina

▶ Four kilometres west of the town, on the banks of the Trebišnjica, is the **Tvrdoš Monastery** (*Manastir Tvrdoš*), which dates from the 15ᵗʰ century and is the centre of Herzegovina for the Serbian Orthodox faith. The monastery, which is still active, has been renovated in recent years and is open to visitors. One can buy original icons in the monastery's small gift shop.

adition to his literary career, was also a diplomat in the first Yugoslavia (see p. 29). He died in 1943 in exile in America but his remains were transferred to Trebinje in 2000. The city park is home to the **Serbian Orthodox Church** (*Saborna Crkva*) of Trebinje. Construction of the colourful church was completed in 1908; its interior shines in blue and gold luster.

▶ The new landmark, dominating the town from

The 15ᵗʰ century Tvrdoš Monastery

▶ Also well worth visiting in the vicinity of Trebinje, is the **old Arslanagić Bridge** (*Arslanagića Most*), which spans the Trebišnjica. The bridge is now also known as the Perovica Bridge. It was built in 1574 during the reign of Mehmed-paša Sokolović, who also presided over the building of the bridge at Višegrad (see p. 237). After the Second World War, during the construction of a new dam, the bridge had to be moved several hundred meters. Today its span of four arches connects the villages of Gradina and Police.

The Arslanagić Bridge, built during the reign of Mehmed-paša Sokolović

2 Neum

▶ With barely 20 kilometres of Adriatic coastline Bosnia and Herzegovina manages to officially position itself amongst the select group of European countries with a Mediterranean coast. The coastline of the city of **Neum** and the Klek peninsula is cut off from the rest of the country, surrounded as it is by the Croatian Pelješac peninsula and Croatian cities Ploče, in the north, and Dubrovnik, in the south. Normally Neum is reached through Croatia, through the Croatian town of Metković, along the main road 8A. But it is also possible to reach Neum from Bosnia, along an old road via Hutovo Blato and over the Žaba mountain, but it is time consuming and a bit of an adventure (see p. 77).

Unlike most other cities on the Adriatic Neum has no harbour and no historical old town. This is due to the fact that Neum was built in the socialist era and was designed from the drawing board. From 1950, a state-planned holiday destination for working people emerged. Neum was

The positively Mediterranean atmosphere of Neum in summer

built from the ground at the same time as the main Split-Dubrovnik road (now in Croatia) was expanded. The development focused on providing large numbers of lodgings and relied heavily on the twin pillars of socialist era urban design, concrete and functionality. The large hotels were built and financed by government agencies and trade unions which wanted to provide a holiday destination for their employees or members. The steep hill down from the highway, completely built up with concrete buildings and roads, is devoid of nature.

One of the large hotels in Neum

Neum only has around 4,000 permanent residents but these are joined by thousands more during the summer. The number of hotel beds is estimated at about 7,000 and new facilities and hotels are constantly added. Taking this construction boom and Neum's history into account, the chances for a relaxing and peaceful holiday are rather low. But Neum as a holiday resort is significantly better and above all more relaxed than you expect; in short, Neum is still well worth a visit.

From June to September the atmosphere of happy holidaymakers fills the hotels, cafes and restaurants of the town, lending it a relaxed and positive feel. The majority of the town's visitors are people who cannot really afford a seaside holiday. Some manage to save a few hundred Convertible Marks during the year and Neum is the sort of place a few hundred Marks is enough for a few days of beach holiday. The resultant jubilant and joyful holiday mood, crammed full of appreciation for the little things, becomes contagious and easily spreads to all other visitors.

Despite its small size, Neum contains a private hospital, police and fire stations, as well as a plethora of restaurants, cafes, supermarkets and nightclubs. Hotels in the town range from large concrete monstrosities from socialist times to numerous small private apartment complexes. The big hotels have sought in recent years to renew their dusty interiors, a process

A view of Neum

that is already largely complete. The many private apartments offer a more comfortable stay. Along the straight and long Primorska Street in the north, there are many private hotels and apartments, which correspond to European standards, and which are usually enhanced by small private beaches.

Neum is deceptively quiet at night

Palm trees sizzle in the summer heat

The beach in Neum is disfigured by concrete but there are some pebble beaches and the unspoilt Klek peninsula offers many opportunities for a natural descent into the sea. Neum's steep descent towards the sea offers just about every terrace and balcony classic Mediterranean views of Klek and Pelješac.

3 Čapljina

▶ The small town of **Čapljina**, with only 7,000 inhabitants, is one of the most visited cities in Herzegovina. On the one hand, this is because of the stunning landscapes of the Neretva River, Trebižat, and Bregova Krupa and on the other hand it is because it is on the road that leads to the Croatian Adriatic coast. Čapljina has a majority Croatian population and is in the Federation.

▶ Although the fertile valley of the Neretva has yielded arable land since Roman times, the oldest buildings in modern-day Čapljina date from the period of Hapsburg rule at the turn of the 20th century. On the square in front of the yellow **Town Hall** building (*Općina*) is a large statue of the Croatian King Tomislav. The statue is 4 metres tall and weighs about 3 tons. The pedestrianised street, Matije Gupča, leads to the Catholic Church of St. Francis of Assisi (*Crkva sv. Franja Asiškog*).

▶ Čapljina may be a relatively new town but only 3km northeast of the centre is the historic site of **Počitelj**, a fortress built in the early 15th century by the Hungarians, who dominated the region at that time, to defend against the advancing Ottomans.

The ruins of the fortress at Počitelj

Built on a hill overlooking the Neretva, the strategic importance the Počitelj fortress once had is still evident today, however, it was not enough to prevent the Ottoman advance. From 1471 the Ottomans began an expansion of recently conquered Počitelj. The mosque (*džamija*), educational institution (*medresa*), baths (*hamam*), inn (*han*) and clock tower (*sahat kula*) can still be visited today.

The medieval ruins at Počitelj

During Ottoman times Počitelj was the centre of the region. During the Ottoman wars at the end of the 17th Century, Venice was able to bring Počitelj briefly under its control. Ultimately, however, the town was re-conquered by the Ottoman Empire and remained under its control until the Congress of Berlin in 1878.

Počitelj lost its strategic value after the arrival of the Hapsburgs and the construction of new military and urban centers in the region, such as Čapljina. Although almost completely preserved as a city and one of the largest and most important historical sites in Bosnia and Herzegovina, Počitelj has fallen into a slumber. In recent years, Počitelj is experiencing a mini-Renaissance as an artists' colony and some private admirers of old architecture have moved in. A small restaurant has also opened in between the old walls.

▶ The **Kravica Waterfalls** are located 15 kilometers north of Čapljina, on the Trebižat River. The waterfalls form a semicircle around the limestone cliffs and send a tumult of water plunging over a cliff-face 120 meters wide and 26 metres deep. The noise is deafening and the water splashes up to the recently constructed panoramic viewing platforms, throwing up sublime rainbows when lit by the sun.

The Kravica Waterfall on the Trebižat

Below the waterfalls the Trebižat flows on towards Čapljina; ideal for a calm canoe trip.

▶ The Lakeland **Hutovo Blato** is situated a few kilometres south of Čapljina. Bird lovers and photographers have been able to enjoy this nature reserve, protected since 1995. Hutovo Blato consists of several interconnected lakes. In the region around this lake district, millions of Central and Northern European migratory birds hibernate between fall and spring.

Wooden boats on Hutovo Blato

Witnessing the colourful birdlife is worthwhile not only for specialised ornithologists and biologists, but also for the untrained visitor.

4 Mostar

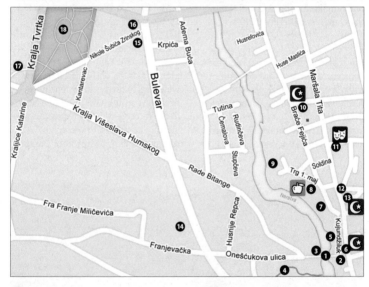

1. The Old Bridge
2. Tara Tower
3. Halebija Tower
4. The Crooked Bridge
5. Kujundžiluk
6. Čejran-Ćelijina Mosque
7. Koski Mehmet-paša Mosque
8. Tepa Market
9. The Biščević House
10. Karadjozbey Mosque
11. The National Theatre
12. The Clock Tower
13. Nasuh-aga Vučijaković Mosque
14. Franciscan Monastery
15. The Old High School
16. The Spanish Square
17. Croatian Cultural Centre
18. Zrinjevac Park

▶ **Mostar** is the capital of Herzegovina. The city is perched 60 metres above the banks of the Neretva River and, thanks to its proximity to the Adriatic Sea, has a climate and scenery that feel Mediterranean. The town is surrounded by mountain peaks reaching up to 2,000 meters high such as Hum, Prenj, Velež and Čapulj, and with the Neretva valley opening out to the Adriatic coast in the south. The railway line from Sarajevo to the Adriatic goes through Mostar, just like highway

The city of Mostar from the air

The Old Bridge from city the town gets its name

17, which connects Central Bosnia with Croatia. Mostar is part of the Federation of Bosnia and Herzegovina and its population of just over 110,000 people is mostly composed of Bosnian Muslims and Croats.

▶ The history of the city of Mostar is so closely connected with the history

of its bridges as to be near enough inseparable. The name of Mostar is derived from the Slavic term for bridge (*most*) or bridge guardians (*mostari*). Bridges have been built across the Neretva and the Radobolja, which also flows through Mostar, since Roman times. Proper urban development began, however, with the arrival of the Ottomans in 1468. The new rulers immediately began to expand Mostar and, in just a few decades, a city with developed infrastructure and a marketplace (*čaršija*) emerged. **The Old Bridge**, built in 1556, has helped the city to fashion a great reputation that has spread beyond the borders of the Ottoman Empire. Mostar grew to become the largest and most important city in Herzegovina and, in addition to the establishment of important Islamic places of worship, also became a centre for increasingly

The Old Bridge

On behalf of and in honour of Ottoman Sultan Suleiman I, architect Mimar Sinan designed the single-arch bridge spanning the Neretva, the bridge was built in 1556. The bridge almost immediately became a symbol of Mostar and is now a UNESCO World Heritage Site. The bridge is just over 28 meters long and hangs 19 meters above the Neretva, a very impressive structure for the time it was built and still impressive today!

In 1993, during the Bosnian Civil War, the bridge was completely destroyed but its reconstruction began immediately after the war, using the original Ottoman-era plans and elements of the original bridge. The grand re-opening of the restored Ottoman bridge was held in 2004.

important Catholic and Serbian Orthodox institutions. By 1767 Mostar had become the seat of the Serbian Orthodox Metropolitan and, in 1847, also of the Catholic Bishop.

In 1878, Mostar became part of the Hapsburg Empire, ending 400 years of Ottoman rule. The fundamental aspects of life in the formerly Ottoman city became little more than memories – but memories that live on to this day. As Bosnia and Herzegovina developed economically under the Hapsburgs, Mostar was connected to the growing railway network and has now been on the important route between Sarajevo and the Adriatic for over 100 years. Besides the railway line, the Hapsburgs left numerous other structural improvements, principally buildings such as a hotel, a high school, swimming baths etc. This development was concentrated on the western side of the Neretva, while the eastern side of the city remained dominated by traditional Ottoman architecture and a largely Muslim population. The western side of Mostar, with a predominantly Christian population, began to develop into a modern city.

During socialist Yugoslavia, Mostar continued to develop economically and socially. A large aluminium plant created thousands of industrial jobs and the multicultural population of the city was known nationally for their tolerant coexistence. Sadly, the war of the 1990s struck Mostar particularly heavily and changed all that, essentially stripping Mostar of much of its multicultural heritage. Even today the city is divided into a Croatian west side and a Bosnian Muslim east side.

During the summer months large numbers of coaches full of tourists from the nearby Croatian resorts descend on the town. During the day the town overloaded with tourists and it is, therefore, worth taking a walk around the town is in the evenings, once the tour groups have left, or the early mornings, before the onslaught begins.

NEAR THE OLD BRIDGE

▶ Mostar's main landmark is the **Old Bridge** (*Stari Most*). Owing to its location on a rocky outcrop above the blue-green waters of the Neretva and its oriental, white limestone design, the Old Bridge is unique. The sheer magnitude of the work and craftsmanship required to build a bridge at this location can leave no visitor unimpressed. If you can, try to get a view of the bridge at night when it is brightly lit and reflected in the river below. The best view of the bridge, day or night, is from just below on the banks of the river, where the tiny Radobolja flows into the Neretva. The

An evening walk through the old town

The Halebija Tower on guards the western entrance onto the Old Bridge

bridge itself is guarded by two towers, **Tara** and **Halebija**. The tower named Tara, on the eastern side of the Neretva, houses the Old Bridge museum. When it was built, back in 1676, the cone-like tower was used as a munitions

The Crooked Bridge was a model for the Old Bridge

depot, which is why it has walls about 3 metres thick facing the bridge. The tower on the opposite side, Halebija, dates from 1716 and once served as a prison guard tower; nowadays it houses the bridge jumpers' club.

▶ Close to the Old Bridge is the town's second historical bridge, the **Crooked Bridge** (*Kriva* Ćuprija), which spans the Radobolja. The single-arch stone bridge is actually slightly older than

the Old Bridge itself and served as a model for its larger cousin. In the historic buildings just by the Crooked Bridge one can find a restaurant and also, the Kriva Ćuprija Hotel, the best hotel in Mostar. The hotel's beautifully designed rooms have a great view of the Crooked Bridge.

THE EAST SIDE: OTTOMAN MOSTAR

On the eastern side of the old bridge is **Kujundžiluk**, the historical street of the merchants. The cobbled street dating from the 15th century runs parallel to the Neretva. At its heyday, upto 500 artisans and merchants had shops on Kujundžiluk. Many traditional

Traditional copperware on sale at Kujundžiluk

Goods on sale in Kujudžiluk

▶ Next to the mosque is **Tepa Market** (*pijaca*), where local trade has always flourished. In contrast to the tourist-orientated dealers and craftsmen on Kujundžiluk alley, Tepa Market is full of local farmers selling local fruit and vegetables to the local population. In the tourist bustle of Mostar, the market has a much more serene, down-to-earth atmosphere and offers a rare glimpse into the everyday life of the locals.

craftsmen still ply their trade in the little stone houses along Kujundžiluk street. In addition to the traders and craftsmen numerous Islamic institutions are located on Kujundžiluk and Velika Tepa (the name of the same street a little further along). One of these, the **Čejvan Ćehjina Mosque**, is the oldest mosque in Mostar, it dates from 1552/53. The Turkish Consulate also has its address on Velika Tepa.

▶ The **Koski Mehmed-Paša Mosque** is, however, the most famous mosque in Mostar because of its prominent location on the Neretva. A copper dome covers the two-storey interior of the mosque, which was built in 1619. Many tourists are happy to pay 4 Marks to enter the mosque for the view of the Old Bridge from its minaret.

The Muslibegović house – one of three traditional Ottoman homes open to visitors

▶ Close to the market is one of the three traditional Ottoman houses accessible to visitors. **Biščević House** (*Biščevića Kuća*) was built in 1636 and is the best preserved of the three. The two columns reaching down to the Neretva that hold up part of the house

A view of the Koski Mehmed-Paša Mosque from the Neretva

The Karadjozbey Mosque is one of the most important Islamic institutions in Bosnia and Herzegovina

make for a popular photo opportunity. Household items from Ottoman life can be viewed also in the traditional homes of the families Kajtaz and Muslibegović. These are also located in the eastern part of Mostar.

▶ The **Karadjozbey Mosque** (*Karađozbegova Džamija*) from 1557 is one of the most important Islamic institutions in Bosnia and Herzegovina, second only to the Mehmed Pasha Mosque in Sarajevo. On the site located next to the mosque library is a traditional educational institution (*medresa*). The dome covers the square interior of one of the largest mosques in South Eastern Europe. The Karadjozbey Mosque was severely damaged during the civil war in the 1990s but the reconstruction was successfully completed. We are lucky that the colourfully decorated interior, with its monumental chandelier, welcomes all visitors, including non-believers. Opposite the mosque is one of the oldest cemeteries Mostar.

▶ Turning east, away from the Neretva, one can reach the start of Marshal Tito Street (*Ulica Maršala Tita*) from the Karadjozbey Mosque.

Marshal Tito Street is the town's main thoroughfare and this is where one can find the city bus station, the railway station and also the hospital, the library and the municipal theatre. The **National Theatre** (*Narodno Pozorište*) was founded in 1949 as and was the first theatre in the newly established Yugoslav republic of Bosnia and Herzegovina after the Second World War. The Theatre has its own in-house ensemble and boasts two stages for performances. The theatre was also badly damaged during the 1990s civil war and, unfortunately, a full restoration is yet to be completed. In contrast to religious buildings and places of worship, little money seems to be available for the arts.

▶ Close to the Theatre are an Islamic cemetery and two significant buildings dating from Ottoman times. The first is the nearly 15 meter-high **clock tower** (*sahat kula*) built in 1636, its first bell remained intact and rang regularly for nearly 300 years. Just opposite is the **Nesuh-aga Vučijaković Mosque**, built in 1654, popularly known mosque under the lime trees. It too was destroyed during the recent civil war and was rebuilt in 1997/1998.

THE WEST SIDE: MODERN MOSTAR

▶ Western Mostar has little in common with the more famous

The Millenium Cross, erected in Western Mostar, is still divisive

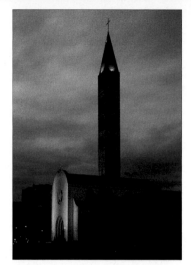

The impressive 107 metre tall tower of the Franciscan Monastery

Ottoman, eastern part of the city. Western Mostar sits beneath Hum Hill and, since the war, has slowly been developing more and more into the actual centre of Mostar; new shops, shopping centres and office buildings have been built. While the eastern part of the city has increasingly focused on tourism and the preservation of Ottoman architecture, the western part is following the model of modern Western European urban planning.

▶ The landmark of this, the younger half of the city, is not a historic building, but a 33 meter-high **white cross** mounted on the hill above the town. Brightly lit at night, the Millennium Cross was erected in 2000 and serves as an identifying symbol for the Catholic part of the town. The cross is still seen as a controversial symbol in this divided and war-scarred city.

▶ In terms of architecture, the symbol of Western Mostar is the **Franciscan Monastery**. The monastery and the accompanying Church of Ss. Peter and Paul was built in 1866. The Monastery Library boasts

a collection of more than 50,000 documents and books. As with so many of Mostar's most attractive religious buildings, the monastery was particularly badly damaged during the 1990s civil war. So much so, in fact, that the present church is a new building; its 107 metre bell tower is the tallest structure in Herzegovina.

▶ Western Mostar's busiest thoroughfare, the Boulevard (*Bulevar*) begins from the Franciscan Monastery. The cities main institutions, including the city Health Centre (*Dom Zdravlja*) and the freshly refurbished Town Hall (*Gradska Viječnica*) line up along the Boulevard. The main characteristic of the yellow Town Hall building from the Hapsburg era and the **Old High School** (*Stara Gimnazija*) is their pseudo-Moorish architecture. The High School, the work of Czech architect, František Blazek, built in 1898, was the first institution of its kind in Herzegovina. Again, the school was badly damaged during the war and was rebuilt in 2004. The building is once again used as a school and includes boarding facilities.

▶ Further up the Boulevard is the **Spanish Square** (*Španski Trg*), which was inaugurated by His Royal Majesty Juan Carlos, the King of Spain, in 2012. The square was built as a reminder of 21 Spanish soldiers who were killed in the civil war; in honour of their fallen compatriots the Spanish Government, in cooperation with the City of Mostar, erected a monument in the square. The square is furnished

The Old High School

A view of Western Mostar with the Spanish Square and the Old High School in the foreground

workers, today it hosts many cultural events and the Writers' Association of Herzegovina has its seat there. The name of the building has changed during the turbulent recent history of Mostar several times. First it was the House of Culture, then the House of Youth and now the home of the Croatian Cultural Centre. The building was heavily damaged during the war and has subsequently been rebuilt.

in an elegant, contemporary style with bright marble, park benches, solar powered lighting, a water feature and a portico. The flags of Spain and Bosnia and Herzegovina flutter together by the monument.

▶ Directly behind the Spanish Square is the newly rejuvenated **Zrinjevac Park**. The car-free Nikole Šubića Zrinjskog Avenue, which forms the western end of the triangular park, is lined with many magnificent Hapsburg-era villas. The Avenue and the Park are popular with locals as a great place for a relaxing evening stroll.

▶ The Nikole Šubića Zrinjskog Avenue ends on Rondo Square, where six plane tree-lined avenues meet. The Herceg Stijepan Kosača **Croatian Cultural Centre** (*Hrvatski Dom*) was built here in 1959. Originally built as a house of the

The Croatian Cultural Centre

BLAGAJ

▶ A trip to Blagaj the source of the Buna River and to the **House of Dervishes** (*Tekija*) is very highly recommended. Blagaj is just south of Mostar and can be reached from the town by car in about 10 minutes. The **source of the Buna**, a tributary of the Neretva, is inside a cave that reaches deep into the mountain. The source of the Buna is one of the most powerful karst springs in Europe, with the stream of water emerging at an astounding 43 metres per second. The temperature of the spring water is never more than 10 degrees C°, making it less than ideal for a swim. The spring cave, which is located at the foot of a 200 meter-high, nearly vertical cliff-face, can be visited in the summer and fall months by means of small boats. In

The Dervish *Tekija* at Blagaj

Whirling Dervishes

Dervishes, members of a religious and spiritual movement from Asia Minor, settled in Bosnia and Herzegovina during the Ottoman era. They quickly became the most famous religious community in the country and based themselves in a *tekija* at the source of the Buna, near Blagaj. Known for their strict religious discipline the Islamic movement practiced Sufism, a spiritual orientation of Islam. The lives of the Dervishes and monastic rules of their order are similar to those of Christian monks. As elsewhere in the world the Blagaj dervishes are famous for their ecstatic, trance-inducing dance, which serves as prayer and contact with God.

the spring, after the snow melt, such a boat trip is simply not possible due to the huge quantity of water gushing from the mountain.

▶ The potent and mesmerising source of the Buna inspired the 16th century Ottoman rulers to build Herzegovina's first **Tekija**, a kind of dervish monastery, at the point where

Velagić House (*Velagića Kuće*) near Blagaj

it emerges from the mountain. The Tekija, built in an Ottoman Turkish Baroque style dates from the 17th century and is still very well preserved today as a museum. It was renovated in 2012 with funding from the Turkish Government and is a popular Muslim pilgrimage site. Numerous cafes and restaurants have also sprung up around the *Tekija* and the source of the Buna.

▶ Close to the Tekija is the **home of the Velagić family**, a typical Muslim household

dating from 1776 and still preserved today, including the original interior of the house. A mill, directly powered from the Buna, is part of the house complex.

▶ The ruins of a castle are perched on the rocks that loom above the village of Blagaj. A castle has been here since Roman times and has been in use by every ruling army in the region until it was destroyed by a major earthquake in 1835. It is named after Duke Stjepan Vukčić Kosača, the last Christian Duke of Herzegovina before the Ottoman invasion in 1465. The ruins are sadly closed to visitors due to the possibility of mines from the civil war still being present here.

▶ In recent years, some good campsites have sprung up around Blagaj, making it a good base for a visit to Mostar and the rest of Herzegovina.

The ruins of the fortress at Blagaj

5 Medjugorje

▶ **Medjugorje** is a small village in the municipality of Čitluk - located between Mostar and Čapljina on a high, barren plateau far from civilisation. This unassuming village has in recent years become a magnet for a very special kind of visitor. Reports of a vision of the Virgin Mary draw tens of thousands Catholic pilgrims every year.

▶ The first reports date back to the spring of 1981, when a few local youngsters claimed that the Virgin Mary revealed herself to them every day for 7 consecutive days. The Virgin Mary, with an infant in her arms, preached to them about the power of love and faith. From this phenomenon a veritable cult of the Virgin Mary has developed over the last few years.

The Catholic church in Medjugorje

A statue of the Virgin Mary in Medjugorje

Almost every day thousands of pilgrims flock from around the (Catholic) world in order to ask the Virgin Mary for healing, grace and clemency.

▶ While the Catholic Church does not recognize Medjugorje as an official pilgrimage site because of doubts about the veracity of the story, the town has developed into a

professionally operated and high-volume centre for believers seeking healing. The infrastructure around **St. Jacob's Church** and the Cross on Cross Mountain is extended annually. This once sleepy town now has many hotels, guest houses, pubs and souvenir shops. The streets are like a colourful, enterprising fair with BBQ stalls and ATMs. The pilgrim tourism has developed into a lucrative business for the local population.

▶ The objective observer could easily find this extreme mix of superficial religiosity and hypocritical profiteering exhausting. Nevertheless, one must recognise

Religious memorabilia on sale in Medjugorje

that the cult of the Virgin Mary in Medjugorje has brought economic prosperity to an area that would otherwise remain relatively poor. And most pilgrims do not visit only Medjugorje but travel to other destinations in Herzegovina, helping to spread income from tourism throughout the region.

Catholic pilgrims from all over the world visit Medjugorje

6 Livno

The Town Mosque (*Čaršijska Džamija*), one of fourteen mosques in Livno

▶ The northernmost city in the Herzegovina is located in close proximity to the border with Croatia and sits at an altitude above sea level of 710 metres. Livno has about 10,000 inhabitants and is a predominantely ethnically Croatian town. It is the capital of the Livno Canton, and is part of the Federation of Bosnia and Herzegovina. The surrounding area is extremely mountainous, the summits of Cincar, Tušnica and Velika Golija range to well over 2,000 meters. The Bistrica River, with its source in Livno and the large Buško reservoir keep the otherwise barren area relatively fertile.

▶ The architecture of the centuries-old **Old Town** is heavily influenced by Ottoman styles. Many of the buildings have been well preserved and the Oriental architectural style of the historical centre, which was once graced by 14 mosques, has been well maintained.

▶ The **Old Bridge** on the Bistrica (*Stari Most na Reci Bistrici*) below the ruins of a Roman fortress, also dates from the period of Ottoman rule. The Hapsburgs also left their mark on Livno's architectural landscape, including the Town Hall (*Viječnica*) and other administrative buildings and educational institutions.

▶ In Livno, the **places of worship** of Bosnia and Herzegovina's three major religions are represented. The Franciscan Monastery of Ss. Peter and Paul with a church dating from 1854, forms the centre of the town. The Serbian Orthodox Church was built in 1859 but contains icons from as far back as the 15th century. The oldest surviving house of worship in Livno is, however, the Beglučka Mosque in the Old Town. The original mosque dates the 1567 but has had to be renovated more than once following the devastation of the Second World War and the 1990s Civil War.

The Franciscan Monastery of Ss. Peter and Paul

the centrepiece of the square, was built in 1925 to commemorate the one thousand year anniversary of the birth of medieval Croatian King, Tomislav. The square around the obelisk and the main street were neatly renovated in 2008.

King Tomislav Square

▶ The core of the town consists mainly of the shopping street, Knez Mutimira, and **King Tomislav Square** (*Trg Kralju Tomislavu*). A nine meter high obelisk,

▶ The **Livanjsko Polje**, the largest karst field in Bosnia and Herzegovina, extends from just outside the city's outskirts and covers an area of 458.7km². The area lies at an altitude of 720 metres above sea level and is the ideal type of karst. The trough-shaped hollow of Livanjsko Polje is surrounded by steep-sided formations of Dinaric mountains and, just to the south, is bordered by **Buško Lake** (*Buško Jezero*). The karst field is fed by the rivers Sturba, Bistrica,

Probably Herzegovina's most beautiful karst field, Livanjsko Polje

Livno Cheese

The famous cheese from Livno (*Livanjski Sir*) has been produced on the Livno plateau and to the same recipe since the end of the 19th century. In 1885 the Hapsburg authorities built a dairy on the slopes of Cincar mountain to which the highland farmers would deliver their milk for processing into cheese. Sheep and cow milk is ripened here for a period of 60-66 days and is then made into cheese with the addition of "secret" ingredients that make the Livno cheese special. This golden yellow and very special cheese with its small holes became popular all over the former Yugoslavia and provides an indispensible source of revenue for the rural population around Livno.

Brina, Plovuča, Jaruga and Ričina, an underground river with plenty of water, feeding diverse flora and fauna in this otherwise arid area. In the 60s this landscape became the backdrop for the filming of "The Last of the Renegades", a movie about Karl May's Winnetou. This almost uninhabited land is also a retreat for some of Europe's endangered species; wolves, bears and wild horses live here. The horses originate from the rugged Bosnian mountain horses and, up to the time before WWII, they served as beasts of burden. As agriculture became increasingly industrialised, these workhorses became unnecessary and were often "dismissed". Thanks to their survivability they have thrived and hundreds of wild horses now live on the Livno karst field.

A view towards Buško Lake

AUTHOR'S PICK: HOTELS & RESTAURANTS

Due to the abundance of hotels and restaurants on offer it would be impossible to list them all and to keep the list current. Instead, please find below a selection of hotels and restaurants recommended by the author:

HOTELS

Trebinje	**Platan Hotel**	The best hotel and restaurant in Trebinje, located in a renovated historic building on the market square, under the plane trees	Cvijetni Trg 1, Trebinje +387 59 270 420
Neum	**Villa Nova Hotel**	With its own private beach and rooms overlooking the Adriatic, just 500m from the centre of Neum	7 Primorska St., Neum +387 36 885 220
Neum	**Posejdon Hotel**	Just 10 metres from the beach, boasting airconditioned rooms and beautiful sea views as well as satellite TV and Wi-Fi	Primorska 61b, Neum +387 36 885 112
Čapljina	**Mogorjelo Hotel**	Spacious rooms with views of the banks of the Neretva and the Čapljina bridge	Ulica Kraljice Katarine, Čapljina +387 36 810 815
Mostar	**Hotel Kriva Ćuprija 1**	Housed in an Ottoman-era building by the Crooked Bridge, under German management and with a beautiful restaurant terrace	Onešćukova 23, Mostar +387 36 360 360
Mostar	**Old Town Hotel**	A great boutique hotel near the Old Bridge - has parking facilities	Rade Bitange 9a, Mostar +387 36 558 877
Livno	**Park Hotel**	The Park Hotel has 60 rooms and is located in the city park – it also has a restaurant with garden terrace and parking facilities	Ulica Kneza Mutimira 56, Livno +387 34 202 149

Hotel Kriva Ćuprija

BOSANSKA KRAJINA

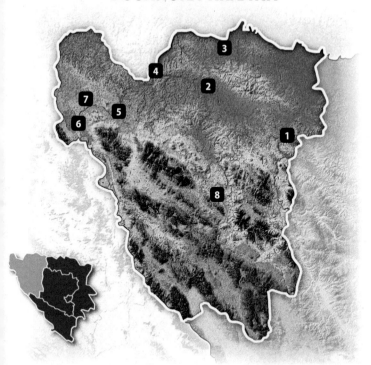

1 BANJA LUKA

2 PRIJEDOR

3 KOZARSKA DUBICA

4 NOVI GRAD

5 BOSANSKA KRUPA

6 BIHAĆ

7 OSTROŽAC

8 KLJUČ

✛ The Bosanska Krajina region (meaning Bosnian borderlands) is characterised mainly by its rivers the Una, Sana and Vrbas. Diverse river landscapes, forested highlands, extensive karst fields and a number of remote caves make the Bosanska Krajina a natural paradise – with the Una National Park as its main attraction.

✛ Krajina means border region and refers to the fact that this area was historically marked by the shifting boundaries between the Ottomans and the Hapsburgs, the Orient and Occident. Bosanska Krajina extends to the west and north of Bosnia and Herzegovina, along the border with Croatia. In the east, the borders of the region are formed by the Vrbas

The River Una

The 70 metre high Bliha Waterfall

and the steep slopes of the Čemerica Mountains, and in the south, by the karst fields.

+ Banja Luka is the administrative centre of Bosanska Krajina and the city of 200,000 on the Vrbas is also the economic and academic centre and transport hub of the region. Thanks to its hiking trails and ski slopes the nature park in the Kozara Mountains, located between Prijedor and Kozarska Dubica, is the main tourist destination of the eastern Krajina region.

+ The southern Krajina region around the cities of Mirkonjić Grad, Ključ and Sanski Most draws visitors to the landscape gouged out by the region's rivers. Hiking through the canyon of the Vrbas to the karst springs, swimming under the 70 meter high Bliha waterfall, rowing on the Sana or a trip to the stalactite-filled world of Hrustovačka cave are just a few examples of active holidays in the southern regions of Bosanska Krajina.

+ The Una National Park stretches across 20,000 hectares of the scenic and natural diversity of the region. Located in the western Bosanska Krajina and surrounded by the cities of Bihać, Petrovac and Drvar it can be tentatively compared to its Croatian counterpart, the Plitvice National Park. Bihać, Bosanska Krupa and Novi Grad lie on the Una, and a visit to these cities can be combined well with a rafting trip along the river.

1 Banja Luka

1 City Park
2 Krajina Square
3 Gospodska pedestrian zone
4 Square of Serbian Rulers
5 Town Hall
6 Presidental Palace
7 Church of Christ the Savior
8 Museum of Contemporary Art
9 National Theatre
10 Museum of Republika Srpska
11 "Banski Dvor" Cultural Centre
12 Square of the Victims of Jasenovac
13 Kastel fortress

▶ Banja Luka is the second largest city in Bosnia and Herzegovina, the capital of the Republika Srpska and the centre of the Bosanska Krajina region. The city on the Vrbas river has 200,000 inhabitants and is situated 163m above sea level. Besides Sarajevo, Banja Luka is the only city in Bosnia and Herzegovina which can be described as anything approaching a metropolis. The city's economy has grown and its infrastructure has improved significantly in recent years, especially in comparison to other cities in Bosnia and Herzegovina. This university town is also now more easily accessible thanks to a new motorway linking it to Croatia.

▶ As the seat of government of Republika Srpska, the city is home to almost all state institutions and cultural institutions of the Serb entity. There is a rich and constructive competition between Banja Luka and Sarajevo with respect to urban development and modernity.

▶ The name Banja Luka is derived from the Bosnian word for spa (*banja*) and points to the fact that this is a region where there are thermal springs to be enjoyed. Both the Romans and the Ottomans have used the thermal springs for healing and recuperation. The present state of the baths is unfortunately rather modest and they offer only limited potential for spa tourism.

The young people of Banja Luka at a pop concert

▶ Banja Luka University attracts young people from across Bosnia and Herzegovina and also from other countries of the former Yugoslavia adding to the sense that Banja Luka is an active and modern city. The city's the nightlife – not just for students – is nationally renowned and the women of Banja Luka are considered to be the most beautiful in the Balkans.

A fresco from a Serbian Orthodox church in Banja Luka

▶ The name Banja Luka was first recorded in 1494 and at a time when the city was ruled by the Hapsburg Empire. The origins of the town, however, go back to the time of the Illyrians and the Romans. Traces of these cultures, such as the fortress, are still visible today. Even the Ottomans were present for a time from 1528 and Banja Luka has retained some cultural and architectural heritage from this period.

▶ Following the Congress of Berlin (p. 28), Banja Luka was placed under the dominion of Vienna. Many of the buildings erected during this period, lasting only 40 years until the end of the First World War, still remain intact; including fine examples such as the Parliament and the Museum of Republic of Srpska. In the years after the First World War Banja Luka served as the centre of a new *Banovina*, an administrative sub-division of the Kingdom of Yugoslavia. During this time, Banja

Luka experienced a real boom and a period of rapid modernization. Even in socialist Yugoslavia, in spite of damage caused by a major earthquake in 1969, Banja Luka was one of the economic and cultural centres of the country.

▶ The war in the 1990s completely transformed the social structure of Banja Luka. From a multicultural entity it has become an almost exclusively Serb-dominated city. The war-damaged mosques and Catholic churches have indeed largely been re-built but the Muslim and Catholic communities have yet to return.

▶ Approximately 20 km north of the city is **Banja Luka Airport** (BNX), which makes the capital of the Bosanska Krajina formally a city with an international airport however a look at the flight schedule betrays that the wide world only occasionally extends to Zurich. The highway to the Croatian border and the town of Gradiška was completed in recent years and makes Banja Luka economically attractive. Many companies and businesses have in recent years settled along this highway that leads to the north. This serves as the basis of an economic recovery of the city.

Banja Luka Airport

The church of Christ the Saviour at night

THE CITY CENTRE: ALONG GOSPODSKA STREET

▶ Banja Luka is anything but compact, nevertheless, it is still best to explore the city on foot or by bicycle. Start your tour of the city at the recently

Krajina Square is at the heart of Banja Luka

renovated **City Park** (*Gradski Park*), located in the centre of Banja Luka. The modern café Staklenac at its centre is one of the city's trendiest locations, and you will see a monument which commemorates Petar Kočić, a writer born in 1877 in Banja Luka. Close to the park, there is a tourist information centre (at number 87 on Kralja Petra I Karađorđevića Street).

▶ Opposite the park, on **Krajina Square** (*Trg Krajine*), is the venerable Palace Hotel. The heavy use of concrete betrays the square's socialist era roots. The nearby Boska shopping centre with integrated cinema has been renovated and is now popular with the younger generation. Krajina Square is also the hub of the city's bus network, while the clock in the middle of the square is a popular meeting spot for young people.

▶ A pedestrian zone begins from Krajina Square, officially called Velika Masleše but popularly known as **Gospodska** (which translates approximately as Gentlemens' Street). The majority of single-storey Art Nouveau buildings from the period between the two world wars have been restored in recent years and the

Gospodska, the pedestrianised street at the heart of Banja Luka

well-kept downtown areas, especially boutiques, banks and cafes mark some of the other parts of the city centre.

▶ Administrative buildings for Banja Luka and Republika Srpska are located in the middle of Gospodska on the **Square of Serbian Rulers** (*Trg Sprskih Vladara*). A monument to Ban Milosavljević, the governor of the Banovina of Banja Luka, in the period between the two world wars, has been erected on the square. The **Town Hall** (*Gradska Palata*) and the Banski Dvor Cultural Centre date from that time and together with the **Presidential Palace** (*Predsjednička Palata*) frame the square. The Banski Dvor Cultural Centre hosts concerts, lectures and exhibitions. The Presidential Palace was built in 1936 in the Bauhaus style.

The church of Christ the Saviour was completed in 2009

▶ The **Orthodox Church of Christ the Saviour** (*Saborni Hram Hrista Spasitelja*) was completed in 2009 and is one of the largest buildings in the city. Originally a church in that space from the 1920s, was destroyed in the spring of 1941 by the German Air Force. It took 70 years for this important Serbian Orthodox church to be rebuilt. Its golden dome has a floor area of 225 metres; the interior is dominated by giant golden chandeliers.

▶ Opposite the church stands the Bosna Hotel, once the best hotel in town but now past its heyday. Next to the hotel is the **Museum of Contemporary Art** of Republika Srpska (*Muzej Savremene Umetnosti Republike Srpske*). The entrance to the museum, once Banja Luka's railway

The Museum of Contemporary Art of Republika Srpska

station, is free of charge, the opening times are from 10am to 10pm.

▶ As you walk further along Gospodska, you arrive at the **National Theatre** of Republika Srpska (*Narodna Pozorište Republike Srpske*). The theatre was founded in the fall of 1930 as a national theatre of the Vrbas Banovina. Further along the Gospodska Street you will find the town library,

The Square of the Victims of Jasenovac and the Parliament of Republika Srpska

a building created and designed by Joseph Goldner. The theatre has an in-house ensemble and boasts two stages for performances.

NOVA VAROŠ & BORIK

▶ The Theatre building represents the end of the pedestrian zone and the city centre. The district of **Nova Varoš** starts at the Square of the Victims of Jasenovac (*Trg Žrtava Jasenovačkih*). On the other side of the street, a Serbian Orthodox and a Catholic church stand next to one another. Along Dr. Mladen Stojanović Street there are various government institutions and international embassies. This magnificent avenue

through Banja Luka is named after a glorious Yugoslav partisan and surrounded by numerous villas of the Hapsburg period.

▶ Also, the **Government of Republika Srpska** (*Vlada Republike Srpske*) was built in Nova Varoš along Dr. Mladen Stojanović street. The tallest building in the city has 17 floors and comprises 50,000 m² of governmental office space. It was completed in 2007 and is home to most government institutions of Republika Srpska. The construction of the futuristic high-rise complex took two years and cost about 100 million Euros, a hefty sum for such a poor country. Nevertheless, Banja Luka is

Mladen Stojanović Park

proud of its new landmark of glass on the **Square of Republika Srpska** (*Trg Republike Srpske*).

▶ Beyond the Square of Republika Srpska and the Government tower is the largest park in the city, named after the heroic partisan of the Second World War, Mladen Stojanović. In this wooded, shady park you can see older men

Borik district

playing chess, while the green lungs of Banja Luka also serve as a home to the so-called Wimbledon Tennis Club. The city's football stadium, where the Borac Banja Luka (Banja Luka Fighter) football club plays its home games, is also located close to the park. The stadium was built in 1937 and can host nearly 10,000 spectators.

▶ The stadium forms the transition to **Borik**. This district is just east of the downtown area and is framed by the Vrbas on its southern and eastern edges. Borik emerged following a devastating earthquake in 1969. The aim of the socialist city planners was to give homeless earthquake victims a new home. The whole area was designed from the drawing board and already in the 1970s offered a new home for almost 10,000 people. With sufficient green areas in Borik there was also space for recreational facilities, such as the large Aqua Park and the University of Banja Luka.

ALONG THE VRBAS

▶ From Borik one can easily reach the banks of the River Vrbas. As is the case with many cities in Bosnia and Herzegovina, the centre of Banja Luka is not located directly on the river, instead the Vrbas is east of the city and somewhat separate from it. On the town side of the river there is no waterfront walk, instead there is a large green area on the opposite side. Crossing the Kabia bridge you reach the Obilićevo district, where some of the Faculties of the University are located.

▶ Following the Vrbas upstream, you can reach the historical highlight of Banja Luka, a **fortress** (commonly known as the Kastel) which covers a huge area of 50,000m² on the eastern bank of the Vrbas. Its origin and the name of this sprawling fortress date from the Roman period. The Ottomans expanded the site to its

The fortress at Banja Luka elegantly adorns the Vrbas

present size. Two gates lead through the fortress wall into the great indoors. Many buildings are still in good condition and the fortress wall can be climbed. In between the historic buildings a park has been created more recently as well as an open-air theatre which hosts a theatre festival every July. The best preserved fortress in Bosnia and Herzegovina contains within its walls one of the leading restaurants in the city.

The Kastel contains a park, particularly beautiful in springtime

▶ Half way back towards the city centre is the **Museum of Republika Srpska** (*Muzej Republike Srpske*). Except for the occasional special exhibitions it holds ethnographic, historical and archaeological collections. The museum is open daily from 8am to 8pm.

▶ A trip to the **Serbian Hot Springs** (*Srpske Toplice*) is definitely worthwhile but especially in summer. The springs are located just 10km outside of the city towards Krupa and Jajce. The water of the eight, 30° Celsius, hot springs flows directly into the cold waters of the Vrbas. Bathing in these waters of varied temperatures is a truly special experience and is not to be missed.

② Prijedor

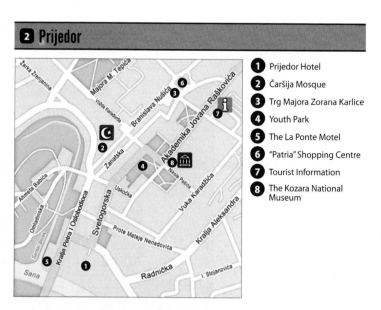

1. Prijedor Hotel
2. Čaršija Mosque
3. Trg Majora Zorana Karlice
4. Youth Park
5. The La Ponte Motel
6. "Patria" Shopping Centre
7. Tourist Information
8. The Kozara National Museum

▶ Prijedor on the banks of the river Sana is home to 65,000 people and the municipality includes 70 villages and other settlements with a total area of 834 km^2 and a population of 105,000. A large part of the current population arrived during the chaos of war in the 1990s. The city is in Republika Srpska, and is inhabited by a majority Serbian population. The Kozara National Park is located on the territory of this municipality.

Prijedor town centre

▶ Prijedor was mentioned by name for the first time at the end of the 17th century. Due to its favourable geographical location on the river Sana and protection offered by the Kozara Mountains, the city developed rapidly in the 18th and 19th centuries. It was connected to the centre of the region and was one of the first cities in Bosnia and Herzegovina to be on the railway network. The train routes from Banja Luka to Novo Mesto and Zagreb from Sarajevo made the city a major transportation hub.

▶ During the war years of the 1990s Prijedor always remained under Serbian control and as a result many Serb refugees from other parts of Bosnia and Herzegovina found shelter here. The Bosnian Muslim and Croatian population, however, was almost completely expelled. Prijedor's countryside bears witness to massacres during the war and captured images of prisoners in the prison camp Omarska, Trnopolje and Keraterm were beamed around the world. No fighting took place inside the city itself, so the infrastructure Prijedor is now in good shape.

▶ Free parking spaces for a visit to the city are located in front of the large building of the **Prijedor Hotel**, in the

Like something from of a dystopian vision of the future, the Prijedor Hotel

southern half of downtown Prijedor. From there, via a small bridge, you can reach the banks of the river Sana. These have been refurbished in recent years into a leisure and sports complex with tennis courts, swimming pool and beach bars and cafes. In the summer months here you will find the most popular swimming destinations in Prijedor.

The socialist-era monument in the Kozara National Park

▶ On the way back to the city across the Sana you will pass the Le Pont Motel. The Berek, a tributary of the Sana, flows along the left-hand side of Prijedor's main road, **King Peter I, the Liberator** (*Kralja Petra I Oslobodioca*). After a few meters Kralja Petra I Oslobodioca becomes a pedestrian zone. This was redesigned in recent years, so you will find marble benches under young trees which provide shade and relaxation. The façades of the older houses on the right side of the street have been restorcd, while the leſt side of the *Kralja Petra I Oslobodioca* is lined with smaller shopping centres.

▶ In the shopping street is also a national monument of Bosnia and Herzegovina – the Čaršija **Mosque** from the 17th century. It was destroyed in 1992 during the war and rebuilt during 2003 to 2008 using the original plans so it looks the same as it was before the war.

▶ The city's main square, **Trg Majora Zorana Karlice**, near the mosque, is called by the locals just the Square. The Square is dominated by the former shopping centre Patria. The façade of this decaying relic from socialist times is now crumbling in many places, while the orange lettering is reminiscent of Pop Art from the 1970s. To the left, behind the Square, in Nušićeva Street, are the locations of the Municipal Theatre (*Pozorište*) and the St. Joseph Catholic Church (*Crkva Sv. Josipa*).

▶ Leaving the Square eastwards via Miloš Obrenović Street you will arrive at Prijedor's administrative district. Here you will find the Tourist Office (at number 18 on Akademija Jovana Raškovića Avenue) and the museum of Kozara National Park on Akademika Jovana Raškovića Avenue. Opposite **Youth Park** (*Omladinski Park*) and Svetosavska Road we return to our starting point, the car park of Hotel Prijedor.

▶ The **Kozara National Park** is one of the most popular destinations in Bosnia and Herzegovina and it is visited by 80,000 people annually. The Kozara mountain is located 30 minutes drive north-east of Prijedor. Kozara is part of the Dinaric mountain range and extends to a length of 75km between the rivers Sava, Vrbas, Una and Sana. The various peaks of the Kozara mountains are all just under 1,000 metres high. Within the mountain is an area of 3,300 hectares that has been under special protection since 1967. As is often the case with national parks in Bosnia and Herzegovina, the original motivation to appoint Kozara as a national park was the memory of a battle in World War II. At the top of Mrakovica plateau there is a monument created by sculptor Dušan Džamonja from Zagreb which commemorates the Battle of Kozara. Tens of thousands of civilians – most of them young people – from the local area lost their lives in this battle.

A view across the Kozara National Park in summer

▶ The locals call them the "Beautiful Green Mountains" of Kozarska Krajina. In addition to hikers, the forests also attract hunting enthusiasts. 18,000 hectares of the Central Mountains are registered as available for hunting. Particularly deer, wild boar and hare can be found on the menus of the hunting lodges and in the Kozara restaurant in Prijedor. In the winter, alpine skiing is possible thanks to a ski-lift. Kozara is a member of the European Association of National Parks – EUROPARC.

3 Kozarska Dubica

▶ The northernmost city in Bosanska Krajina is Kozarska Dubica. It is home to slightly more than 10,000 residents, which makes it a small town, located on the banks of the River Una, near its confluence with the Sava. Its name comes from its geographical proximity to Dubica Kozara National Park. A bridge crossing the border connects Kozarska Dubica with Croatia. Before the Civil War of the 1990s, Kozarska Dubica was called Bosanska Dubica (Bosnian Dubica), with its twin city of Croatian Hrvatska Dubica (Croatian Dubica) across the bridge. Kozarska Dubica is part of Republika Srpska and is majority Serb populated. The town on the Una is about 70km north-

Kozarska Dubica town centre

The Kozara National Park

west of Banja Luka and 30km north of Prijedor. Highways M14 and M15 intersect at Kozarska Dubica.

▶ Kozarska Dubica and its region are very rural. Although along the highways there are a few smaller factories and manufacturing plants, the majority of the population earns its living from the cultivation, processing and marketing of agricultural products. Besides traditional farming on the fertile fields along the Una, it is especially cattle farming and recently established grape farming and wine production that generate the livelihood for its population. Fishing on the Una is now almost completely for the populations own consumption. The same applies to hunting in the wild forests on the slopes of the **Kozara National Park** (*Nacionalni Park Kozara*).

▶ The town of Kozarska Dubica was first settled around 900AD, however, the first written reference dates back to 1197, as Dubica was at the time part of medieval Bosnia. The town fell to the Ottomans in 1538 and, because of its position on the border between the Ottoman Empire and the Hapsburg Empire, the history of Kozarska Dubica is one of repeated military conflicts. This is especially

so during the last Austrian-Turkish war of 1787-1791, when most of the decisive battles were played out in and around Kozarska Dubica. Hapsburg troops under Emperor Joseph II succeeded in using this geographically advantageous location on the Una as a base from which to venture further into the territory of Bosnia and Herzegovina. However, the peace of Sistova in the summer of 1791 saw a retreat of the Hapsburgs from Bosnia and Herzegovina, so Kozarska Dubica – just like the rest of Bosnia and Herzegovina – remained part of the Ottoman Empire until the Congress of Berlin in 1878.

▶ During World War Two, Kozarska Dubica and Mount Kozara, just to the south of the town, were hotly contested. In the summer of 1942 this was the site of one of the most decisive battles between the fascist forces of the Germans and Croats and the Yugoslav communist Partisans. The Jesenovac concentration camp, which had a branch in Kozarska Dubica, was just 10km away. The events of World War II are commemorated on Mount Kozara with a socialist-era memorial.

▶ In the town, a small plaque in the city park commemorates the victims of the Second World War. The small

In striking contrast to the rest of the town, the Zepter Hotel

Town Park (*Gradski Park*) in the centre of Kozarska Dubica, with its shady trees and a fountain, invites numerous visitors to linger and relax – especially in the summer.

▶ Opposite is David's Square (*Davidov Trg*) and the City Courthouse, east of which is the recently redesigned **Zepter Plateau**. This modern central square is circled by numerous cafes and two-storey retail and office buildings. Also, the new space located behind the hotel is named after the founder and the most famous son of the city, Philip Zepter. In addition to its comfortable rooms, the Zepter Hotel has a spacious terrace where drinks are served and where you can enjoy gorgeous views across the Una.

The town Health Centre

▶ From the hotel you can walk to the small frontier bridge and to a **promenade** along the Una. On the banks of the Una you can find some areas which serve as small beaches, which, in the summer months, are very frequently visited by the town's young people. During the weekends, the restaurant-boat, St. Nicholas (*Sveti Nikola*), turns into a floating disco.

▶ Opposite the Zepter Plato is the pedestrianised street and shopping district of Kozarska Dubica, **Svetosavska Street**. Next to the public library and the Town Hall is the reconstructed Čaršija Mosque (*Čaršijska Džamija*) with its impressive wooden minaret. The car-free shopping street is where you will find a surprising number of local retail stores. The architecture style of the buildings in Svetosavka – as well as throughout Kozarska Dubica – is varied and ranges from socialist-era concrete and modern commercial buildings, to classical burghers' houses from the turn of the last century. You can see the best examples of the colourful town houses if you go to the end of Svetosavska Street and turn left towards the town Health Centre (*Dom Zdravlja*). This friendly residential area is characterised by well-kept houses and, with its many trees and gardens, reminds one of a bygone era. From the health centre you can return to the banks of the Una.

▶ Around Kozarska Dubica, below Mount Kozara, is the medieval Orthodox Christian **Moštanica Monastery**, dating from the 12th century. This Serbian Orthodox pilgrimage site in the valley of the river Moštanica is also an extremely scenic spot.

▶ Halfway to Prijedor is the **Mlječanica Spa**. The spa's waters are believed to have healing powers and a quick renovation of the swimming facilities would certainly not hurt the local tourist trade.

The Moštanica Serbian Orthodox Monastery

Zepter

In Kozarska Dubica you will encounter the name Zepter all over the place. Both the new hotel and the great square and urban space bear this name. Furthermore, many social and sport clubs in Dubica have Zepter as a benefactor and donor. In all cases this refers to Philip Zepter. A man whose given name is Milan Janković and who was born here in 1950. While not born in Kozarska Dubica, it is here that he spent his childhood before he went to study in Belgrade.

Janković founded a company called Zepter in 1986, which specialized in the production and sale of high quality household goods and luxury items. Zepter was based in Europe from the beginning and produced his products in Germany, Italy and Switzerland – as well as in Kozarska Dubica. Zepter shops can now be found in over 40 countries around the world. Zepter is considered one of the richest man of Serbian nationality. Although, he hasn't lived in the region for decades he has actively engaged in the development of his homeland with numerous philanthropic ventures. Without his involvement Kozarska Dubica would undoubtedly be a very different town today.

❹ Novi Grad

▶ Novi Grad is located at the confluence of the rivers Una and Sana and sits on the border with Croatia. Before the 1990s civil war the town was called Bosanski Novi. And some of the street signs still display this name. Novi Grad, which is part of Republika Srpska, is situated at about 122 metres above sea level and has around 15,000 inhabitants.

▶ Novi Grad was first mentioned in 1280 under the Latin name, Castrum Novum. The town's fortress, on the hill above the confluence of the Una and Sana, played a major military role in the Middle Ages, during the struggle for Bosnia's independence. During this period a town developed in the shadow of the fortress and became known as Under Fortress (*Podgrad*).

A view across Novi Grad

The Ottomans rebuilt the fortress after their takeover of the town in 1557 and the first bridge over the Una dates from this period. Novi Grad became an important strategic location for the Ottoman Empire and its march towards Vienna. As the balance of power between empires shifted, Novi Grad passed from Hapsburg to Ottoman control but after the Congress of Berlin in 1878 the town fell under Hapsburg rule and was transformed as a town. The Hapsburg rulers dismantled the fort and other buildings from the Ottoman era and used the 'liberated' materials to build a new, modern town.

▶ Today, the town of Novi Grad is also characterised with buildings from the socialist era. The **Promenade** on the Una leads from the border bridge to the confluence with the Sana. In numerous places pebble beaches and beach volleyball courts have been created and, on a peninsula at the confluence of Sana and Una, you will find an interesting restaurant and guest house, the "Mill on the River Island" (*Mlin na Adi*). The terrace of *Mlin na Adi* offers lovely views of the town and the river.

▶ Along Mladen Stojanović Street and behind the *Mlin na Adi* restaurant you reach the foot of the hill bearing the the former Ottoman fortress. At the summit there is a memorial to the Partisan Mother (*Majka Partizanka*), erected in memory of the victims of the Second World War in the region.

▶ From Novi Grad it is worth taking a short trip to the town of **Kostajnica**. The town is also located right on the river Una and from Novi Grad it is a 20 minute drive following the wild meanders of the river.

The town of Kostajnica on the banks of the Una

5 Bosanska Krupa

▶ Bosanska Krupa is located in the valley of the rivers Una and Krušnica and is a good 25km north of Bihać, on the M14 highway. Bosanska Krupa is part of the Una-Sana Canton, itself part of the Federation of Bosnia and Herzegovina. The town is just called Krupa by the locals, who number approximately 15,000. The surrounding villages belonging to the Bosanska Krupa municipality bring the number up to around 30,000 and

A Catholic church in Bosanska Krupa

the municipality is one of the major centres of Bosanska Krajina. Because of its location in the valley and the source of the Krušnica, the town is one of the most scenic destinations in Bosanska Krajina. Krupa is also home to one of the tidiest and best kept campsites in Bosnia and Herzegovina.

▶ The town's origins date back to the Roman times and excavations in Ljusina unearthed tombs and many other traces of Roman buildings. The first written records of Krupa date back to the Middle Ages, when Krupa was part of the Croatian Kingdom. The first records mentioning Krupa, in the 13th century, refer to a fortress on a small hill above the Una. Until the Ottoman conquest of Bosnia and Herzegovina Bosanska Krupa was part of the Croatian medieval kingdom. The Ottomans rebuilt the fortress at the Una into a stately castle and held it until the 19th century. After the 1878 Congress of Berlin Krupa, then a small town of just 2,000 inhabitants, passed to Hapsburg control. The Hapsburgs had no longer had any use for the medieval fortress, so it fell out of use.

▶ Bosanska Krupa and its surroundings have been the scene of gruesome massacres and heavy fighting – both during the Second World War and during the civil war of the 1990s. A commemorative plaque has been placed in the Una Valley, in the direction of Bihać, the site of the execution of many Partisans by German troops. During the war of the 1990s Bosanska Krupa was one of the most contested places in Bosnia and Herzegovina. The border and thus the front line between the Bosnian Muslim and Serbian forces cut through the town for three years, from 1992 to 1995. Only in the last days of the war, before the signing of the Dayton Agreement, did Bosnian Muslim forces succeeded in taking the town. Atrocities and destruction

The wooden footbridge leads to an island on the Una

carried out by both sides have left a town devastated and ruined by war.

▶ Although, traces of the war are still visible in Krupa, many parts of the town have been renovated and are going through a bright new beginning. In the historic **Old Town** (*Stari Grad*) around the mountain fortress, the hustle and bustle of everyday town life has returned and the wooden footbridge (*Međumostovi*) across the Una to the river island practically turns into a fashion catwalk in the summer months when the town's young people gather to see and be seen. A Catholic church, a Serbian Orthodox church and a mosque were built close to each other in the old town. A fountain and marble plaques commemorate the fallen Muslims in the community. From the fortress you can enjoy a wonderful view of the surrounding forested mountains, and of the powerful blue colours of the waters of the Una. In Bosanska Krupa, the Una reaches an impressive expansion and sometimes seems almost like a calm lake. Fun and activities, especially rowing, are very popular in Bosanska Krupa and below the wooden bridge you can find a riverside public bathing area.

▶ The main attraction in the area of Bosanska Krupa is the **source of the**

The commemorative fountain in the heart of Bosanska Krupa

Krušnica. This can be hiked to on foot from the town. About an hour should be enough for the 6km walk along the Krušnica at a relaxed pace. The source itself is in a cave around which several myths and legends have grown. The exact dimensions and the depth of the cave are not yet known. In 2008 an international group of divers managed to penetrate 112 metres into the cave interior, however, they did not reach the cave's deepest point.

▶ Bosanska Krupa is recommended to lovers of camping. The **Una campsite** is located in the direction of Novo Mesto near the river. In addition to numerous plots on lush green lawn, the campsite also offers three bungalows. The sanitation facilities in the camp are also new and in good condition. A shaded terrace right on the river Una is available to all guests. The campsite is an ideal starting point and destination for rafting and rowing trips. A bicycle rental offers mobility to explore the surrounding area. In the summer months the friendly camp warden cooks for his guests and will gladly take guests across to the other bank of the Una in his boat, if necessary. As a sign of its quality, the Una camp has an award from the German automotive association, and costs just €4 per person per night.

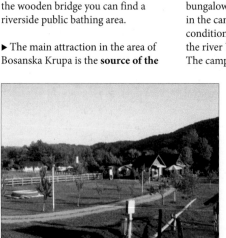

The Una campsite

6 Bihać

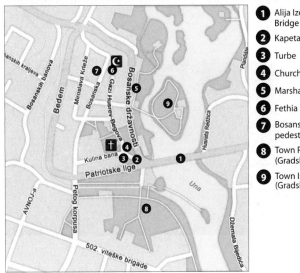

1. Alija Izetbegović Bridge
2. Kapetanova Kula
3. Turbe
4. Church of St. Anthony
5. Marshal Tito Square
6. Fethia Mosque
7. Bosanska street pedestrian zone
8. Town Park (Gradski Park)
9. Town Island (Gradski Otok)

▶ The town of Bihać, in the northwest of Bosanska Krajina, is the first point of contact with Bosnia and Herzegovina for many European visitors arriving by car. Directly on the border with Croatia and only a stone's throw from Croatia's world famous Plitvice Lakes National Park, the city on the banks of the Una offers travellers a good insight into what to expect in Bosnia and Herzegovina – and especially in Bosanska Krajina – unspoiled nature and cultural diversity. This makes Bihać and its surroundings an ideal place to begin a visit to Bosnia and Herzegovina.

▶ Bihać is located just north of the Una National Park, the only National Park in the Federation of Bosnia and Herzegovina, and the city serves as the starting point for excursions into the beautiful natural environment of

A winter view of the Una as it passes through Bihać

A view of Bihać

the park. Bihać itself offers the visitor an interesting juxtaposition of history and modernity, historical architecture and modern infrastructure. Unlike other towns and cities in Bosnia and Herzegovina, Bihać has successfully integrated the Una river into its urban landscape.

▶ Bihać is the capital of the Una-Sana Canton, part of the Federation, and has just over 60,000 inhabitants. About 90% of the inhabitants are Bosnian Muslim. The city was strongly contested during the Civil War in the 1990s and the once large Serbian Orthodox community has only a few members left today.

▶ As it enters Bihać, the Una stretches through a broad valley – above and below the city it passes through narrow gorges. South-east of Bihać, the peaks of the Grmeč mountains rise to about 1,100 metres above sea level and to the west is the Plješevica mountain range, which simultaneously forms the Croatian border. The highest peak in Plješevica reaches up to 1,649 metres. The municipality of Bihać stretches 40km to the south in a curve along the Croatian border and includes the Una National Park, which ends with the village of Martin Brod.

▶ The historic origins of the city go back at least to Roman times but the existence of Bihać was first documented in 1260 when a city here was recorded in a document of the Hungarian-Croatian king, Bela IV, with the Latin name Castrum Bichiciense, as the property of a Catholic monastery. The town walls of Bihać dating from this period are still visible today. Until the 16th century the city council, predominantly Croat, held meetings in the highest Croatian body, the *Sabor*. At the end of the 16th century Bihać was conquered by the Ottomans. Because of its location on the military frontier of the Hapsburg Empire and its Catholic tradition, Bihać was often on the front line in the many armed conflicts between the Ottoman and Hapsburg empires. Despite numerous attempts and short-term successes of the Hapsburg Monarchy to integrate Bihać into its territory, the city remained part of the Ottoman Empire until the 1878 Congress of Berlin and the final withdrawal of Ottoman forces.

▶ During the Second World War, in the spring of 1942, Tito's Partisans succeeded in liberating Bihać from its fascist occupiers for a short period and proclaimed the Free Republic of Bihać. At the end of November 1942, the first inaugural meeting of the Anti-Fascist Council for the National Liberation of Yugoslavia (*Antifašističko Vijeće Narodnog Oslobođenja Jugoslavije* or AVNOJ for short) was held in Bihać and formed the basis for the post-war government of Tito's Yugoslavia. Soon after this meeting, however, the German *Wehrmacht* managed to retake Bihać but the Partisans' success had an important psychological effect on the courage of the communist resistence. In Tito's Yugoslavia Bihać enjoyed a special role because of its efforts during the war and was thus treated preferentially in the establishment of industrial and military facilities after the war.

▶ Bihać is one of the most important cities of Bosnia and Herzegovina, not only in terms of its population, but also because it is the capital of the Canton of Bihać and has a well developed urban infrastructure; such as hospitals, a university and a number of local government offices. Sports facilities also can be found in abundance in this, the largest city on the river Una – for example, Bihać is considered the centre of tennis in Bosnia and Herzegovina.

THE CENTRE

▶ The starting point for a walking tour of Bihać's downtown is the **Alija Izetbegović Bridge**. Part of the M5 highway (*Magistrala 5*) that runs through Bihać connects the neighborhoods Prekounje and Brklja with the centre. From the bridge you can see numerous small islands on the river Una. The largest island, *Gradski Otok* (City Island), can be reached from both sides of the river via a footbridge.

▶ The rise in the Old Town (*Stari Grad*) begins at the Alija Izetbegovic Bridge, from here you can reach the top by way of a set of stairs. The Old Town is laid out as a park with green spaces between the historic buildings serving as a popular rest and meeting places. The most visible sight is **Kapetanova Kula**, a tower that dates from the early 13th century, when Bihać was still a part of the Hungarian-Croatian Kingdom. It was part of the medieval fortifications and served as a prison – Kapetanova Kula is today a museum.

▶ Opposite the tower is a **Turbe** and several myths about the history and origin of this mausoleum have

The Alija Izetbegović Bridge leads to the City Island

The 13th century *Kapetanova Kula* and Ottoman-era *Turbe*

developed. The only thing we can confidently say is that it originated from the period of Ottoman rule over Bihać and was built as a tomb for two pashas. During the civil war in Bosnia and Herzegovina in the 1990s the Turbe was unfortunately largely destroyed – it has, however, since been restored and remains an interesting monument.

▶ The third historic building on the hillock of the Old Town is the **Church of St. Anthony** from the 19th century. The large church has some 900m² of floor space that, combined with a striking bell tower, make it one of the largest buildings of its time in Bosnia and Herzegovina. The construction of the Catholic Church began immediately after the beginning of the Hapsburg administration in 1878 to serve as visual proof of the return of Christianity. In the Second World War the church itself was razed to the ground, an event that just the bell tower survived, and was never rebuilt. The tower still stands as a reminder of what was once the largest church in the city.

▶ Along the paved Gazi Husrevbegova alley you return to the banks of the Una and **Marshal Tito Square** (*Trg Maršala Tita*). On this busy urban square you will find a bus terminal, the University Library and a marketplace (*pijaca*). Local tradesmen sell fresh regional produce at the market and, due to the proximity of the Adriatic, there are also many Mediterranean foods on sale here.

▶ A staircase ascends from here to reach the Džemaludin Čaušević

The bell tower of the Church of St. Anthony

Square. Here you will see the **Fethija Mosque**, one of the best preserved mosques in Bosnia and Herzegovina. In 1592, when the mosque was built, Bihać was an Ottoman town and one of the first acts of the new regime was to turn churches into mosques. This is what was done with what was once the church of a Dominican monastery; the walls of the original Gothic church from the 13th century were largely preserved by the Ottoman builders. It now has a Muslim minaret as well as a Christian bell tower. A number of traces and structural elements which point to the original Christian church can still be seen today.

▶ Opposite the mosque there is the renovated Una Theatre. This is where Bihać's pedestrian zone begins, it is called just Bosanska and leads past the Town Hall and to an unspectacular modern town square, to Alija Izetbegović Avenue and the City Park. The pedestrianised **Bosanska Street** is brought to life by numerous cafes and small boutiques; regional handicrafts and honey are also sold on the space in front of the Town Hall. In the information centre of the Una National Park (at number 1 Bosanska Street) information can be obtained about the region and the national park.

▶ The **City Park** (*Gradski Park*) of Bihać is the most extensive urban park in Bosnia and Herzegovina. Especially during the mist-shrouded morning hours, the leafy park has a charming peaceful atmosphere and is a perfect place for a stroll down to the river. A canoeing course has been installed on a small side channel of the Una, just by the park. The paved path along the river, which continues across to one of the islands on the river, with numerous refreshments on offer, simply invites you to go for a liesurly walk at any time of day.

BEYOND THE CENTRE

▶ In a small park just south of the downtown area, at the foot of

The Fethija Mosque

Plješevica, a **Partizan** memorial commemorates the fallen Partisans in World War Two. The stadium of the city's Jedinstvo (Unity) football club lies just opposite and the park also features a children's play area.

▶ The remains of the medieval **Sokolac** fortress still stand on a summit to the south of the city and can be reached by a 15 minute climb from the Golubić district. Sturdy footwear is advised given the steep path. The unusual triangular ruins with two main towers were once one of the many strongholds of the 14th century medieval Bosnian kingdom. The Sokolac fortress also served as a stronghold for the Ottomans from 1592. Today the site offers magnificent vistas over the Una valley and the wooded Plješevica mountain range in the west.

▶ Besides the natural beauty of the Una National Park, there are two other recommended excursions from Bihać. The first is the Ostrožac fortress (see p. 172) to the east of Bihać and the second is the village of **Gravice**, which contains a Partisan monument. Gravice is just 4km northwest of the city and can easily be reached on foot.

7 Ostrožac

▶ The Ostrožac fortress and palace complex is one of the most impressive historical buildings in Bosnia and Herzegovina. Originally dating from the Middle Ages and adapted by Ottoman rulers and subsequently, the Hapsburgs in the 19th and 20th centuries, the sprawling complex displays the rich architectural traces of many ages. The location of Ostrožac, 200 metres above the valley of the Una, offers fantastic views of the varied and colorful landscape of Bosanska Krajina.

▶ Ostrožac is located on the outskirts of Cazin, 15km northeast of Bihać. To get there by car from Bihać you have to take the M14 highway in the direction of Bosanska Krupa. Just past the Strbački Bug hotel turn left over the Una and then follow the serpentines until you reach Ostrožac. In the village bearing the same name and in front of the mighty entrance there is plenty of parking space available.

▶ The name Ostrožac was first recorded in 1286 as the seat of the Croatian noble family, Babonić. The massive defensive tower, through which one enters into the facility, dates from that period, however, the origins of Ostrožac are significantly older. Historians believe that some structural components date as far back as 500BC. The **Romans**, whose road network crisscrossed Bosanska Krajina most probably made use of this strategic location.

▶ The courtyard of the fortress, 175 metres long and 50 metres wide, is surrounded by a wall 6-8 metres high. The defensive ramparts date from the **Ottoman era** – the Ottomans ruled Ostrožac for exactly 300 years from 1578 to 1878. Apart from this defensive wall, all other traces of the Ottomans were eliminated after their withdrawl and when the Hapsburgs took control of the fortress after the Congress of Berlin.

▶ The **Hapsburgs** could not, however, make use of the fortress for military purposes. Instead, they installed a military governor in Bihać, Lothar von Berks, who treated Ostrožac as his private architectural playground. He had a palace built for his family

The main tower of the Ostrožac fortress

here in 1900 and the palace still stands directly above the valley of the Una. Until just before the Second World War, the von Berks family lived in this traditional Austrian pleasure palace. This Bosnian version of Neuschwanstein Castle may have seen better days but it still retains a certain ramshackle charm.

▶ Since the end of World War Two, Ostrožac has been owned by the state. Since the 1960s, a new tradition was initiated in which a new stone sculpture is erected in the complex's sprawling courtyard every year. Artists from around the world participate in this annual tradition. The entrance to the palace costs 4 Convertible Marks. Although the ticket booth is mostly unoccupied the phone number of the 'Castle caretaker' can be found on a sign at the entrance. He is very happy to receive a phone call and has great anecdotes to tell about the colourful history of Ostrožac.

The Ostrožac fortress

7 Ključ

▶ Ključ, on the River Sana forms the southernmost tip of the Bosanska Krajina region. Before the war in the 1990s, Ključ was regarded one of the largest communities in Bosnia and Herzegovina; after the Dayton Peace Agreement, however, the community was divided. The eastern part,

The *Stari Grad* fortress at Ključ

The 14th century Old Fortress at Ključ

incredibly popular with the region's anglers as the crystal-clear rivers have made the region famous, especially among fly fishermen. In 2010, the European fly fishing championships took place in the region around Ključ. This emerging fishing-tourism boom has also led to an increase in the accommodation on offer along the Sana, Sanica and Ribnik rivers.

which was, before the war, inhabited almost entirely by Serbs, is now part of Republika Srpska and has been renamed Ribnik. The remainder of the town, still called Ključ, belongs to the Federation of Bosnia and Herzegovina, and about 90% of the approximately 6,000 inhabitants are Bosnian Muslims.

▶ Ključ lies in a green valley at a bend of the Sana. Outside the city, the river cuts an impressive canyon through the steep mountain range and divides it into the Breščica Massif in the west and the Ljubinska mountains to the east. For centuries the gorge held a key position on the trade routes of the region. The name of the town, Ključ, is Bosnian for 'key'.

▶ Due to the low population density of the area, the diversity of the surrounding landscape including the river habitats of the Sana, Sanica and Ribnik remains largely untouched, making Ključ great destination for nature lovers and hikers. Ključ is also

▶ The **Old Fortress** (*Stari Grad*) was probably established in the first half of the 14th century and is built on a spectacular position above the present town. Here the last Bosnian king, Stjepan Tomašević, was captured in 1463 by the Ottoman army and taken to a location near Jajce where he was executed (see p. 190). By 1838 an Ottoman garrison was stationed in the fortress in order to control the trade routes through the Sana Valley. The path leading to the partially restored fort is steep but paved and well marked and the climb is well worth it if only because of the enchanting view of the Sana Valley.

▶ Walks to the sources of Sana, Sanica and Ribnik rivers in the area around Ključ are highly recommended. All three are karst springs which are typical for the region and which spring with crystal clear, shimmering, turquoise coloured but bitterly cold water (see p. 78).

The spring of the Sana

AUTHOR'S PICK: HOTELS & RESTAURANTS

Due to the abundance of hotels and restaurants on offer it would be impossible to list them all and to keep the list current. Instead, please find below a selection of hotels and restaurants recommended by the author:

HOTELS

Banja Luka	**Banja Luka Hotel**	With its 200 rooms this is the largest hotel in Banja Luka, offering a central location, parking, a restaurant, a night club and a casino	Kralja Petra I Karađorđevića 97 Banja Luka +387 51 215 775
Banja Luka	**Palas Hotel**	A historic but recently renovated hotel with 69 rooms, underground parking and a restaurant	Kralja Petra I Karađorđevića 60 78000 Banja Luka +387 51 218 723
Banja Luka	**Cezar Hotel**	A modern business hotel close to the Government, 42 rooms with Wi-Fi and parking as standard	Mladjena Stojanovića 123, 78000 Banja Luka +387 51 326 400
Prijedor	**Motel Le Pont**	21 rooms right on the banks of the Sana with a terrace, restaurant, parking and Wi-Fi	Kralja Petra I Oslobodioca 1, Prijedor +387 52 234 788
Kozarska Dubica	**Zepter Hotel**	A brand new hotel on the Una with a very good restaurant, Wi-Fi, car park and 19 comfortable rooms	Svetosavska 2, 79240 Kozarska Dubica +387 52 424 242
Bihać	**Kostelski Buk Hotel**	Wonderful hotel 8km from Bihać with views of the Una, a restaurant, a petting zoo, Wi-Fi and parking	Kostela bb, 77000 Bihać +387 37 302 340
Bihać	**Pavilijon Hotel**	Located in the city park, close to the Una, this small hotel has a restaurant and large terrace as well as parking facilities	Aleja Alije Izetbegovića bb 77000 Bihać +387 37 224 194
Bihać	**Opal Hotel**	Just north of the centre and with a restaurant overlooking the Una, this hotel also offers parking facilities and Wi-Fi	Krupska bb 77000 Bihać +387 37 228 585
Ključ	**Konak Crvena Jabuka**	Private accommodation with 7 rooms, quiet and great location above the Sana, Wi-Fi and multi-lingual host	79280 Ključ +387 37 663 579
Sanica	**Villa Oaza Mira**	The "Oasis of Peace" has 4 bungalows with 20 beds, a small swimming pool and spectacular views of the Sanica Valley	Željeznička 24 79285 Sanica +387 37 671 462

RESTAURANTS

Sanica	**Restaurant Ribnjak**	100 metres from the Sanica River this open-air restaurant serves the most delicious grilled trout in the country	Source of the Sanica 79285 Sanica +387 61 697 162

CENTRAL BOSNIA

EASTERN BOSNIA

Maglaj

BOSANSKA KRAJINA

Vitez

EASTERN BOSNIA

HERZEGOVINA

1 TRAVNIK   **4** JAJCE   **7** KONJIC

2 ZENICA   **5** BUGOJNO

3 VRANDUK   **6** VISOKO

✠ Central Bosnia is defined by the river from which the country draws its name, the Bosna. The source of the Bosna (see p. 122) is the Olympic mountain, Mount Igman, from where she flows through the region's largest cities and on to its northern borders. Central Bosnia, the industrial heartland of Bosnia and the cradle of its history, is also the centre of the country's Islamic community and Ottoman heritage. The region was the inspiration for the country's only Nobel Prize winning author, Ivo Andrić (see p. 182). A recently 'discovered' pyramid is undoubtedly

Zenica

The Bosnian 'Pyramid'

the wackiest tourist attraction in Bosnia and Herzegovina (see p. 198).

✦ Zenica, the capital of the region has been evolving since the late 19th century into a centre of heavy industry and its mining and steel works are both a blessing and a curse for the town. Science and commerce are developing gradually as alternatives to heavy industry in this exciting city, however, the war of the 1990s has unfortunately left deep scars here too.

✦ Jajce, the city with the spectacular waterfall on the River Vrbas, was the medieval capital of the Bosnian kings and important fortresses were also located in Vranduk and Visoko. The Ottomans turned Travnik into one of their central trading centres in Europe and in Konjic they constructed an architecturally inspiring bridge.

✦ The Ottoman legacy in Central Bosnia can be clearly seen and felt. Zenica, Bugojno, Travnik and Konjic are strongholds of Bosnian Islam,

with mosques extensively renovated and new ones being built all the time and veiled women are a more common sight in these towns than in other regions of Bosnia and Herzegovina. Tourism in this region is relatively under-developed but it offers a view onto an enchanting and mysterious tradition of European Islam.

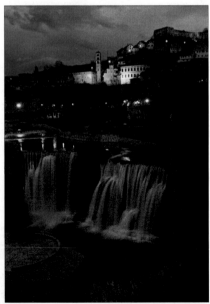

Jajce with its spectacular waterfall

1 Travnik

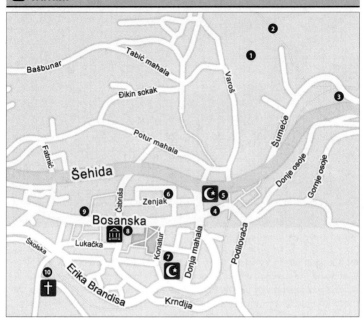

1. Old Town (Stari Grad)
2. Plave Vode (Blue Water)
3. Ibrahim Paša Medresa
4. Donja Čaršija
5. Suleiman Mosque
6. No. 13 Zenjak street: Birthplace of Ivo Andrić
7. Konatur Mosque
8. City & Regional Museum
9. Consul Caffe
10. Catholic Church

▶ The town of Travnik on the River Lašva was once the capital of Bosnia and Herzegovina and is one of the most beautiful cities in the country and one of the most worth taking the time to visit. Travnik is a town of about 20,000 inhabitants that has largely retained its historic character. Its 16 mosques, several Ottoman *Turbe* (Turkish mausoleums), Islamic education centres and cemeteries serve to maintain the delightful Oriental atmosphere of the city. The birthplace of Nobel Prize winning author, Ivo Andrić, Travnik still retains the atmospheric charm that captivated the main characters of Andrić's main novel set in the town, "The Bosnian Chronicle".

▶ Travnik is situated on the road from Sarajevo to Banja Luka and almost the all the passenger and freight traffic between the two cities runs through the nearby Lašva Valley. Fortunately, the highway does not lead through the city centre of Travnik and the old town is spared traffic of the main road. The mountains around Travnik are ideal

The streets of Travnik

A night view of the fortress at Travnik

for hiking in summer and skiing in winter and the standard of facilities for visitors is comparatively high both in the town and the surrounding area.

▶ The history of the city and region can be told most clearly through the **Old Town** (*Stari Grad*) of Travnik. The Old Town is encapsulated in a fortress overlooking the town, protected by steep cliffs that run down to two rivers, the Hendek and the Šumeće. The first written records of the town were created with the arrival of the Ottomans in 1463, however, the origins of Travnik stretch much further back than the 15th century.

The fort is 130 metres wide and 60 meters long, significant dimensions for a fort built in the Middle Ages. At the beginning there were 47 houses - 11 Muslim and 36 Christian in the Old Town but the town's true heyday came in the late 17th century when Travnik served as a residence for the Ottoman Vizier of the region. The French and Hapsburg consulates were established in the early 19th century in Travnik and the lives of the first diplomats in Bosnia and Herzegovina was beautifully recorded in the literary works of Ivo Andrić, especially his novel "Bosnian Chronicle", also known as "The Chronicles of Travnik".

The Blue Water (*Plava Voda*) spring in Travnik

▶ The Old Town in Travnik has in recent years been completely renovated. Today, the area is home to an information centre, a museum, the old minaret, and is used again for cultural events that are held on a small outdoor stage during the summer months. The entrance to the Old Town costs 2 Convertible Marks and you can reach the historic Old Town on foot from the city centre in 15 minutes.

The Suleiman Mosque, with its decorative arcades

▶ Below the fortress is the much-visited source of the Šumeće river. Because of the bluish colour of the spring water this place is also called **Blue Water** (*Plava Voda*). In the summer buses from all over Bosnia and Herzegovina line up in the car park for the multitude of restaurants and souvenir stands. Opposite the source is the **Ibrahim Pasha Medresa**, this educational institution was built in 1705 is still used today as an Islamic school. Together with the Šumeće spring, Plava Voda is an Islamic pilgrimage site for the tombs (*Turbe*) of Mufta Muhamed and his wife.

▶ The centre of Travnik is not far from the Plava Voda spring. An archway leads into the traditional bazaar district **Donja Čaršija** (*Lower Market*) and there are numerous *ćevapčići* stalls, small shops and boutiques plying their wares, including gold

jewellery and leather goods. Please note that the Islamic city regulations prohibit the sale of all alcoholic beverages in Donja Čaršija.

▶ In the square following the Čaršija is the colourful **Suleiman Mosque**. After a fire at the beginning of the 19th century, the colourful mosque was rebuilt based on the original blueprints which date from 1757. The wood-panelled arcades of the beautifully decorated mosque contain a number of small shops. The town's main street, Bosanska, begins by the mosque.

▶ The **birthplace** of the most famous son of the city, Ivo Andric, who was born in October 1892, is close to the Suleiman Mosque at number 13 Zenjak Street. The building where he was born is now a small museum hosting exhibitions, books, writings and images from Andric's life. The interior dates from the time when the writer's family lived here and the typical Bosnian courtyard (*avlija*) now houses a restaurant. The entrance fee for the museum is 2 Convertible Marks.

▶ Back on Bosanska and a few metres to the left is the small city park. At the top of the park is the town hall and the 17th century **Kanator Mosque** with its remarkable wooden minaret.

The house in which Nobel Laureate, Ivo Andrić, was born

The Travnik Regional Museum

▶ **The City and Regional Museum** (*Zavičajni Muzej Travnik*) is one of the country's oldest having existed since 1921. It hosts an exhibition of embalmed exotic and domesticated animals on the ground floor and a traditional Bosnian drawing room, which has been recreated with historical household items and weapons from the Ottoman period, on the second floor. The drawing room also serves as a registry office. One area of the museum has been set aside for exhibitions by contemporary artists from the region. The Museum is open on weekdays from 9am-3pm and on weekends from 10am-2pm.

▶ Also worth visiting is the **Consul Cafe** in Bosanska; be sure to take time out to relax on the terrace of the ivy covered house with a Bosnian coffee and a copy of Ivo Andric 's "Bosnian Chronicle". The Consul is in the traditional guest house that is mentioned in the book and the Catholic Church where Ivo Andrić was baptised 1892, is also located just down the street.

▶ The area around Travnik is also well worth visiting. **Mount Vlašić**, just on the outskirts of the town possesses an authentic rural charm and is a great location for hiking, mountain-biking and other leisure

No one has ever reckoned the number of hours of sunlight which nature has withheld from this town, but it is certain that here the sun rises later and sets earlier than in any other of the numerous Bosnian cities and small towns. The people of the town – Travničani – do not deny it either, but they claim that, while it shines, it does so with a light that no other town can boast of.

An extract from "Bosnian Chronicle" by Ivo Andrić

Ivo Andrić

The most famous person from Bosnia and Herzegovina is Nobel prizewinning author Ivo Andrić. He was born on 9 October 1892 in Travnik, where one of his most famous novels and "Bosnian Chronicle" is set. Andrić attended school in Sarajevo and studied philosophy in Zagreb, Vienna, Krakow and Graz. After the First World War Andrić subsequently graduated into a diplomat for the new Yugoslav state. At the outbreak of the Second World War, he was the ambassador in Berlin. Henceforth Andrić devoted his life primarily to literature and during the war created his two masterpieces the Consul and Vizier and the Bridge on the Drina. Both works are set and deal with events in his homeland. The epic narrative of Bosnia and Herzegovina is one of the leitmotifs for Andric, who was awarded the 1961 Nobel Prize for Literature.

Skiing on Vlašić

activities. The highest peak of the nearby Vlašić mountain range is Paljenik, which is just shy of 2,000 metres. The name Vlašić comes from the Slavic patronymic form of 'Vlach' (*Vlah*). The Vlachs in the area around Travnik became known for their innovative sheep breeding skills and from this tradition a special sheep husbandry dates back centuries. The local *Pramenka* sheep's milk is still the basis for a delicacy well-known throughout the former Yugoslavia: **Valšić Cheese** (*Vlašićki Sir*).

▶ The Vlašić Mountains also offer a wide variety of winter sports activities. In Babanovac there are two drag-ski-lifts and a host of large hotels and private accommodation. This small, ageing ski resort also has an unusual curiosity, the ruins of a destroyed ski-jump (see p. 58). During the summer months the Vlašić Mountains are especially good for mountain biking and many of the routes are well signposted.

In reality, this town of theirs was a narrow and deep gorge which successive generations had in the course of time built up and brought under cultivation, a fortified passageway where had paused and then settled down permanently, adapting themselves to it and it to themselves down the centuries. On both sides, mountains tumble down steeply and meet in the valley at a sharp angle, leaving barely enough room for a thin river and a road running beside it. It all reminds one of an oversize half-open book, the pages of which, standing up stiffly on each side, are generously illustrated with gardens, streets, houses, fields, cemeteries and mosques.

An extract from "Bosnian Chronicle" by Ivo Andrić

2 Zenica

1. Square of Bosnia & Herzegovina
2. Bosnian National Theatre
3. Marshal Tito pedestrian zone
4. Kočeva Mosque
5. Market
6. Synagogue
7. Čaršija
8. Sultan Ahmed Mosque
9. Riverside Boulevard

▶ Zenica, with a population of over 130,000 inhabitants, is the largest town in the central part of the Federation of Bosnia and Herzegovina, yet, despite its size, legacy of economic prosperity, university and its central location, the city is alas neither prosperous nor beautiful. Modernization of socialist-era heavy industry has only partially succeeded, yet the post-WWII concrete structures reaching for the sky like the ruins of dystopian fortresses still dominate the cityscape, while the River Bosna follows a subdued and lifeless path through the town. A visit to Zenica should not be motivated by aesthetic concerns, instead one should go there for a sense of the country's lost socialist and industrial past. One thing is for sure, Zenica is one of the cities in Bosnia and Herzegovina with the greatest potential for change.

▶ Situated 320 metres above sea level in the valley of the Bosna river, Zenica is surrounded by high, forested mountains whose peaks Kapak and Hum and Mount Ravna reach heights of up to 1,300 metres. The mountain

A view of Zenica

The Bosna rolls through Zenica

peaks, coupled with a skyline of once potent heavy industry, the horizon over Zenica is a very special sight. The nearby mountains, just beyond the city limits, are popular destinations for excursions and local residents enjoy the varied recreational opportunities they offer the whole year round.

▶ The history of the town and its surroundings dates back to the Bronze Age, and archaeologists have unearthed tools and skeletons from this period in nearby Drivuše and Gradišća. The Romans too left their mark in the wide valley of the Bosna. In Bosnia in the Middle Ages, Vranduk, near Zenica, was an important stronghold and played a major role in defending the area against the Ottoman onslaught. The first written records of Zenica date as far back as March 1436 – nowadays Zenica celebrates the anniversary of its founding every year on the 20th of March. Following the arrival of the Ottomans, however, Zenica ceased to be the important strategic location it once was. Away from the county's main communication lines, the city's development slowed drastically. Only with the start of Hapsburg rule in 1878, did a modern city begin to develop. Zenica's industrialisation began in 1892 when the first steel mill was founded here. When the town was linked to a growing international rail network the population grew to more than 10,000 and the standard of living increased.

▶ The Second World War caused great material damage to the budding town; both in terms of destroyed industry and in terms of the human cost. The outcome was that in 1948, the population numbered just 12,000 inhabitants and the city needed to be reborn yet again. In socialist Yugoslavia it was decreed that Zenica would become a centre for heavy industry and many factories were built, the most significant being the large steel works. Zenica was adapted to the needs and expectations of industry and a rapidly growing

The socialist-era high-rises of Zenica are a legacy of its once prosperous past

number of workers. Large blocks of flats were built for young families and functional leisure and sports facilities were created. To serve the needs of the increasingly industrial city, new educational institutions with a focus on industry were established. Zenica grew enormously during the decades of socialism in Yugoslavia and 40 years after the Second World War, its population was ten times what it had been when the war ended. Some 25,000 people were employed just by the Željezara steel mill. Zenica was a thriving new model socialist city.

As with so many buildings in Zenica, the National Theatre has seen better days

▶ The city's economic and social prosperity ended abruptly in the early 1990s. The collapse of the socialist state-managed economy was followed by mass unemployment and the war destroyed the fabric of social cohesion in this ethnically mixed city. Zenica has sadly yet to recover from these catastrophic events. The unemployment rate remains high, indeed the highest in Bosnia and Herzegovina. There are, however, some positive developments; the steel plant was privatised in 2004 and is again the largest employer in the region; the university broadened its range of subjects and is again attracting students from all over Central Bosnia and the highway to Sarajevo is, in theory at least, close to completion.

▶ A stroll through Zenica leads one from the most central square of the city, **the Square of Bosnia and Herzegovina** (*Trg Bosne i Herzegovine*) near the river Bosna. Over time many important institutions have settled in the square; the City Hall (*Zgrada Opštine*), the Court (*Sud*), the headquarters the steel giant, ArcelorMittal, and the Town Kafana (*Gradska Kafana*) – all four buildings have seen better days. The four buildings and the square itself date back to the glory days of socialist-era urban planning. Concrete dominates the landscape and green spaces were only marginally integrated, a small fountain looks a bit lost amongst the gray buildings.

▶ The **Bosnian National Theatre** (*Bosansko Narodno Pozorište*) is also located on the square, the building is a 1950s design and from the unremarkable exterior there is no indication that a rich programme of cultural events is still held inside. The in-house troop of theatre performers are well known even beyond the region and perform on a number of stages. The theatres programme is augmented with guest performances by international theatre companies.

▶ From the Square of Bosnia and Herzegovina the Islambegović Road (*Islambegovića Put*) leads to the central shopping area. The pedestrianised zone still carries the name of **Marshal Tito** (*Maršala Tita*) and has been refurbished in recent years. It is inhabited by numerous cafes, small boutiques and local shops. Global brands like MacDonald's are refreshingly absent and we are instead enticed to sample local delights such as *burek* and *ćevapčići* (see p. 91).

The Kočeva

The Sultan Ahmed Mosque

▶ If you follow Marshal Tito Street in a southerly direction to the river Bosna, you will come to the **Kočeva Mosque** (*Kočevska Džamija*). This, one of the oldest mosques in Zenica, owes its name to a tributary of the River Bosna, the Kočeva, whose route through the city has been channelled into a straight, concrete-lined canal that runs through the centre of town.

▶ The mosque stands almost immediately next to the municipal **Markct** (*Pijaca*). On its sprawling grounds many types of fruits, vegetables and meats are sold and farmers from Central Bosnia bring fresh local produce daily. The atmosphere at the *pijaca* reflects the dominance of the Islamic population in Zenica, where veiled women are a common sight and pork a rare one.

▶ Slightly beyond the bridge across the Kočeva, Marshal Tito street meets Jevrejska Street. At this point the straightened river runs parallel to the road and leads to Zenica's **Synagogue**. The synagogue was built in 1906 and is one of the most magnificent and most impressive buildings in the city. It testifies to the wealth and influence of the Jewish community during the period before the First World War. The synagogue building today serves as the City Museum (*Muzej Grada*). The museum is open on weekdays from 9am to 4:30pm, Saturdays 9am-3pm and on Sundays the museum is closed.

▶ At the end of Jevrejska, the Čaršija begins. The Ottoman term for city or market is used as a term the Old Town. This area is characterized by the numerous cafes and restaurants and on the weekends becomes rich with local nightlife for the town's younger residents, as well as a shopping street. The buildings of the Čaršija originate primarily from the Hapsburg period and form a contrast to the more socialist character of urban development from the period after the Second World War.

▶ In the Čaršija you will also find the **Sultan Ahmed Mosque** (*Sultan Ahmedova Džamija*). The mosque from 1676 is one of the most important and beautiful Islamic places of worship in Central Bosnia. It is a listed building and is also known as the Čaršijska mosque due to its location.

▶ From the mosque you can see the River Bosna, the main river of Central Bosnia, which meanders in a U-shape around the Old Town. The **Riverside Boulevard** (*Obalni Bulevar*) has not yet been pedestrianised, but its numerous roadside trees make it a magnificent avenue, while the sidewalk cafes create a lively Mediterranean atmosphere.

Kamberovića Polje

▶ On the opposite side of the river, the largest green area of the city is **Kamberovića Polje** with its sports grounds, playgrounds and park benches, it is as a favourite retreat and place for recreation for the local population. Three bridges connect the city of Zenica with the park.

▶ By following the course of the Bosna along the Riverside Boulevard on your right side you will come to the First High School (*Prva Gimanzija*) and the Dubrovnik Hotel. The hotel was opened in 2008 and is the best hotel in town. From there you can take Školska Street back to the Square of Bosnia and Herzegovina.

▶ The **University** which was only founded in 2000, but was based on Zenica's existing College of Metallurgy now consists of 13 faculties and offers the typical Zenica technical and industry-related courses as well as law, medicine and economics and other subjects. The university has no less that 16,000 students enrolled in more than 50 courses of study, making Zenica, one of the major university towns in Bosnia and Herzegovina. The university buildings are located west of the downtown area, along Fakultetska (Faculty) street.

▶ The city's football club *Nogometni Klub* Čelik *Zenica* (the Zenica Steel Football Club), named in honour of the city's industrial past, plays its home games at the 18,000 capacity Bilino Polje stadium. The club was founded in 1945 and plays in the top flight of the Bosnia and Herzegovina football league. The stadium was built in 1972 and the national team of Bosnia and Herzegovina plays most of its home games here. The atmosphere in the stadium is usually chaotic and bubbling with excitement.

The exhilarating atmosphere at a *Čelik Zenica* game

❸ Vranduk

▶ The most impressive location in Central Bosnia, historically and architecturally, is the fortress of Vranduk. The fortress, perched on steep slopes above the Bosna, dates from the 14th century and is in the care of the city museum of Zenica. Due to its location, Vranduk is also called the **Gate of Bosnia** (*Kapije Bosne*).

▶ Vranduk was first mentioned in 1410 and, due to its unique strategic position, we can assume that at this point earlier fortifications were also

In the Middle Ages, Vranduk was an important stronghold

built here. Vranduk was one of the main centres of medieval Bosnia in the early 15th century. On the slopes around the fort a small town grew, agriculture flourished and the **Church of St. Thomas** (*Crkva Sv. Tome*) was built. Vranduk was a self-sufficient, almost impregnable castle.

▶ The Ottomans, however, were not to be deterred by thick walls and high cliff faces. The fortress, like the whole of Bosnia and Herzegovina, fell to the Ottomans and the new rulers immediately set about expanding Vranduk; a mosque was built and later a prison for political prisoners. The Hapsburgs had no use for a medieval fortress and since 1890, Vranduk was no longer used as a military installation.

▶ This medieval fortress, 10km north of Zenica, is now a museum. In the 35m by 22m courtyard jousting competitions take place and cannons point out from the castle walls toward the Bosna Valley. The castle tower contains many finds and objects from the Middle Ages and the Ottoman period, such as: coins, tools, jewellery, tableware and numerous weapons.

▶ The fortress and the mosque are well worth visiting. The **Sultan Fatiha Mosque** was built in 1463 directly after the fortress was captured by the Ottomans. The mosque is made mainly of wood and has two roads leading out - one to the south and the other in an easterly direction.

▶ The small village on the hillside below the castle is still inhabited. 84 families live in small, mostly traditional cottages above the river Bosna. Vranduk is open to visitors daily from 9am to 8pm and the castle restaurant serves food. Take the M17 highway from Zenica in the direction of Doboj and you will be at the Gate of Bosnia in just ten minutes.

The small mosque in Vranduk

4 Jajce

The town of Jajce overlooks a spectacular waterfall

▶ Jajce is the Central Bosnian town with the greatest potential for attracting visitors. The old town is nestled between the Vrbas and Pliva rivers, whose spectacular confluence is a 27 meter high waterfall. Furthermore, Jajce was once the capital of the medieval Bosnian kingdom and also a very important chapter in the establishment of socialist Yugoslavia was completed here in the fall of 1943. All these historical and geographical features are enhanced further still by the beautiful location Jajce finds itself in, huddled down between forested mountains with peaks reaching up almost 1,500 metres.

▶ Jajce is located 70km south of Banja Luka and 40km west of Travnik at the confluence of the Vrbas and Pliva rivers and is part of the Federation of Bosnia and Herzegovina. Approximately 28,000 people live in the town, mostly Croats and Bosnian Muslims. The town's name derives from the Slavic word for egg (*jaje*), an allusion to the shape of the town. The Old Town winds in a spiral fashion upwards and to the castle hill, on top of which stand perched the remains of the medieval fortress.

▶ Jajce and the region have been inhabited since the Roman times. The actual founding of the town, however, dates from the 14th century. Throughout Jajce you will encounter numerous places bearing the name **Duke Hrvoje Vukčić Hrvatinić**; he was the founder of the town. In 1396 the Duke decided to expand a small fortress on the hill at the confluence of the Vrbas and Pliva rivers and named it Jajce. In the course of the 15th century a town developed below the fortress and was secured by sturdy town walls. These are mostly still visible today and the historic buildings and churches also date from this period. The Bosnian king Tvrtko II made Jajce his royal residence in 1421 - the economic and political heyday for the town.

▶ The boom years of the first capital of Bosnia were abruptly brought to an end as early as 1463, when the Ottomans defeated King Stjepan Tomasević here. In the centuries that followed, Jajce was mostly under Ottoman rule, however, Croatia and Hungary have also left their mark. By then the political and strategic importance of Jajce was largely lost and this did not change when, in 1878, Bosnia and Herzegovina fell under the Austro-Hungarian rule according to the terms of the Congress of Berlin.

▶ Jajce's return to the centre of the action came in November 1943, during the Second World War, when this liberated city was the stage of the second part of the declaration that was to form the basis of socialist Yugoslavia (AVNOJ, see also p. 30). In socialist Yugoslavia the **29th of November** was one of the most important national holidays and Jajce became a sort of pilgrimage site that just about every schoolchild in Yugoslavia visited.

▶ A tour of Jajce begins at the highest point of the town. The foundations of the **Fortress** (*Tvrđava*) were laid in the 13th century but the real

A view of Jajce at dusk

The Tower of St. Luke

expansion of the fortifications came during the reign of Hrvoje Vukčić Hrvatinić, in 1396. As Jajce was the seat of Bosnian King Tvrtko II from the 1320s additional grand buildings were constructed - unfortunately only the ruins of these remain today. The fortress, which affords a sweeping view of the landscape of Central Bosnia, is open to visitors.

▶ From the fortress there is a small street leading downhill, which goes past the Female Mosque (*Ženska Džamija*) and the bell tower (*Sahat Kula*) to the ruins of the **Church of St. Mary** (*Crkva Sv. Marije*). This church was where the last of Bosnia's independent medieval kings was crowned in 1461 by papal emissaries. After the conquest of Jajce by the Ottomans the church was converted into a mosque and the bell tower became a minaret. Following the final departure of the Ottomans and some fire damage it was never rebuilt. Since the mid-19th century, it is left to

The Esma Sultanija Mosque and the houses of Jajce

The Old Town

its fate. The foundations of the **Tower of St. Luke** (*Toranj Sv. Luke*) are still well preserved.

▶ A few steps away from the church tower are the **Catacombs** (*Katakombe*). This underground church was also built by Hrvoje Vukčić Hrvatinić, who wanted to build a proper burial place for himself and his descendants. The interior of the catacombs, which are open for visitors daily from 8am to 4pm, contains an underground church, an altar and a chapel. The catacombs were literally built into the rock and the entrance to the catacombs and the stone stairs to the underground church were built in the late 19ᵗʰ century.

Esma Sultanija Mosque was built in 1750 and is the largest mosque in the city. It owes its name to the wife of the Ottoman governor Mehmed-Paša Muhsinović, who dedicated the house of God, and two bridges over the Vrbas, to his wife. Esma Sultanija Mosque in Jajce was one of the last mosques built by the Ottomans in Bosnia and Herzegovina. During the civil war of the 1990s, the mosque was almost completely destroyed but was rebuilt and refurbished in 2002.

▶ Opposite the mosque there is a memorial for the victims of the 1990s war in Croatia. The monument, with a massive cross as a centrepiece, stands on the forecourt of the city shopping centre, which is architecturally reminiscent of an Islamic market. Also, the municipal **theatre** (*pozorište*) is here.

▶ At the bottom of the hill below the Old Town the **Travnik Gate** (*Travnička Kapija*) allows one through the city wall towards the waterfall. This gate, together with the city's other gate, the Banja Luka Gate (*Banjalučaka Kapija*), was one of only two entrances to the well-fortified medieval capital of Bosnia. In 2011, a bridge across the Pliva was built behind the Travnik Gate. The river flows along an artificial bed, while its left and right banks form the City Park (*Gradski Park*).

The AVNOJ museum in Jajce

The Pliva plummets down 27 metres into the Vrbas

▶ The sports hall in which Tito and his Partisans approved the establishment of the socialist Yugoslav state on the 29th of November 1943 is on the river bank opposite the town. Today the sports hall is a **museum** where one can see original objects and documents from the declaration – including the chair on which Tito sat when the declaration was signed! The walls of the museum are hung with portraits of the former allies of the guerrillas, including Stalin and Churchill. The museum is an important part of Yugoslav cultural memory.

▶ About 250 metres behind the museum, the Pliva rushes into the

Vrbas. Below the 27 meter high **waterfall** (*vodopad*), an artificial island was created. The view of the waterfall and Jajce's Old Town makes for a classic photo opportunity.

▶ A highlight of the region is located about 5km from the centre, on the right bank of the Pliva and Pliva Lake: the **water mills** of Jajce. The wooden Ottoman-era mills, many of which stand on stilts in the water, were once used for washing, grinding and collecting water. The historic water mills can be reached from the centre of Jajce on foot and, along the way, you will see the varied flow of the Pliva, which is characterised by rapids and small waterfalls. Halfway to the mills

Ottoman-era water mills on the Pliva

is the **Slapovi** (Rapids) Restaurant, which serves fresh fish from the clear waters of Pliva. There is also a perfectly serviceable campsite near the mills.

The astounding natural beauty of the Pliva Lake (*Plivsko Jezero*)

5 Bugojno

A view of Bugojno

▶ The town of Bugojno, with a population of approximately 40,000 people, in the south-western part of Central Bosnia, hugs the upper reaches of the River Vrbas and is surrounded by the mountains Crni Vrh (1514m), Stozer (1757m) and Rudina (1385m). Tito once hunted deer in the woods around Bugojno and today, this region is one of the centers Bosnia and Herzegovina's population of brown bears.

▶ Bugojno is part of the Federation and is populated almost exclusively by Bosnian Muslims. This part of Central Bosnia is one of the poorest in the whole country and even during the socialist era the region was economically underdeveloped. The war in the 1990s, which was particularly intense here, has further exacerbated the area's troubled economic situation.

▶ Bugojno's history dates back to Roman times when it was an important node in the Roman road network through the Balkans Bugojno. The town was once the meeting point of roads coming from

central Dalmatia (in modern-day Croatia) and from the Pannonian Plain. The Bosnian and Hungarian/ Croatian kings of the Middle Ages also appreciated the strategic position of Bugojno. In 1463 the Ottomans built a new Islamic centre here, which can still clearly be seen today.

▶ The **Sultan Ahmedova Mosque**, from 1693, is the symbol of the town

The Sultan Ahmed Mosque in Bugojno

and of its Ottoman heritage. The large interior of the mosque is rectangular in shape and covers an area of some 200m². In 1888, the entrance to the mosque was expanded making the Sultan Ahmdedova Mosque one of the largest mosques in the country. War damage inflicted during the 1990s has subsequently been repaired. Opposite the mosque are the Islamic Cemetery (Šehidsko *Mezarje*) and the Youth Park (*Omladinski Park*), two of the largest green spaces Bugojno.

▶ The Sultan Ahmed road, the town's central pedestrian zone, begins at the mosque and is known as the **Korzo** (Promenade) by locals. This boulevard was redesigned in September 2012 in a modern architectural style with futuristic street lamps, white benches and jolly paving stone patterns, in order to enliven the town and give it a more contemporary appearance.

The city's main **marketplace** (*pijaca*) is halfway up the pedestrian area, directly behind a monument with three pillars. The stalls shelter under wooden roofs and the local farmers offer fresh regional goods, while Chinese traders offer affordable, plastic household items.

▶ The Street of the Golden Lily (*Zlatnih Ljiljana*) forms the second part of the Korzo. There you will find the most beautiful Hapsburg-era building in the city; the **Municipal High School**, built in 1901 in a pseudo-Moorish style. In part, the school was used as a post office and a library, however, today, the building with its yellow and brown facade again fulfils its proper function as an educational institution. On the square in front of the school, a memorial, with three busts of socialist leaders, commemorates fallen fighters in World War II.

▶ The **Rostovo Hotel**, built in 1984 for the Winter Olympics, graces the upper end of the Street of the Golden Lily. The hotel stands as a reminder of the fact that there is a nearby ski resort, the Rostovo ski resort. Rostovo is halfway towards Travnik at an altitude of 1,400 metres and is equipped with all of the facilities, which skiing enthusiasts need to enjoy their winter sport and during the summer the area is popular with hikers and mountain bikers.

Sultan Ahmed street in Bugojno at night

6 Visoko

A view of Visoko

▶ The town of Visoko is located at the confluence of the River Fojnica into the Bosna, 25 kilometres northwest of Sarajevo at a height of 422 metres above sea level. The municipality (*općina*) belongs to the Federation and covers an area of 232 km² and has a population of approximately 40,000 inhabitants, 15,000 of whom live in the town itself. The A1 motorway from Zenica to Sarajevo leads past Visoko, from where you can see the true symbol of the city: the Bosnian Pyramid.

▶ Archaeological excavations in the area around Visoko have found remains of Roman origin and, on the nearby Visočica mountain, the remains of a town wall. In the Middle Ages, in a town once called Mile (now part of the Arnautovići suburb) King Tvrtko Kotromanić I, Bosnia's medieval ruler, was crowned in 1377. His uncle Stjepan II Kotromanić, the last king of Bosnia, used Visoko and its mountainous surroundings as a residence and a retreat. In 1463 the Ottoman Turks built what was to

become the actual town of Visoko. The first bridge over the Bosna was erected, as were an Islamic school and a mosque. The town, strategically located between the main cities of Ottoman rule, Sarajevo and Travnik, became a regional trade and administrative centre.

▶ During Hapsburg rule in Bosnia and Herzegovina from 1878, the town's significance declined continuously and when the new railway bypassed Visoko, the town was also, figuratively speaking, bypassed by the modern world. In the autumn of 1911, a fire ravaged much of the city and about 400 traditional Ottoman houses were destroyed. In socialist Yugoslavia, Visoko once again became the regional centre, the establishment of a textile and food industry made for industrial jobs and as a result, new buildings for education, administration, and security were created. The 1990s civil war raged violently in and around Visoko.

▶ The **Mustafa-Pasha Babić Madrasa** is one of the most renowned Islamic

A view of the 'Bosnian Pyramid'

schools in Bosnia and Herzegovina. It was built in 1838 and expanded, a short time later, to include a library. Since the school's violent destruction in the 1990s, it has been completely renovated and today the Mustafa Paša Babić Madrasa is still a successful Islamic boarding school. Seven hundred students are taught in this historic educational institution, which also includes a sports field and a mosque.

▶ The **Serbian Orthodox Church** (*Crkva Sv. Prokopija*) was established in 1857 and is located at the foot of the Visočica Mountain in the direction of Kiseljak. The church was destroyed and then rebuilt in both the recent conflicts in the 1990s and in the Second World War. The church, which houses hundreds of historical icons and a cemetery, has the status of a protected cultural monument of Bosnia and Herzegovina.

▶ Druing the mid-2000s Visoko suddenly became known internationally when the 'discovery' of a man-made **pyramid** caused the international media and their readers to raise a smile. A local businessman and amateur archaeologist claimed to have discovered a concealed, ancient pyramid under the Visočica mountain during his excavations. According to

Kiseljak

Bosnia and Herzegovina's most popular bottled water comes from Kiseljak, in the immediate vicinity of Sarajevo. The place name comes from the time of the Ottomans and means, more or less, soda fountain. Water from Kiseljak has been bottled and distributed since the late 19th century. These days, the company Sarajevski Kiseljak is now part of the Croatian Agrokor Group and remains as popular as ever, the distinctive green water bottles are found throughout Bosnia and Herzegovina.

his theory, he christened it the Pyramid of the Sun and dated its construction to the time of the Illyrians. Excavations of the area did not support the theory that a pyramid was hidden beneath the mountain and further reports of pyramids in the local area proved to have no basis in reality. Nevertheless, a certain pyramid cult has developed with tourists jokingly hiking to the Pyramid of the Sun and adventurers digging deeper into

The Serbian Orthodox Church (*Crkva Sv. Prokopija*)

Visoko's local mountains looking for further proof of the Bosnian Pyramid.

7 Konjic

▶ The town of Konjic is in the valley of the Neretva River, just over 50km southeast of Sarajevo, along the No. 17 highway, surrounded by the Bjelasnica and Prenj mountains, reaching over 2,000 metres high. The town's 10,000 inhabitants, almost exclusively Bosnian Muslims, live in the Federation of Bosnia and Herzegovina. Konjic is on the geographical border between the regions of Central Bosnia and Herzegovina, which gives the town a mixed Mediterranean and Continental climate. In addition to its Ottoman Old Town and the historic bridge across the Neretva the area is especially suitable for outdoor sports activities, which makes Konjic an attractive tourist destination.

▶ Konjic and the region around it is one of the oldest settlements in

A view of Konjic

Central Bosnia. Archaeological finds from the pre-Roman Illyrian era are evidence of early human settlement in this fertile farming region. Konjic itself was first mentioned in 1382, when it was part of the independent kingdom of Ragusa (today Dubrovnik). After the arrival of the Ottomans, Konjic experienced an economic and urban development boom, with the Old Bridge on the Neretva and the Old Town being built.

▶ The Hapsburgs connected the Neretva Valley town to their growing railway network and the trains from Sarajevo to the Adriatic Sea still stop in Konjic even today (see p. 73). The Second World War and the civil war of the 1990s both ravaged the city thoroughly. In the final days of the war, in the spring of 1945, the German army destroyed the Old Bridge and the town's strategic location, combined with the fact that it housed a munitions factory and a large barracks, meant that Konjic saw too much armed conflict in the 1990s too. The consequences of the war are still visible in many places but an optimistic spirit is palpable amongst the local population.

▶ The main landmark of Konjic is the **Old Bridge** (*Stara Ćuprija*) over the Neretva. The bridge leads over the river exactly where the territories of Bosnia and Herzegovina meet. The Old Bridge was built in 1682-83 by the Ottomans and consists of six arches of unequal length, each spanning widths from 6.72 to 13.56 metres. In total, the bridge is 86.20 meters long and 5.35 metres wide. Until its destruction it was considered one of the best preserved and most beautiful Ottoman bridges in South Eastern Europe. The German army blew up the Old Bridge in March 1945, just before the final liberation of the city by the Partisans. It took until 2009 for the bridge to be restored to its original condition. The restoration project was financed and carried out by the Turkish government.

▶ As part of the restoration of the Old Bridge, the historic town centre was also rebuilt and restored. The street known as **Old Market** (*Stara Čaršija*), on the eastern bank of the Neretva, today shines in a new splendour and an entire neighbourhood was built in the traditional Ottoman style. The

The Ottoman bridge across the Neretva at Konjic

Mountain biking in the area around Konjic

pedestrianised street is home to a mosque, a local museum (*Zavičajni Muzej*) and the traditional Konak restaurant and guesthouse. On the western side of the river, parallel to the new, Ottoman-style neighbourhood, a complex was built in the mountains with Ottoman-style houses, boutiques and cafes. A stone staircase leads to a small **viewpoint** (*vidikovac*).

▶ The local shopping centre and the real centre of Konjic are on the western side of the Neretva. This socialist-era centre was built in the 1960s and 1970s and has little charm. However, there is hardly a town in the country that has such a wide range of recreational activities in the beautiful scenery of its wooded hills and mountains.

▶ The Neretva river and the lake it feeds, **Boračko Lake**, offer plenty of opportunities for water sports and swimming. Around the lake, which can be reached from Konjic in about 30 minutes by car, there are numerous

campsites, some of which also offer bungalows for rent. As a starting point for hiking and mountain biking, the lake is well positioned and paragliders have increasingly started to make use of this area.

▶ Rafting trips on the upper reaches of the Neretva River, the canyon between Bjelasnica and Prenj, usually begin and end in the village Glavitičevo Džajići shortly before Konjic. Several rapids and small waterfalls make a summer boat trip on the cool and fresh Neretva an exciting adventure. A number of

Jablanica Lake from the air

agencies offering rafting tours can be found in Sarajevo and Konjic.

▶ In addition to Boračko Lake, **Jablanica Lake,** which lies just south of Konjic, is one of the largest and most well known lakes in the country. The dam on the Neretva, close to Jablanica, turns the river into a lake for 31 km upstream of Konjic. The hydroelectric plant was built in the time of Tito's Yugoslavia, between 1954-1958, and consists of six power generation units, generating a total of 25 Mega Watts of electricity. When it was completed in the late 1950s, the Jablanica power plant was one of the most technologically advanced hydroelectric plants in the world and a showcase of what the Yugoslav leadership could achieve. The lake is a popular excursion and holiday destination and its location between the steep mountain slopes of Čvrsnica and Prenj gives it a visually impressive appearance. It's wealth of fish is known far and wide and attracts fishing enthusiasts and lovers of freshly caught carp, trout and stickleback. The **Garden City Hotel** at the

Skiing on Čvrsnica

headwaters of the Neretva River on the eastern edge of Konjic, is one of the better hotels in Bosnia and Herzegovina. Part of the Garden Group hotel chain, the 4★ Garden City Hotel has 38 rooms and features a large wellness centre and sports area. It is generally recommended for seminars and conferences but is a good base from which to explore the area around Konjic.

Local Hero: Hasan Salihamidžić

This most famous son of the Jablanica is a former professional football player and a Champions League winner. He was born in Jablanica on New Year's Day 1977. At the age of 10, Hasan joined his local club, Turbina Jablanica, and it was immediately obvious that he was going to be a special player. He developed quickly and became one of the most successful young players in the clubs history. At 14 he moved to best club in the region at the time, Velež Mostar, and was also picked for the national youth team of Yugoslavia. When the war broke out in 1992, 15-year-old Hasan fled to Hamburg to live with relatives. He was snapped up by the local club, Hamburger SV, where he played for youth B-side and, in 1995, he was offered his first professional contract. After three years as a pro at HSV, Hasan moved to Bayern Munich and also served as a key player for the national team of his native Bosnia and Herzegovina. His greatest achievements came as part of his club career in Germany where he managed to win a total of 6 German Championship titles, four German Cups and, in 2001, he was the first player from Bosnia to win the Champions League. In the memorable Champions League Final against AC Milan, Hasan scored during the nail-biting, nerve-wracking penalty shootout. Towards the end his career Salihamidžić, whose nickname is Brazzo (from the Bosnian *Braco*, meaning 'little bro'), also played for Juventus and Wolfsburg and has also received 43 international caps. Hasan still lives in Germany but also frequently visits his hometown so you stand a good chance of bumping into him.

AUTHOR'S PICK: HOTELS & RESTAURANTS

Due to the abundance of hotels and restaurants on offer it would be impossible to list them all and to keep the list current. Instead, please find below a selection of hotels and restaurants recommended by the author:

HOTELS

Travnik	**Aba Motel**	Small hotel near Plava Voda offering Wi-Fi and parking	Šumeće 166, Travnik +387 30 51 14 62
Vlašić	**Blanca Hotel**	Brand new luxury hotel at the Vlašić ski resort with 56 rooms and a spa centre	Babanovac bb Vlašić +387 30 519 900
Zenica	**Dubrovnik Hotel**	Integrated 4★ hotel, part of Zenica's new shopping complex with 33 rooms	Školska 10, Zenica +387 32 202 700
Jajce	**Stari Grad Hotel**	Nice, friendly city centre hotel with 9 rooms, a sauna and a restaurant	Svetog Luke 3, Jajce +387 30 65 40 06
Jajce	**Plivsko Jezero Apartments**	A modern apartment complex located by the water mills near the peaceful Pliva Lake, includes a campsite	Pliva Jajce +387 30 65 40 06
Konjic	**Garden City Hotel**	Huge hotel and sports complex with swimming pool, tennis courts and restaurant located close to the Neretva River	Trbića Polje b.b. Konjic +387 36 71 28 00
Šipovo	**Pliva Resort**	Recently refurbished hotel close to the Pliva, 8 bungalows for 6-8 people, 2km from the popular fly-fishing location at the source of the Pliva	Fly fishing center Pliva Pljeva, Šipovo +387 50 320 000

Hotel Blanca

EASTERN BOSNIA

Bosanski Šamac
Orašje
Modriča

1. BIJELJINA
2. BRČKO
3. POSAVINA
4. DOBOJ
5. GRADAČAC
6. SREBRENIK
7. TUZLA
8. ROMANIJA AND PALE
9. ZVORNIK
10. SREBRENICA
11. VIŠEGRAD
12. GORAŽDE
13. SUTJESKA NATIONAL PARK

✦ The Sutjeska National Park in Eastern Bosnia is one of the most beautiful and enticing areas for nature lovers in the whole country. Generally speaking, Eastern Bosnia is neither the best known nor the most historic region of Bosnia and Herzegovina, however, the region's lack of urban appeal in the form of historic towns is more than made up for with untouched natural landscapes and the opportunity to experience a traditional rural way of life.

✦ The River Drina is the defining element of Eastern Bosnia. Its source rises in the karst mountains along the border with Montenegro and the river meanders through the fertile

A lake in the Sutjeska National Park

The world famous bridge across the Drina at Višegrad

Sutjeska National Park is home to bears and wolves, and contains the ancient, primeval Perućica Forest, one of the last remaining natural forest reserves in Europe.

✦ The cities and towns of Eastern Bosnia are heavily influenced by commerce. In addition to Tuzla, the largest city in Eastern Bosnia, the cities of Brčko and Bijeljina leave an especially busy, bustling and sometimes chaotic impression. In the northern fertile Posavina and Semberija plains, about 50 percent of the working population are employed in agriculture while Tuzla and Doboj are the industrial centres of the region. The salt capital of Tuzla has been home to major manufacturing plants for generations and its power plant contributes significantly to the energy production of the country.

Semberija lowlands where it flows into the Sava. The Drina combines the contrasting characteristic of Eastern Bosnia's varied landscapes. Emerald green, mostly icy cold and crossed by centuries-old bridges, the Drina winds through historic towns such as Goražde and Višegrad.

✦ In addition to the Drina, Eastern Bosnia is characterised by its hills and mountains. In the north, between the towns of Tuzla and Gradačac, the green wooded mountains Trebovac, Ozren and Majevica rise over 1,000 metres. The mountains around the town of Vlasenica – Javor and Javorniki Dervetnik – project up to nearly 1,500 metres. To the west the Romanija mountains with high, barren plateaus, a direct contrast to the scenery they lead to, the highest mountains in Bosnia and Hezegovina. Above 2,000 metres, there are the craggy peaks of Maglić (2386m), Volujak (2336m), Velika Ljubušnja (2238m) and Zelengora (2014m). The

✦ Further south, in the increasingly forested and mountainous areas, the population density decreases significantly. Small towns like Kladanj, Vlasenica, Han Pijesak and Sokolca have yet to recover from the effects of war, rural depopulation and unemployment. A 'beneficiary' of this process is the natural environment, which has begun to undergo a process of rewilding now that many of the people have departed.

A view of the Drina as it flows into Višegrad

1 Bijeljina

A view of Bijeljina's central square

▶ Bijeljina is the centre of the Semberija. The **Semberija** lowlands are part of the Pannonian Plain, which stretches from Hungary to Serbia and Croatia to the north-east of Bosnia and Herzegovina and is one of the largest sedimentary basins in Europe. Bijeljina, and nearby towns Ugljevik and Lopare, are part of these flat, fertile lowlands. Due to its geo-strategic location – between the Drina and Sava rivers, at the foot of the Majevica Mountains – Bijeljina has attracted settlement and agriculture since time immemorial and archaeological finds trace human settlement back to Celtic times.

▶ With about 100,000 inhabitants, Bijeljina is the second largest city in Eastern Bosnia and the Republika Srpska of which it is a part. Despite its sprawling vastness – Bijeljina covers an area of 734km² – the town is chaotic and the traffic always seems about to collapse. On weekdays, non-existent parking spaces and endless traffic jams are the norm rather than the exception. Both in the town and in the urban periphery extensive trade is the main economic activity. Agricultural

equipment, construction materials and automotive spare parts are readily available and Bijeljina seems like a colourful bazaar. Besides the local population from the Semberija, some Serbs and Croats also come to Bijeljina from the neighbouring countries to shop.

▶ The architectural cityscape of Bijeljina reminds one more of the regions of Croatian Slavonia and Serbian Vojvodina, which have also been shaped by centuries of Hapsburg rule. The influence of the Hapsburgs on local architecture is unmistakable, and especially so in the town centre around Vuk Karadžić Square. A typically Hapsburg, Art Deco, **Town Hall** (*Opština*), completed in 1910, sits on Karadžić Square directly behind a monument to a Serbian King, Peter I.

▶ A modern **library** building, named after epic poet and writer Filip Višnjić (1767-1834), is just opposite the Town Hall. On a block of marble before the entrance of the library a stone visage of the bard sits with lute in hand, looking towards the Town Museum. The **Atak Mosque**, the largest mosque in the

The Hapsburg Town Hall in Bijeljina

city, whose original construction is dated to the mid-16th century, is also on the square.

▶ A memorial commemorating the victims of the war in the 1990s from Bijeljina can also be found on **Vuk Karadžić Square**. Across Nikola Tesla street, you discover the municipal vegetable market (*zelena pijaca*) partly hidden behind numerous cafes and bars.

▶ The **City Park** (*Gradski Park*) with shady trees and well-tended flower beds can be reached if one follows the newly paved Jovan Dučić street, coming from Vuk Karadžić Square.

▶ As elsewhere in Bosnia and Herzegovina many new places of worship are under construction in Bijeljina. The Catholic Church, the Serbian Orthodox Church and the Muslim community, appear to be very active when it comes to renovation and construction of new religious buildings. The most striking and also currently the largest church project of the Serbian Orthodox Church in Bosnia and Herzegovina is the **Monastery of Saint Parascheva of the Balkans** (*Manastir Sveta Petka*). Built on the northwestern outskirts of Bijeljina in 2004, the new monastery includes a stunning 25 meter high golden-domed church (visible for miles around), an amphitheatre, a lake and an orchard. The monastery and audaciously domed church are open to the public.

▶ North of Bijeljina, driving towards Croatia, on the right hand side you will come across the **Stanišić "ethno village"**. Several artificial lakes have been created to form part of the 5-acre village complex and these are surrounded by replicas of

The leafy City Park

The ostentatious domes of the Monastery of Saint Parascheva of the Balkans

traditional wooden houses, where craft techniques from the 19th century are presented to visitors. The "ethno village" has a hotel complex with a restaurant and several function rooms for parties, a church and a miniature railway. The whole resort is carefully designed and the accommodation available is of a very high standard. However, the Stanišić "ethno village", with its commercial approach, reminds one more of Disneyland than a traditional Slavic village. Wedding parties are a regular occurrence, particularly in the summer months and on weekends.

▶ By driving west of the town, in the direction of the Serbian border, you will find tranquillity in the natural surroundings of the charming landscape of the river Drina. Along the river, walkers and water-lovers will also find plenty of places to find refreshment. The highlight is the first weekend in August, when thousands of visitors participate and watch the annual regatta on the Drina.

The Stanišić "ethno village" at dusk

2 Brčko

The central promenade in Brčko

▶ Brčko, a town of 40,000 at the confluence of the river **Brka** into the Sava, is the only town in Bosnia and Herzegovina that is neither part of the Republika Srpska nor the Muslim-Croat Federation. In terms of how it is governed, Brčko is unique in Bosnia and Herzegovina. During the negotiations to end the civil war in Dayton in 1995 no agreement can be found on which side should control the strategically important town of Brčko and the surrounding area. Both of the entities insisted on a transit corridor to avoid splitting their territories into two and it was, therefore, finally agreed to leave Brčko under international supervision. Today it belongs to neither side or to both. The so-called Special Administrative Region of **Brčko District** is administered as a merging of both entities.

▶ The border between Croatia and Bosnia and Herzegovina begins immediately after Brčko's main shopping street, behind the **Square of the Young** (*Trg Mladih*), right in the middle of the city. The border bridge over the Sava can be easily crossed on foot or by bicycle and it is often used by residents of the Croatian border town Gunja on the other bank of the Sava, especially for shopping,

as alcohol and cigarettes are much cheaper in Bosnia and Herzegovina. Generally bilateral trade still blooms here, making this border town a place of trade and transit.

▶ While Brčko is located on two rivers, one will search in vain for a municipal use of the riverbanks, or even a recreational area. The town and the Sava are geographically close but misguided urban planning means they are not really linked together. The town gains no benefit from its proximity to the Sava, the river is banished to the suburbs and is not an inviting place to linger. Also, the preserved historic buildings are located close to the shore on **Vuk Karadžić Street**, so one could imagine a friendly and accessible area extended and upgraded to form part of the town's central pedestrian zone.

▶ The newly restored Serbian Orthodox Church and also the renewed **Posavina Grand Hotel** are also located on the Square of the Young. These two representative buildings are a clear indication of the great potential the city has architecturally. On the lawn area in front of the hotel there are monuments that commemorate the victims of the war in the 1990s. As is the case almost everywhere in Bosnia and Herzegovina, the three main ethnic groups do not mourn their loss together, instead each ethnic group mourns separately – but in close proximity to their former opponents.

▶ The pedestrianised street, **Silver Bosna** (*Bosne Srebrne*), directly to connects to the Square of the Young and looks no different to most other commercial streets in the country. Besides the

Brčko Park

many lively bistros and boutiques, the town's young men can be found in the many betting shops, forever waiting for that big win. The architecture is mixed, ranging from Hapsburg Art Nouveau on the square itself, to the practical functional buildings of socialist days in the surrounding streets. If you follow the pedestrian zone from the direction of the Sava, you reach Brčko's large City Park (*Gradski Park*) behind Miroslav Krleža street. On the triangular, landscaped park, surrounded by street cafes as well as a children's playground, people of all ages and walks of life come to rest and relax. South of the park is **New Brčko** (*Novo Brčko*), which also contains the city coach and train stations.

▶ The well known, in South Eastern Europe at least, **Arizona Market** is on the territory of the Brčko district. The large market area extends over two hectares in the village of Dubrava, 10 km south of Brčko, where about 2500 (although it feels like twice as many) small shops and stalls sell just about everything that the (former-Yugoslav) heart desires, from wedding dresses and fake brands to puppies and spare car parts. The name Arizona was chosen as a reference to the anarchic Wild West atmosphere that once prevailed here. Even though the chaotic, lawless times have been left behind, the dealers are registered and pay their taxes, you can still feel something of the charm of the disordered optimism of the post-war years in the mid-1990s so a visit to Arizona is well worth it, even if you are not out to buy some cheap textiles or turbo folk DVDs.

The River Sava near Brčko

❸ Posavina: Orašje, Bosanski Šamac & Modriča

A view of Orašje

▶ The Sava River Basin extends through Eastern Bosnia from Odžak up to Brčko. Three smaller towns Orašje, Bosanska Šamac and Modriča and numerous villages dot this fertile region. Posavina literally means 'along the Sava' and is thus denotes the region's defining characteristic, the River Sava. However, the Sava, which forms the border with Croatia, is of only very limited interest for visitors to the area. Lovers of fishing are offered numerous opportunities for a good fishing spot on the Sava and another popular activity in the Eastern Bosnian Posavina is hunting.

▶ Driving through the Posavina, one embarks on a constant switching between Republika Srpska and the Muslim-Croat Federation. The region was highly contested during the war in the 1990s and was claimed by all three ethnic groups. The Posavina is an ethnic patchwork, a diversity that was supported by the Dayton Peace Accord and also accounts for the fact that the two Entities share power, as in the case of Brčko, and ownership changes "on every other street corner". Socially, too, the image of the Sava River Basin was greatly changed by the war. Many people, mostly Bosnian Muslims, left the Posavina in the 1990s and fled to Western Europe. Today, the return of these former refugees from host countries in Europe and North America is one of the dominant images of the region as, in the summer months, more than 50% of car number plates are of foreign origin. Most of these returnees, who mostly found homes in Sweden, Germany or Slovenia, show off their relative wealth by driving around the region in their shiny new cars and by building themselves expansive holiday homes.

▶ Especially in the town of **Orašje**, which is also the administrative centre and thus the capital of the Canton of Posavina, the economic emigrees seem

A fishing lake in Orašje

Hunting in the Posavina region draws enthusiasts from all over Europe

to have taken over completely. Their often tacky buildings dominate the cityscape and license plates from Germany dominate the market. This 'wealth' in a town of only 20,000 has made Orašje a town of contradictions. The city's **Freedom** Square (*Trg Slobode*) and the concrete waterfront not invite you to linger, yet serious efforts to change this are clearly underway. As a border town and a town that relies on cross-border trade, Orašje has some smaller hotels and motels as well as a multitude of petrol stations.

▶ Visually, there is almost nothing sexy about the town of **Bosanski Šamac**. Located almost directly behind the confluence of the Bosna into the Sava, on first glance there is nothing to feel or see in Bosanski Šamac. Neglecting the confluence of two major rivers of Bosnia and Herzegovina the town is located off to one side. An overgrown field separates the waterfront from the

town, therefore there is nothing to see in the town itself. The architectural potential of the city is, however, clearly visible. Even here, functional socialist buildings dominate the cobbled **Town Square** (*Gradski Trg*), somewhat apart from this, however, there are many residential and commercial buildings from the Hapsburg era. Although the houses all seem to be about to collapse, one can imagine how Bosanski Šamac once looked and how it might look once again. And as in most other towns in Bosnia and Herzegovina, several monuments commemorating the victims of the wars of the 20th century can be found in the town center. Certainly the most exciting monument is in the park, a white marble tower dedicated to the victims of the Second World War.

▶ Bosanski Šamac is also the birthplace of two major politicians relevant to the recent history of the former Yugoslavia. Both the late Serbian Prime Minister, Zoran Djindjić, and the former President of Bosnia and Herzegovina, Alija Izetbegović, were born in Bosanski Šamac. Neither, however, spent their childhood here, but in Belgrade and Sarajevo, respectively.

▶ If you travel out of Bosanski Šamac in a westerly direction, just beyond the town you will encounter the train station on the left hand side and on the other side a huge industrial area. Both the run-down freight and passenger station and the abandoned, destroyed, or barely usable industrial buildings, are reminiscent of better

Bosanski Šamac

economic times. Wood, textile and glass industries were once located in Bosanski Šamac and provided work for thousands of the townsfolk.

▶ A similarly structured industrial past is also evident in the town of **Modriča**, 20 km to the south west. Every child in the former Yugoslavia knew the jingle of the TV advert for the popular Optima motor oil from Modriča. And today Modriča is still associated with the oil producer, Optima, a formerly state-owned refinery, which is now operated by a Russian investor.

▶ The small town, situated within close proximity to the Bosna, has a car-free shopping street, Svetosavska, which is peppered by street cafes and betting shops. Large shady deciduous trees give character to this otherwise rather austere pedestrian avenue. At the upper end of Svetosavska the small, square City Park contains a monument to fallen Partisans from World War II.

▶ A short trip to a cemetery in no man's land between Doboj and

A life-size soldier guards this grave near Doboj

Modriča can be an interesting diversion; the cemetery is approximately half way between the two towns, on highway M17. Between the normal grave stones an unusual sculpture stands out: a life-sized armed soldier guarding his own grave, serving as a reminder of the recent war.

4 Doboj

A view of Doboj

▶ Doboj forms a geographical transition to the regions of Bosanska Krajina and Central Bosnia. Doboj sits on the border between the three regions and the north-south M17 highway, together with the confluence

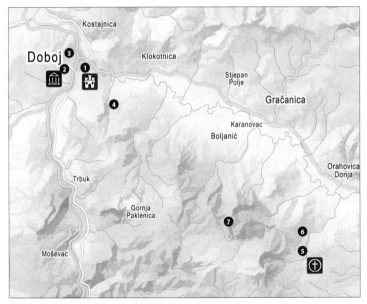

1 Doboj Fortress

2 Doboj Regional Museum

3 Town Park

4 Goransko Jezero

5 Monastery of St Nicholas

6 Eagle Lake

7 Ozren

of the rivers Usora and Spreča into the Bosna, makes the town one of the main transport hubs in the country. It is not surprising, therefore, that the railway company of Republic of Srpska has its headquarters in Doboj.

▶ Approximately 35,000 people live in Doboj, and about twice as many people inhabit the surrounding villages. Doboj is part of Republika Srpska and is home to some of the entity's university faculties as well as a private university. The town is also home to the recording studios of the entity's main broadcaster, *Radio Televizija Republike Srpske* (RTRS).

▶ In the 1st century AD the Romans built a fortress at the strategic confluence of the Usora into the Bosna, near the present-day town. Over the centuries people sought shelter beneath the walls of the fortress and the

resulting town slowly grew into one of the largest settlements in the region. The importance of the fortress and the settlement didn't change when it fell to the conquering Slavs, nor when it became part of the Byzantine Empire and the medieval Kingdoms of Serbia and Bosnia. Due to its important strategic location, Doboj has always been a coveted and therefore fiercely contested objective.

A view from Doboj Fortress

▶ The historical importance of Doboj is still evident today when one looks upon **Doboj Fortress** (*Dobojska Tvrđava*) towering over the town. Built in the 13th century on the ruins of a Roman fortification by the Bosnian Kotromanić dynasty, the structure of the fortress is still well preserved. A view from the highest point of the fortress, down into the valleys the Spreča and Bosna, perfectly illustrates the brilliant strategic location of the town and the fortress. A visit to the fortress is recommended not only to every visitor Doboj, but also to everyone who finds themselves passing through Doboj along the highway. A stop off here is particularly appealing in the summer months when literary and dramatic performances are often held in the fortress amphitheatre. The fortress also has a shop and a café that provide refreshment should you wish to stay longer. Furthermore, the Doboj tourist organisation clearly works hard at attracting more visitors – a model other local tourist organisations in Bosnia and Herzegovina would do well to follow – and organises events such as jousting tournaments and thematic exhibitions

The Doboj Fortress overlooks the town

in the fortress. The entrance fee of 2.5 Convertible Marks is, thanks to the well maintained fortress and the wealth of activities on offer, certainly a worthwhile investment.

▶ In the **Regional Museum** (*Regionalni Muzej Doboj*) there is a fairly comprehensive account of the history Doboj in English and both the castle and the region are presented

The Regional Museum, Doboj

City Park, Doboj

very clearly. The museum, located at the intersection Svetog Save and Vidovdanska in the city centre, was founded in 1956 and has been lovingly preserved – it is open Monday to Friday from 7am to 4pm.

▶ Opposite are the Rectorate of the Pavlović University and the municipal library. The intersection of the two main roads, Svetog Save and Nemanjina, closes the shopping district off with a **market** selling fruit and veg (*zelena pijaca*) and numerous shops and cafes.

▶ The present day town centre of Doboj is in stark contrast to the 13th century fortress. Lacking a historic old town or any interesting architecture, the downtown area is far from attractive. This lack of substance is compensated mainly by the large **Town Park** (*Gradski Park*) where you will not regret stopping off in the shade of the lush trees, especially in the warmer evenings. As you will see the locals also appreciate the lungs of their town. An elongated landscaped fountain and the obligatory memorials for the civil war and World War II, as well as a children's' playground, give the park character.

▶ The park is surrounded by the main administrative buildings of Doboj. In addition to the Town Hall there are the local parliament, the **Art Gallery** (*Umjetnička Galerija*) and the Park Hotel. The hotel was renovated and re-opened in 2012. The two main shopping streets, Svetog Save and

Art Gallery, Doboj

Goransko Jezero has excellent facilities for recreation and relaxation

Nemanjina, are adjacent to the city park. Both streets are pedestrianised but somehow leave one with a lively, but unfortunately, a vaguely unwelcoming impression.

▶ At the bottom of Svetog Save is the main administrative building of the **railway company of Republika Srpske** (Željeznice *Republike Srpske*) and, in front of the building a blue, white and red steam locomotive recalls the early days of rail transport in Bosnia and Herzegovina. The Doboj coach station is also located along Svetog Save.

▶ As already mentioned, Doboj is a transport hub, especially rail transport. Apart from the main railway company of the Republic of Srpska, the tradition of mobility is maintained by the Faculty of Transportation and the train station, which is located outside the city centre on the other bank of the Bosna. Of the former factories of the railway industry, unfortunately none have survived until the present and the railway station seems like a graveyard of discarded, rusty train engines and carriages. Nowadays transport policy is rather different. For train lovers, however, this unhappy graveyard could be a fantastic opportunity to see trains that no longer exist anywhere else in Europe.

▶ About 5km from the railway station, near the village of Josava, is the artificial lake **Goransko Jezero**. The road to the lake passes through a pine forest and is well signposted from Doboj, a short mountain-bike ride is suitable for this trail. The popular, but rarely crowded beach area offers two smaller water slides and a diving tower, a children's playground and barbecue facilities and also a restaurant. A stay at Goransko Jezero is also ideal for travellers who do not want to take a break from driving in one of the musty motels/restaurants on the main road but prefer to be in more natural surroundings. The rather wonderful lakeside picnic spot, known as *Preslica*, is nearby and lends itself wonderfully to this.

The Serbian Orthodox Monastery of Saint Nicholas

▶ The pine forest that surrounds Goransko Jezero is part of the foothills of the Ozren mountains which spread long the Spreča east of Doboj, in the direction of Tuzla. The Ozren mountains offer a number of opportunities for both active and passive recreation and relaxation. The highest point of the low mountain chain is completely covered by pine and oak forests and rises to a mere 918 metres.

The wild forests of the Ozren mountains

▶ The cultural highlight of the Ozren mountain range is the Serbian Orthodox **Monastery of St. Nicholas** (*Sveti Nikola*) about 20km east of Doboj, on the boundary of the municipality Petrovo. Though it was built in the 13th century, the first records of the sprawling monastery complex date from 1587. Delightful, well-kept flower gardens and a number of monastic administrative and residential buildings cluster around the main stone church. A monastery orchard is hidden in a clearing in the forest that the monastery calls its own. The monastery of St. Nicholas has, since 2003, been a listed building and is listed as one of the National Monuments of Bosnia and Herzegovina. Just a few metres away from the monastery is the sleepy mountain village of Kaludjerica, which is an ideal starting point for hikes in the area. The campsite situated in the village is unfortunately only open during the Ozren Mountaineering Marathon in early June.

▶ Halfway between Petrovo and the monastery is **Eagle Lake** (*Orlovo Jezero*), surrounded by dense woods. The lake is uniquely idyllic, lying away from any traffic noise, but has been deprived of much of its natural beauty by the construction of a flashy modern building. It is still of course a fine place for a bathe and small reed huts offer protection from the sun in the summertime. Other distractions include bathing near Ozren spa, located in the valley, with its thermal water rich in calcium, sodium and magnesium. For 3 Convertible Marks you can visit a nearby communist-era water amusement park. Latest European standards are not met, however, the pool still enjoys great popularity amongst the local population. Even though the pool isn't the world's most attractive, the temperature of the water is almost 40° C and the view of Ozren is magnificent.

▶ Mount Ozren provides ideal conditions for those who love the great outdoors. In recent years, the mountains between Tuzla and Doboj have increasingly become a centre for mountain biking, BMX sports, paragliding, hiking and climbing. The

Eagle Lake

Paragliding is an increasingly popular pastime in the area around Doboj

participating local municipalities are also behind this trend and are busy signposting hiking and cycling trails and the route of the annual Ozren Mountaineering Marathon, which is enjoying something of a revival of its popularity not only during the race weekend but also during the first week of June. The marathon, with its four categories – from 5km to 100km – attracts mountain sports lovers from all over Europe. A social framework program, with the active involvement of local people, completes the highlight of Bosnian and Herzegovinian mountain sports. Private agencies and organisers inform nature-lovers about the growing number of activities on offer and are continuously increasing the number of guest rooms and gastronomic options of the Ozren mountains.

5 Gradačac

Gradačac

▶ Along the banks of the Gradišnica is the small Islamic town of Gradačac. Positioned away from busy traffic flows, nestled between the mountains Trebava and Majevica, Gradačac is a treasure trove of architectural remnants of the later parts of Ottoman rule. The 19th century local ruler, General Husein Gradaščević (see box), who became known as '**The Dragon of Bosnia**' (*Zmaj od Bosne*), and whose influence is still evident in the town, once lived in the fortress perched on the mountain in the middle of the Gradašac. The town and the surrounding 38 villages are part of the Federation and number some 55,000 inhabitants. The population of the area is almost exclusively Bosnian Muslim.

▶ Before and during his time as Vizier, the Ottoman governor, Husein Gradaščević, built a number of important buildings in Gradačac – both cultural institutions and military installations – many of which can be visited today. The **Old Town** (*Stari Grad*) of the mountain town consists almost exclusively of relics of the Gradaščević family. The defensive wall which still surrounds the entire old town, can be negotiated via three gates. Two smaller inconspicuous gates were primarily used by servants

as well as an escape route. The third portal, however, is at the lower end of the hill in the middle of the Old Town and, as is clear from its imposing size, was the official entrance to the town for the Dragon of Bosnia. Right next to the entrance is the mighty Husein Mosque with its 20 meter tall minaret. To climb the hill in the middle of the town you need to tackle a wide stone staircase from which you can reach the museum, gallery and library – all buildings commissioned by Gradaščević. The facilities bear his name and some are partly in use even today as Islamic educational institutions. At the highest point of the landscaped park atop the town's central hill is the most visible symbol of Gradačac, the four-story high **Tower** (*Kula*). The tower was built in 1824 as a residence for the Dragon of Bosnia and as a lookout tower. A restaurant on the top floor of the tower today offers traditional Bosnian cuisine and wonderful views of the town and the surrounding areas.

▶ Below the Old Town is the **Town Park**, this can be reached directly through either of the two smaller gates that lead through the town walls. Following a standard feature, the park serves as a repository of cultural memory. Particularly striking

The Dragon of Bosnia

Husein Gradaščević was a leader of Bosnian feudal lords who were dissatisfied with Ottoman rule and who tried to resist the dominance of Istanbul – he came to be known as The Dragon of Bosnia (*Zmaj od Bosne*). In 1831 Gradaščević defeated the troops of the Ottoman governors Ali Paša and Namik and was subsequently elected Grand Vizier at the Emperor's Mosque in Sarajevo. The rebel lords he led desired to establish a vassal relationship with the Sublime Porte, however, the Sultan refused. In another battle the rebels defeated the Grand Vizier Rešid Paša, but Gradaščević lacked the diplomatic skill to use this victory to obtain recognition of his vassal status from the the Sultan. Instead of acquiescing to his demands the Sublime Porte sent Herzegovinian lords, Smail Aga Čengić and Ali Paša Rizvanbegović, to deal with him. Husein Gradašević was utterly crushed on the 4th of April 1832 by the two Herzegovinan lords. Completely defeated and abandoned by his comrades, Gradaščević fled and saught asylum in Austria.

The Vidara Lake at sunset

here, however, is the proliferation of monuments reflecting different cultures and periods. Apart from the obligatory memorials for the victims of the wars of the break-up of Yugoslavia and the Second World War, there are also numerous sculptures and busts – of both Islamic and socialist origin – spread throughout the park. Close to the Town Park is the town's main street – named of course after the most famous son of the city, Husein Kapetan Gradaščević – a local administration building, a cinema and

the Islamic centre of the town are also to be found here.

▶ Two manmade lakes, **Hazna** and **Vidara**, created around Gradačac provide the citizens of the town with an opportunity for refreshment during the heat of the summer. As a tourist destination, however, they are not unavoidable. Also the bath (*banja*) of Gradačac has seen better days and will probably appeal to guests only after a thorough and much needed renovation.

⑥ Srebrenik

▶ The small town of Srebrenik is 35km north of Tuzla and hosts a well-preserved and impressive medieval fortress. The view from the fortress, situated on a rock overlooking the valley of the river Tinja and the heights of the Maljević, Ratiš and Trebava mountains, is in itself worth the visit. The name the Srebrenik fortress and the small community that has grown up below it is derived from the Slavic word for silver (*srebro*). The belief is that this is not a reference to the fact that silver was once mined

here but to the fact that the fortress once had a silvery roof that was visible across the valley.

▶ The first records of Srebrenik date back to 1333, when the fortress was conquered by the Bosnian lord, Ban Stjepan II Kotromanić. Prior to this there are no surviving documents but it is known that the rocky outcrop on which the fortress sits has been used since Roman times as a military fortification. Before the arrival of the Ottomans in Bosnia and Herzegovina,

Srebrenik was the capital of a Hungarian *banat* (a region ruled by a *ban*, a feudal lord), which included the towns of Brčko, Tešanj and Gradačac. From 1512 the Ottomans ruled this part of the country and the fortress was expanded to include a mosque and a white minaret was added to the silver roof of the castle.

The fortress perched above Srebrenik

▶ When the Hapsburgs took control of the hard to reach fortress from 1878 they no longer use for it and it fell into ruin. It was only after the 1990s civil war, that the ruins were restored. Thanks primarily Spanish development aid, the fortress and its wooden draw bridge, are now open to visitors daily from 9am to 8pm. The entrance fee is 1 Convertible Mark.

▶ The climb to the fortress – from the main road coming from Tuzla – begins at the small town of Srebrenik. While the town itself extends on the left side of the main road, along the valley of the Tinja river, you can reach the medieval fortress and the original community by an approximately 10km long mountainous climb along a paved road. Theoretically, the fort can also be reached on foot from the town, but we recommend you drive to the fortress

The medieval fortress at Tešanj

The Majevica mountains

and use it as the starting point for walks in the surrounding area.

▶ The highest peak of the Majevica mountains is **Okresanica** at 815 metres above sea level; it can be reached on foot from the fortress. At the summit there is a mountain refuge (*planinarski dom*) operated by the local hiking and mountaineering club. On weekends in the summer months the mountain cabin is also serves hearty regional dishes and offers stunning views across the valley.

▶ The river Tinja meanders just away from the city centre and the central **Alija Izetbegović** promenade, which is, typically for small Bosnian towns, home to a heady mix of street cafés, betting shops and Chinese merchants selling cheap wares. At the upper end this promenade-cum-shopping street a memorial commemorates the Muslim victims of the 1990s civil war. The plaques list the names of those citizens from Srebrenik who lost their lives. Except for a quarry, which even today is used for the production of building materials and is the largest industrial employer in the town, the natural environment in the area around Srebrenik has not been damaged by excessive human interference. While the natural environment has benefited from this, the same cannot be said for the economic prosperity of the town. Young people from Srebrenik prefer, therefore, to move to nearby Tuzla or to become economic migrants in Western Europe.

7 Tuzla

▶ Tuzla is the largest city in Eastern Bosnia and is a cultural, administrative centre, as well as being a university town and centre of academic learning in the region. Located in the valley of the, sadly mostly concrete, River Jala, the city is at 232 metres above sea level and has more than 100,000 inhabitants, making it the fourth largest city in Bosnia and Herzegovina. The predominantly Muslim-dominated city is part of the Federation of Bosnia and Herzegovina. Tuzla is surrounded by the forested Majevica mountains north east of the city, which separate the plains of Posavina and Semberija in the north and the Spreča lowlands (*Sprečko*

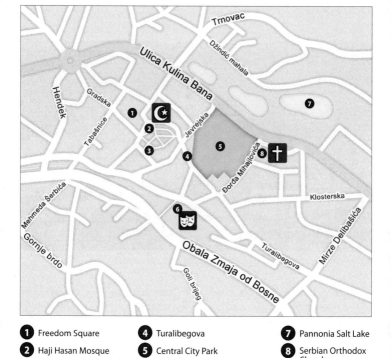

1 Freedom Square
2 Haji Hasan Mosque
3 Salt Square
4 Turalibegova
5 Central City Park
6 National Theatre
7 Pannonia Salt Lake
8 Serbian Orthodox Church

Polje) in the south. The highest point of the Majevica chain is Mount Stolice (916m) near Tuzla.

▶ The first traces of human settlement in Tuzla date back to the 5th millennium before Christ, though the original name for Tuzla dates from the time of the first settlement of Slavic tribes, from the 7th century AD. The city was then called Sali, from the Slavic word for **salt** (*sol*) but when the Ottomans arrived in the 15th century and finally took possession of the town, they replace the Slavic name by the corresponding Turkish word for salt, *tuz*. The name, whether Slavic or Turkish, comes from the fact that the area around Tuzla is rich with saline springs. For centuries, the salt mining

A view across Tuzla at dusk

A forest of socialist-era housing blocks dominates the town's skyline

town and its surroundings, has relied on this resource for revenue. And even today, Tuzla salt is exported all over the world – but of course, primarily to the countries of the former Yugoslavia. Salt and salt mining shape the city to this today – for good or ill – and both the positive and negative consequences of this industry can be seen in many places, among these is the salt lake in the middle of the city.

▶ During nearly 400 years of Ottoman rule, Tuzla was a great commercial and military centre and was responsible for the salt requirement of all Ottoman lands. The Hapsburg takeover in 1878 for Tuzla, as well as for the rest of Bosnia and Herzegovina, represented the beginning of a new economic era. Modern salt extraction methods were introduced and the emerging industrialization also took in Tuzla and areas in its immediate vicinity. To this day, Tuzla remains an industrial city and one of the main products of which, besides the salt, is beer. It is also one of the largest producers of

A view of Freedom Square and the old town from the air

electric power in Bosnia and Herzegovina.

▶ While the salt has been a source of jobs and prosperity for Tuzla and its citizens, it has also had a negative impact too: large parts of the city have been damaged by salt erosion and corrosion and threaten to continue to decline. Mine shafts dug under the city are now empty or are filled with water and put

The fountain on Freedom Square

the city on an insecure foundation. The ground beneath the centre of Tuzla has been weakened over the last decades and there are plenty of buildings drawn into the salty abyss, which is sometimes as deep as 20 metres. This is also the reason why only a small number of historical architectural traces remain of Tuzla's long past. Strolling through Tuzla's pedestrianised zone, a mix of old and new buildings is immediately apparent, as are the town's sometimes astoundingly steep roads.

▶ At **Freedom Square** (*Trg Slobode*), the historic market square of Tuzla,

the slope is extreme. From the somewhat scruffy old Town Hall, the large space declines significantly toward the adjoining Srebrenica Place. The square is named to commemorate the victims of the Srebrenica massacre in July 1995 (see p. 234). In the middle of Freedom Square, next to a brand new effervescent fountain, the newly restored Salt Trading Centre reminds visitors of the city's history. At the bottom of the square is the **Haji Hasan Mosque**. The 12 by 12 metre mosque, originally built in 1548, has been destroyed and reconstructed many times during its long history.

The Hadži Hasan Mosque

The fountain on Salt Square, cheerfully lit at night

▶ A few metres further on you come to **Salt Square** (*Soni Trg*). The square was laid out in its present form in 2004 with a new Salt Museum. The museum presents interested visitors with a graphic representation of the history of salt production in Tuzla as well as various historical salt production methods.

▶ From Salt Square you come to the main pedestrianised shopping street, **Turalibegova**, which takes its shops and cafes housed in a colourful mix of old buildings, on a winding and snaking path up and down the city's steep slopes. Turalibegova leads also to the **Central City Park** (*Centralni Gradski Park*). At the time of writing the whole centre of the city is a construction site as a road tunnel is being built to traverse the city centre.

▶ At the bottom of the shopping street is the **National Theatre** (*Narodno Pozorište Tuzle*), one of the few remaining older buildings Tuzla and one of the oldest theatres in Bosnia and Herzegovina. The theatre was built in 1898 during the Hapsburg rule over Tuzla and made Tuzla into Eastern Bosnia's cultural and social centre. Very close to the theatre is also the former cinema of the city.

Modern shopping along Turalibegova

In the summer crowds of locals and tourists alike flock to the Pannonia Lake

▶ One of the main landmarks and attractions in Tuzla is the **Pannonia Salt Lake**. It serves the population of Tuzla and those living near the town as a leisure and recreation centre as well as a municipal swimming pool. The origins of the lake date back to a collapse in the salt mine; erosion and literally under-mining caused the collapse. The city authorities took the opportunity and enlarged the hole resulting from the collapse to build an artificial salt waterfall and swimming pool. Sports facilities and playgrounds were also included in the plans. A pebble beach and some restaurants surround the round salt lake – in the summer it is hard to find a free space either on the beach or in a cafe.

▶ In addition to the numerous mosques, some Catholic and Orthodox churches are also found in Tuzla. Probably the most beautiful of these is the **Serbian Orthodox Church of the Holy Mary** from 1882, located between Turalibegova and the salt lake. Like most other Christian churches in Bosnia and Herzegovina it was also built after the withdrawal of the Ottomans the country. Right next to the church is also the seat of the Bishop of the Diocese of Tuzla-Zvornik. Thanks to numerous structural stability measures against soil erosion, the Episcopal Church has been preserved until today. The Serbian Orthodox Church is thus one of the oldest surviving buildings in Tuzla.

▶ A trip to the seemingly inviting waters of the Modrac Reservoir, 10km west of Tuzla, located near the community of Lukavac, unfortunately makes little sense. The 17km² lake is the result of a hydroelectric plant and the purity of the water leaves much to be desired, besides, there is no infrastructure to allow recreational use of the lake.

Tuzla's Serbian Orthodox church is one of the town's oldest buildings

8 Romanija and Pale

Romanija

▶ Romanija is the name both of a small town in Bosnia and Herzegovina and of a mountain range. Romanija, the mountain range, extends 20 kilometres east of Sarajevo between the mountain ranges of Ozren in the north and Jahorina in the south. The capital and the centre of the Romanija is not the town of the same name, nor is it the region's largest town, Sokolac, but instead it is Pale, the wartime capital of Republika Srpska.

▶ The Romanija is a distinctive, somewhat inhospitable region that was famous, or infamous, throughout the former Yugoslavia for its stubborn and rustic citizens and for its traditional music and hearty cuisine. If you are prepared to put your trust in these prejudices, it can be said that the inhabitants of the Romanija have adapted to the barren landscape and the harsh, windy climate of the plateau they live on.

▶ The Romanija has always been one of the centres of the Serbian community in Bosnia. During the civil war in the 1990s the Romanija was the seat of power and military base for Bosnian Serbs. Pale, the small town at the foot of Mount Jahorina, once part

The rolling landscape of the Romanija

of the Winter Olympic site, was the capital of Republika Srpska until the mid-1990s. Even before the outbreak of war the 'Autonomous Serb Republic of Romanija' was proclaimed here in the fall of 1991, a proclamation that aggravated already strained ethnic tensions. A Bosnian Serb paramilitary unit that became notorious during the siege of Sarajevo, was also called Romanija.

▶ The highest peak of the Romanija is Great Lupoglava (*Velika Lupoglava*). This extends east from Pale to 1,652 metres in height and is therefore only slightly lower than Sjeniste, the highest peak of the Jahorina mountains just across the valley. The Romanija is also the source of the Miljacka river that flows from its western slopes, downhill through Sarajevo, as well as the Praca, which feeds into the Drina. Remains of Illyrian settlements have been unearthed on the Glasinac Plateau on the eastern edge of the Romanija.

▶ Approximately 30,000 residents live in the Romanija, 10,000 of them in and around **Pale**. Pale is the economic and administrative centre of the Romanija and is also home to the Faculty of Economics of the University of East Sarajevo. As part of the municipality of East Sarajevo, Pale is part of Republika Srpska. In addition to numerous recently built churches,

Pale also hosts a new shopping centre in the middle of the town as well as a number of hotels and restaurants. Pale is the base camp for winter tourism on Jahorina.

▶ There's no denying it, Pale is not overwhelmingly charming. This is mainly due to the many new buildings, erected without any real adherence to a coherent urban image. Pale is, however, worth visiting because of the scenic beauty of the Romanija region. Besides the aforementioned Jahorina mountains there are two interesting caves to be explored.

▶ The first of these, **Novak**, is a cave at 1,515 metres above sea level that is very close to Pale. The path to the cave is well marked, but not necessarily easy to traverse as it follows the river Novak to its source. The cave area is underdeveloped for visitors and untrained or inexperienced cavers should only visit the front part of the cave. This is not the case with the second of Romania's caves, **Orlovača**, located near Sokolac and well known throughout Bosnia and Herzegovina for its many shimmering and colourful stalagmites and stalactites. The Orlovača cave is 2.5 kilometres deep into the Romanija mountains, almost 600 metres of this vast depth is open to visitors. Admission is 4 Convertible Marks.

A view of Pale

❾ Zvornik

Djurdjev Grad overlooks the small Eastern Bosnian town

▶ The name Zvornik is derived from the Slavic word for bell – *zvono*. Due to its important strategic location on the Drina and the protection afforded by the surrounding mountains and forests, Zvornik has always been a coveted military objective and, in the Middle Ages, a bell tower on the mountain town was used to warn of intruders. As with many Eastern Bosnian towns, Zvornik therefore traces its origins to the fortress that overlooks the town.

▶ The ruins of the **Djurdjev Grad fortress** (also often known just as *Kula*: Tower) and a small nearby Orthodox Christian chapel can be reached on foot, in about an hour from the town centre of Zvornik. Should you want to avoid the well-marked trail, it is also possible to drive to the fortress. The climb up the hill is generously rewarded with breathtaking views of the wooded valley of the Drina and the Zvornik reservoir. Although undergoing renovation work at the time of writing, the largely ruined medieval walls of the fortress tell the tale of many different occupations and occupiers. The historical origins of

the fort lay in the period before the Ottoman conquest, however, with the arrival and settlement of the first Ottoman troops on the Drina from the 15th century, the town entered into a golden age. The fortress became an important element of the administrative and military rule of the Ottomans in Bosnia and Herzegovina and Zvornik became a regional capital and a centre of trade. Below the fortress, Zvornik grew during the course of the following centuries and life in the town gradually moved from the mountain to the river. But the fortress remained an important military site even as late as the beginning of the 20th century when the Hapsburgs made use of its sturdy, old walls for military purposes. German language engravings in the fortress walls are a reminder of this time.

▶ Even today Zvornik is an important city in terms of trade and communications. Firstly, the M19 highway through the city connects Sarajevo and Belgrade, transforming it to a place of bilateral trade and transit. Additionally, Zvornik is the only city in Bosnia and Herzegovina that sits directly on the border with

The small Orthodox chapel near Djurdjev Grad

Serbia. An old, steel bridge, a relic of early industrialisation in these parts, connects the city with the Serbian border. The problem-free border traffic to Zvornik's twin town on the Serbian side, **Little Zvornik** (*Mali Zvornik*), offers visitors the novel experience of crossing a border on foot. The border also gives the citizens of Bosnian Zvornik a chance to skip across to Serbia where the shops are often cheaper.

▶ The city of Zvornik runs along the Drina and two main shopping streets, **Svetog Save** and Karadjordjeva, flow out from the main square. The main square is adorned with a memorial to the victims of war of the 1990s and the town hall sits diagonally opposite on the square and offers a small green space with benches, a perfect spot to relax. Below Svetog Save street is a sports and shopping complex that is getting on a bit in years but includes

An old steel footbridge connects Zvornik with Serbia

A view over Zvornik

the 3,000 seater **Drina football ground**. Next to the stadium is the town's coach station, with regular coach services connecting Zvornik to other Bosnian towns and to Serbia. From the bus station you can also get to the pedestrian border bridge that leads to the waterfront.

▶ Unlike most other towns in Eastern Bosnia, Zvornik has succeeded in integrating the river into its urban landscape. Unfortunately, getting to the river is a bit arduous as one has to cross the interceding highway but once this hurdle has been surmounted, the banks of the Drina have much to offer. Locals take to the river for a range of leisure activities and the **promenade** along the banks is a hive of hustle and bustle, day and night. The well lit walkway is also very popular in the evenings when those out for a stroll gradually replace the joggers. In addition to the riverside walkway, the Drina is popular with fishermen and swimmers alike and has become an integral part of the town's day-to-day life.

▶ Walking in a southerly direction along the riverside walkway will bring you to the ancient town walls which once ran from the fortress to the river. Today, the M19 highway winds through one of the medieval gates. Just beyond the town walls is the dam of the hydroelectric power station. In the nearby suburb of **Divić** the Drina pushes up against the dam and forms a lake 2 km wide. For another 25 kilometres upstream the Drina looks less like a river and more like a lake. Divić is a charming village, clamped against the banks of the lake-like Drina and is always worth the short walk from Zvornik because it offers phenomenal views of the Zvornik fortress and the forested mountains on the opposite bank.

❿ Srebrenica

▶ Srebrenica (meaning, approximately, Silver Town) is, next to Sarajevo, the most well known city in Bosnia and Herzegovina. Only a few people, however, connect this small, sleepy Eastern Bosnian town with its long tradition of mining and its rich silver deposits. The scenic nature of the town's idyllic rural hinterland and its mining past have been overshadowed by the now infamous massacre on the 11th of July 1995.

A view over Srebrenica

▶ The massacre that occurred in Srebrenica in the summer of the last year of the war was the most terrible war crime to take place in Europe since the end of the Second World War; an atrocity in which more than 7,000 Bosnian Muslims were killed in the space of a few July days in 1995.

▶ To this day date not all of the victims have been identified and almost every week more bodies are found and exhumed. The laborious and time-consuming work of identifying the victims of the massacre is still far from complete. Even nearly 20 years after the Srebrenica massacre, the event is the subject of political and social discourse worldwide and the international courts have yet to pronounce judgments on many of those involved. A serious debate within the Bosnian Serb society and the Serbian elite itself resulting in an objective and constructive account of the massacre, is still beyond reach.

▶ The terrible events in July 1995, played out right before the eyes of the world media, shook the international community. After Srebrenica NATO became fully militarily and politically involved and forced the warring sides to the negotiating table in talks that resulted in the Dayton Peace Accord. The Serbian side only reluctantly signed the agreement that ultimately led to the division of Bosnia and Herzegovina into the two Entities (see p. 17) along the front lines of fighting, with geographical or cultural divisions hardly taken into account. Nevertheless, the Dayton Peace Agreement ended the fighting immediately. Sadly perhaps, it became the victim of its own rapid success – a confused long term territorial division that does no justice to the victims of the war or their survivors. This is especially true in Srebrenica, which the Dayton Agreement awarded to Republika Srpska. Srebrenica initiated the end of the war in Bosnia and Herzegovina, but this is of little or no comfort to the bereaved families of the many victims. Neither Serbs nor Muslims want to live in this town any longer. Only a few coaches depart from the central coach station for Sarajevo or Belgrade and the inner ring road is home to only a few cafes and shops.

▶ Visits to Srebrenica are an emotionally serious matter. The facts surrounding the massacre are unsurprisingly still incredibly emotionally charged for all Bosnians of whatever ethnicity. On the Serbian side, much controversy still surrounds the events but the historically and socially interested traveler will, as they

The Wall of Names at the Potočari Memorial Centre

travel through the region, want to make their own impressions.

▶ In memory of those killed and as a reminder to future generations, a memorial was built on the outskirts of Srebrenica. The **Potočari Momorial Centre** (*Srebrenica – Potočari Memorijalni Centar*) serves the bereaved as a place of mourning and remembrance. A marble wall on which the names of all the identified victims are listed, frames a large, round space with an open-roofed mosque at its centre. Here funerals and commemorative events are held regularly. Behind the square begins the cemetery, a vast sober space with thousands of white Muslim grave stones strung together. The car park in front of the memorial is filled with cars with foreign plates, mostly from Germany, Switzerland and the Scandinavian countries, an indication that the survivors and their families no longer live in this place.

▶ If you have a bit of time while visiting Srebrenica, take time out to head for Milići – the road to which is only partially paved but is passable. The drive to Milići offers 40 kilometres of idyllic rural roads, through abandoned villages, as well as disused lignite and silver mining districts. This area once teemed with German craftsmen and other immigrants who came in search of their fortunes. Just 10 kilometres from Srebrenica is the town of Bratunac, a place whose vacant factories are a reminder of the area's former productivity and not-so-distant prosperity.

The endless rows of graves at the Potočari Memorial Centre

11 Višegrad

A view of the famous bridge and the town in the background

▶ The world famous novel **"The Bridge on the Drina"**, for which author Ivo Andrić won the Nobel Prize for Literature, has transformed Višegrad from a scenic town in the Drina Valley into a literary monument. The Rzav mountains, the Olujaker rocks and mountains of Lijeska form a ring around the town in which Andrić spent his formative years. A new part of town, built in honour of the writer, is set to fill the sleepy riverside town with a renewed cultural vigour.

▶ Višegrad, which roughly translates as "High Town", now has a 15,000 strong majority Serbian population and the town, part of Republika Srpska, is located just off the border with Serbia. On the Drina, just a few hundred metres from the town, is a hydroelectric plant that controls the flow of the river so that it circumnavigates Višegrad in a slow, leisurely arc around the 'new' old town of Andrićgrad.

The mountains loom over Višegrad and the Drina

The arches of the Mehmet-pasha Sokolović Bridge reflected in the green waters of the Drina

▶ The landmark of the city is the **Mehmed-Paša Sokolović Bridge**. Built from 1571 to 1578 the stone bridge with its 11 arches can be crossed on foot and is closed to traffic. The bridge is 180 metres long and 6 metres wide. Since 2007, the bridge has been listed as a UNESCO World Heritage Site. For centuries the Mehmed-Paša Sokolović Bridge was the only crossing on the upper and middle reaches of the Drina and thus an important connection on the trade route between the Orient and the Occident, between East and West.

▶ At the southern end of the bridge, the original old town begins, however, hardly any historic buildings from the Ottoman era remain. The gardens of the Višegrad Hotel offer wonderful views of the bridge and the mountainous hinterland of the town. The lack of historical buildings could soon be compensated by the town's new emerging cultural district, **Andrićgrad**. The mini town within a town, dedicated to Ivo Andrić, will feature a cinema, a theatre, a hotel (planned) and a literature institute and is intended to breathe new life into the city. The first construction works have been completed and the alleys of Andrićgrad are beginning to take shape. The first bookshops, restaurants and art dealerships are already moving

A statue of Ivo Andrić in Višegrad's new cultural district, Andrićgrad

A painting of Ivo Andrić in a gallery in Andrićgrad

into the new town on the confluence of the Rzav into the Drina.

▶ The **Dobrun Monastery** (*Dobrun Manastir*) is located in the mountains east of Višegrad on the immediate border with Serbia. Built in 1343, the Serbian Orthodox monastery is one of the oldest and architecturally most impressive ecclesiastical buildings in Bosnia and Herzegovina. The monastery, despite also being an active monastery, is open to visitors and houses a small museum. The entrance gate, with its three bells and orange-yellow ornaments, simply invites visitors to go in and explore. Around the courtyard are the monastic residential building, decorated in plain white, the monastery church and the former travel lodge (*konak*) of the royal Karadjordjević family, which still patronises and looks after the monastery. On a rock above the monastery is a large white cross. The monastery can be reached from highway 20 over a small footbridge.

▶ In front of the monastery is a historic Henschel locomotive from 1923. The *Series 19-126 Industrielok* model locomotive once drove on the narrow gauge railway which connected Sarajevo with Belgrade. The railway line, the so-called **Šarganska Osmica** (the Šargan figure-eight), was decommissioned in 1974, however, in the early 2000s film-director Emir Kusturica breathed a new lease of life into part of the old

The railway line, the so-called *Šarganska Osmica*, just across the border in Serbia

Drvengrad, another of Kusturica's projects, this time in Serbia

railway line. Today, in the summer months, old steam locomotives run along the Bosnian narrow gauge between Višegrad and the Serbian village of **Mokra Gora** (Wet Mountain). On Mokra Gora there is a small village, also built by Kusturica, as a studio and film school. The town, Drvengrad (meaning "Woodtown"), has a picturesque feel and, in addition to the wooden station building, it is mainly built in keeping with the tradition of Serbian mountain architecture. It is worth skipping over the border to see it, if you have some time to spare. A ride on the historic steam train from Mokra Gora to Višegrad is an unforgettable experience, and not only for antique train enthusiasts.

Emir Kusturica: film-maker, nationalist and environmentalist

No matter how you imagine the person Emir Kusturica, you will never get it quite right. Kusturica is one of the most controversial celebrities in the region, for some he is a heroic figure and an artistic genius while for others he is a nationalist extremist.

Kusturica was born in 1954 and grew up in Sarajevo where he was able to come into contact with Western culture and art at an early age. He went on to study at the film school in Prague in 1the 1970s and in the 1980s he made his first successful film, "Do You Remember Dolly Bell" ("*Sjećaš li se Dolly Bell?*"). The firm made Kusturica famous throughout Europe in 1981. In the film, Kusturica tackles a young boy's search for identity in 1960s Sarajevo and he continues to deal with social issues Yugoslavia in his other films. His films push political boundaries again and again. Subsequent films such as "When Father was away on Business" ("*Otac na službenom putu*") and his film "Underground" in the mid-90s, made clear but controversial political statements. Later Kusturica devoted his work to the lives of the region's Roma communities. His films "Time of the Gypsies" (1989) and "Black Cat, White Cat" (1998) were also met with international success. The soundtracks of these films became famous well beyond the region and Kusturica has even written songs and performed with Sarajevo band, the No Smoking Orchestra (formerly *Zabranjeno Pušenje* – No Smoking).

Politically, Kusturica has alienated many in Bosnia and in his adopted homeland, Serbia, with his often extreme and controversial views. In interviews and in some songs with the No Smoking Orchestra, he has aligned himself with nationalist pro-Serbian sentiment and shown support for Serbian leaders Milošević and Karadžić. He describes himself as conservative and ecologist.

▶ The journey from Sarajevo to Višegrad along the Drina is worthwhile just in itself. The so-called **Pioneer Road** (*Pionirski Put*), was completed in 1988 and is thus one of the last Yugoslav construction projects to be completed before the break-up of the country. The name is an allusion to the march of Tito's partisans in 1942, in which they walked from Višegrad to Sutjeska to join the famous battle there (see p.

243). From Višegrad to Ustipraca this modern highway follows the line of the Drina and then climbs into the karst mountains where, between some 30 tunnels, you will be treated to spectacular views over the river and the mountain valleys. A monument to the successful construction of the Pioneer Road still stands in Belgrade today in front of the main building of the state television station.

12 Goražde

A view of Goražde and the Drina river

▶ This town of 30,000 hugs the banks of the Drina about 40km upstream from Višegrad. During the Yugoslav civil war in the 1990s, Goražde was one of the Bosnian Muslim enclaves protected by the UN and is, sadly, best known for this outside of Bosnia and Herzegovina. Even two decades later, the aftermath of the war in this former industrial powerhouse, is still seen and felt. Sadly in this small town, surrounded by forested mountains, you will be hard pushed to sense any optimism for the future. The are a number of monuments which make it evident that the people continue to be proud of their successful resistance of Bosnian Serb forces during the

war in the 1990s. Cut off from the rest of Bosnian Muslim territory and protected in name only by the UN, the town offered bitter and ultimately successful resistance to the Bosnian Serb troops led by General Mladić. Goražde is therefore not part of the Republika Srpska, but is the center of one of the Federation's ten cantons (see p. 18). The Podrinje Canton (*Podrinje* means below the Drina) is named after the landmark of the city and region, the River Drina.

▶ Goražde was and is a city of transit. In the Middle Ages, Goražde was an important transport hub between the pillars of Ottoman rule in Bosnia and

The Drina as it passes through the Podrinje Canton

Herzegovina, Travnik and Sarajevo. These days the M20 highway from Serbia to the Adriatic Sea in Croatia and Montenegro flows through the town. This favourable location means Goražde has a large selection of accommodation, mostly catering for Eastern Bosnian travellers. Unlike in the nearby city on the Drina, Višegrad, in Goražde one can choose between several hotels, inns and motels.

▶ Numerous buildings and monuments in Goražde commemorate and create a sense of the period of Ottoman rule. In the 16th century the first printing in Bosnia and Herzegovina, took place in the Serbian Orthodox Church of Saint George.

Also located in Goražde is one of the nation's most historic cemeteries where hundreds of medieval grave stones can be admired. In the traditional Ottoman district there is much to discover in Goražde. Unfortunately, the buildings are located around the narrow streets are mostly in a humble state. The war destroyed mosques have been rebuilt, however, and new ones have been added.

▶ Goražde owes its form and *raison d'être* to the Drina, as it hugs the banks of the widely meandering river. A few kilometres after Goražde, the Drina squeezes between karst formations and assumes its peculiar green colour. In the summer, the urban population uses the Drina as a place to cool off and, on the southern shore, a walkway leads along the banks of the river. Of the three bridges in the city, two are passable by car – the middle bridge can be crossed only by bicycle or on foot. It is named after the first president of post-civil war Bosnia and Herzegovina, **Alija Izetbegović** (*Most Alije Izetbegovića*) and

The Alija Izetbegović Bridge is the central feature of Goražde

forms the central feature of the city. During the day, street vendors ply their wares on the white bridge and in the evenings it is the meeting point of the town's young people. At the small Omladinska street, south of the bridge, there are some office buildings, the sports hall also numerous cafes and bars. The functional buildings date mostly from

Bijele Vode resort

the 60s and 70s and are still riddled with bullet holes as a reminder of the recent war.

▶ The area around Goražde is known for fruit growing. In this part of Eastern Bosnia the apple tree is particularly popular and every year there is an Apple Festival in the autumn. In addition to the enjoyment of local specialties, it is a celebration of the conclusion of the harvest and, of course, it must also be accompanied by the local **apple brandy** (*Jabukovača*). The City Festival in July and the Apple Festival in the autumn are highlights of the town's events calander. Many members of the Goražde diaspora see the celebrations as a good excuse to visit their hometown, and see the town at its most joyous.

▶ **Bijele Vode** (White Water) is a remote recreation area with restaurants and accommodation, about 35km from Goražde. The local water is bottled in the woods above Goražde and sold as having medicinal benefits. The tourist facility, modelled on a ranch, serves mostly as a popular base camp for lovers of hunting. But Bijele Vode is also an ideal point from which to embark on excursions and hikes into the karst mountains of the rugged and sparsely populated hinterland of Goražde for unarmed nature lovers. Due to unresolved problems with landmines, the walks are only recommended if you can be sure not to stray from marked paths. A safer alternative is to hire a local guide and multilingual excursions are organized by the Bijele Vode resort.

13 The Sutjeska National Park

A view across the Sutjeska National Park

The Sutjeska Canyon

▶ The Sutjeska National Park is in the south of Bosnia, close to the mountainous border with Montenegro, and about an hour's drive from Sarajevo. It lies along the banks of the Sutjeska river, a tributary of the Drina. The national park covers an area of 175km² and is home to the highest peaks in Bosnia and Herzegovina, Maglić (2,386 metres) and Volujak (2,346 metres), as well as one of the last remaining primeval forests in Europe, the Perućica Forest (see p. 53). It is also one of the best places to see wolves and bears in Bosnia and Herzegovina (with the appropriate precautions, of course).

The Sutjeska National Park is for all users, a place for recreation, inspiration and the wholesome enjoyment of nature, forest and animal kingdom – an absolutely remarkable destination.

▶ Sutjeska, with its dark green, woody heart at Perućica, has officially been listed as a National Park since 1962. The appointment of Sutjeska as the National Park was only secondarily intended to protect the unique landscape, it was primarily the maintenance of historical memories from World War II. A monstrous monument complex is a reminder of the importance of the memory of the Battle of Sutjeska in socialist Yugoslavia.

▶ The National Park is located entirely within the municipality of Foča. The largest town in the protected area is Tjentište, further settlements include Popov Most and Suba. A total of some 2,500 people live within the protected National Park area. Highway 20, which connects Eastern Bosnia via Trebinje to the Adriatic Sea, crosses the National Park through the Sutjeska canyon. In Tjentište, opposite the monument complex is the **Mladost Hotel** and the headquarters of the National Park, the starting point for all excursions into the park itself.

▶ The highest mountain in Bosnia and Herzegovina, **Maglić**, rises some

A Partisan monument in the Sutjeska National Park

The ascent to the peak of Maglić

2,386 metres above sea level on the eastern edge of the National Park. Its name comes from the Bosnian word for fog (*magla*). On one hand, a linguistic reference to the fact that the summit is often covered in fog. On the other, it can be seen as an allusion to the numerous 'nebulous' stories that have emerged in the shadows of this mountain, straddling the border between Bosnia and Herzegovina and neighbouring Montenegro – and which are readily retold and handsomely embellished by the local National Park guides.

▶ An ascent to the peak of Malgić is possible via a number of different routes. The easiest of these is can be traversed even by inexperienced hikers. Like all trips to the peak, this one day tour begins in Tjentište at the headquarters of the National park and is best undertaken together with local ranchers. There is a 45 minute drive to the starting point of the ascent, which leads through the woods and meadows and over heaths. After about an hour of hiking you reach a plateau at the foot of Maglić where the vegetation starts to change and the rocky climb to the highest mountain in the country begins. Critical points are all secured with ropes and the path is well marked and the accompanying guides always happy to lend a helping hand. After another 90-120 minutes of hike to the top of the Maglić. In good weather you can view large parts of Bosnia and Herzegovina and Montenegro.

A view of the Sutjeska National Park from Maglić

Trnovačko lake, a starting point for one of the routes to the sumit of Maglić

▶ An alternative ascent to the top of Maglić via the Trnovačko lake. For this climb, however, you should allow two days and seek advice from one of the established travel agencies in Sarajevo. Most of the tours involve an overnight camp on Trnovačko lake.

▶ A walk through the primeval **Forest of Perućica** in a 4-hour long hike: The start of the hike is in Dragoš Sedlo and it cuts through the dense forest before reaching the Prijevor plateau. The hike is only recommended in the company of a guide from the National Park. Other attractions in the national park are the 75 meter high Skakavac waterfall, the river within the Perućica forest and of course the canyon of the Sutjeska.

▶ The forests of the Sutjeska National Park were a battleground in World War II and clashes that took place here contributed significantly to the victory of the Yugoslav partisans over the German occupiers. In the early summer of 1943, numerically inferior Partisans managed to break a weeks-long siege by the Germans and their allies in spectacular fashion. Many historians consider this to have been a turning point in World War II in South Eastern Europe. The rise of Tito's partisans as a political and military force and of Tito's unshakable grip on Yugoslavia was established here.

▶ The battle was immortalised in the 1972 Hollywood movie "The Battle of Sutjeska" in which Richard Burton played the title role of Tito. The monument in Tjentište and the National Park itself both celebrate the famous Partisan victory in which over 3000 fighters, mostly very young men and boys, perished. As a symbol of youth, the memorial complex is laid out in the form of a guitar. The 25th of May, Youth Day (*Dan Mladost*), was celebrated annually in the former Yugoslavia and thousands of young people descended on Sutjeska.

The Skakavac Waterfall

AUTHOR'S PICK: HOTELS & RESTAURANTS

Due to the abundance of hotels and restaurants on offer it would be impossible to list them all and to keep the list current. Instead, please find below a selection of hotels and restaurants recommended by the author:

HOTELS

Bijeljina	**Hotel Šico**	Centrally located hotel with secure parking, 17 rooms and Wi-Fi	Ul. Patrijarha Pavla 3, Bijeljina + 387 55 210 952
Brčko	**Hotel Jelena**	Comfortable, tidy hotel with hearty breakfast – has parking facilities	Bulevar mira 3, Brčko +387 49 232 850
Brčko	**Grand Hotel Posavina**	Housed in a historic building from 1891 but renovated in 2001 – has 36 rooms and is centrally located	Trg Mladih 4, Brčko + 387 49 220 111
Doboj	**Hotel Park**	A large new hotel with 112 rooms, parking, swimming pool, Wi-Fi and restaurant just opposite the town park	Kneza Lazara 2, Doboj +387 53 209 300
Tuzla	**Hotel Tuzla**	Large hotel complex, partly renovated, with swimming pool, restaurant and nightclub	Ul. Zavnobih-a 13, Tuzla +387 35 302 600
Zvornik	**Motel Laguna**	A small hotel with 15 rooms located right on the Drina River – restaurant, Wi-Fi and parking	Magistralni put, Zvornik +387 56 210 002
Goražde	**Hotel Behar**	Small but modern hotel with 24 rooms, parking and Wi-Fi – located on the Drina River	Trg branilaca, Goražde +387 38 227 997
Sutjeska	**Hotel Mladost**	A simple but comfortable hotel in the National Park offering stunning views of Maglić – recently renovated top floor and very friendly staff	Sutjeska National Park Tjentište +387 58 233 118 +387 58 233 130

Hotel Mladost

PRACTICAL HELP

Entry Requirements
Travel
Currency & Banking
Communication
Health & Security
Events

Entry Requirements

The Izačić border crossing near bihać

Visitors to Bosnia and Herzegovina from the European Union and Switzerland do not require a visa and can enter the country using just their ID cards. Visitors from other countries will need to check with their Foreign Office. A tourist stay is limited to 90 days; a visa is required for longer stays. Pets do not require a visa or passport. Hard currency amounts over €10,000 must be declared.

If you are arriving in Bosnia and Herzegovina by car you must present a Green Card the border. Due to an extensive free trade agreement between Bosnia and Herzegovina and the European Union border crossings are usually quick. At most, there may be queues during the busy summer months.

Travel

Compared to Western Europe, but also many of its neighbouring countries, the transport network of Bosnia and Herzegovina is in a relatively poor condition. This is a problem not so much because of the condition of existing roads as much as the lack of a real alternative to road transport.

The roads in Bosnia are often make for scenic driving

Car travel in Bosnia and Herzegovina can often be painfully slow, especially for those visitors who are used to Western European roads; the average speed of a car journey in Bosnia and Herzegovina is about half that of Western Europe. Don't expect your average speed during a cross-country trip to go far about 40 or 50 kilometres per hour and calculate your journey time with that speed in mind.

The road network is relatively comprehensive and for the most part the condition of the roads is good. International aid came to the rescue of the road network after the 1990s civil war and the regional highways were the focus of these funds so they are generally in good shape. The construction of motorways is, however, painfully slow. The motorway from Banja Luka to Croatia has indeed been largely completed, however, construction of the Central Bosnia motorway connecting Zenica and Sarajevo is at a standstill. The highway to the Adriatic has yet to progress beyond the drawing board.

When driving through Bosnia and Herzegovina, be aware that the road markings and signs are often hard to see and sometimes misleading. Place names or signs directing you to local population centres are sometimes misleading or absent. It is therefore advisable to carry a map with you at all times.

The railway network of Bosnia and Herzegovina covers a little more than 1,000 kilometres. By comparison, Switzerland, a much smaller country, has more than 5,000 kilometres of railways. The problem in Bosnia and Herzegovina, however, is not just the quantity of railways but also the poor quality. The condition of both the track and the rolling stock – not to mention the inability of the three railway companies (both the Federation and the Republika Srpska have a private state-owned railway company, whose cooperation is guided by a third national railway authority) to make the trains run on time – mean that rail travel is not a reliable way of getting around. Nevertheless, rail travel in Bosnia and Herzegovina can be a very exciting, not to mention cheap, way to get around – but only if you're not in a hurry. The Sarajevo-Mostar (see p. 73) line is especially interesting for its astounding views of the Neretva Valley and is one of the highlights for many a visitor to Bosnia and Herzegovina as well as a treat for all fans of rail travel the way it used to be.

The mass transport role the railways could and should play is instead taken on by coaches. Intercity coaches connect anywhere to everywhere and do so very regularly and on time. It seems as though every sleepy village in Bosnia and Herzegovina has a coach station from which you can go not only to the nearest large town but also to Sarajevo, Zagreb, Belgrade - and often also to Ulm, Lucerne or Vienna.

Train travel is slow and unreliable... but potentially exotic and exciting!

Currency & Banking

A 100 Convertible Mark note

The official currency of Bosnia and Herzegovina is the **Convertible Mark** (*Konvertibilna Marka*) also known as the Bosnian Mark and abbreviated as BAM.

The Bosnian Mark has been valid tender in Bosnia and Herzegovina since the 22nd of June 1998 and has a fixed exchange rate with the Euro of 1.956KM to €1. This corresponds exactly to the value of the German Deutsche Mark, which was the country's official currency until the Convertible Mark was launched.

As was the case with the German Deutsche Mark, the Convertible Mark comprises marks and fenings (derived from the German *Pfennig*). Coinage comes in the form of 1, 2, 5, 10, 20 and 50 fening coins and 1, 2 and 5 Mark coins. Convertible Mark notes come in denominations of 10, 20, 50, 100 and 200 marks.

Theoretically it is illegal to pay for goods or services with any currency other than BAM in Bosnia and Herzegovina, nevertheless, it is possible to pay with Euros almost everywhere, while the Croatian Kuna and the Serbian Dinar are also often accepted in some parts of the country.

The Euro forms a sort of informal second currency in Bosnia and Herzegovina

Communication

The people of Bosnia and Herzegovina must number amongst the most talkative in the world – certainly if judging by the popularity of mobile phones. Mobile phones are a fashion statement and status symbol for the young people and the latest

smartphone is *de rigueur* as much as branded cigarettes and flashy car keys.

Due to the high density of mobile phones, it is not surprising that the good old telephone box is an endangered species. Although found

The three main mobile network operators are: m-tel (Telekom Srbija), BH Mobile (BH Telecom) and HT Eronet

in the larger cities and some post offices still have phone-booths, as a visitor you should not rely on being able to find one of these rare specimens.

Since Bosnia and Herzegovina is outside the EU, the price of calling or receiving calls whilst in roaming is very high. A good option is to get a prepaid SIM card for a local mobile network. Most kiosks sell these for 2-5 Convertible Marks. The SIM cards are sold with some credit on them and with no registration required so all you need to do is plug them in and you're ready to go.

Dedicated internet cafes in Bosnia and Herzegovina are few and far between but Wi-Fi is usually available in hotels, restaurants and cafes – and often without needing a password.

Stamps can be bought in hotels, at some kiosks and in all post offices.

Health & Security

HEALTH

All citizens in Bosnia and Herzegovina are have health insurance provided by the state. Every community and every major district has its own health centre (*Dom Zdravlija*) or hospital (*Bolnica*). The health centres serve as a first point of contact for patients. From these general polyclinics patients are

The comfortingly clean lines of a modern hospital in Mostar

A landmine warning in Bosnia and Herzegovina

Landmines

During the war in the 1990s, thousands of landmines were planted along the front lines. As the front line often changed huge areas of Bosnia and Herzegovina remained infested with landmines. The number of mined areas has since been reduced to little more than 1,300 km². The areas in which there are still suspected to be landmines are clearly marked and are mostly far from populated areas. Hiking trails and even remote country roads, however, are all mine-free and can be used freely and without danger. One must, however, take extreme care to stay on marked footpaths in areas that are marked as still potentially containing landmines. Generally speaking landmines, thankfully, present no real danger to visitors.

referred to specialists, if necessary, or else state hospitals.

Due to the inefficiency of the government health system, a dense network of private clinics and physicians has developed. The costs associated with these private health facilities will not be covered by the state health insurance company and services are to be paid for directly in cash.

There is a general agreement regarding the mutual restitution of incurred medical and hospital expenses between the European Union and Bosnia and Herzegovina. Travellers from the EU

(and from Switzerland) can, therefore, receive medical services in Bosnia and Herzegovina that will be covered by their own national health insurance provider. In most cases this covers treatment in private hospitals in Bosnia and Herzegovina. You should, however, check that this is the case with your own health insurance provider.

In general, travellers are not advised to rely on medical services in Bosnia and Herzegovina – except, of course, in emergencies. Even though the level of medical expertise is remarkable, as are hygiene standards, the technical equipment and the level of care in

Bosnian police cars

Emergency number: 112

(public) health facilities are very modest to say the least.

Travellers are, therefore, advised to take out a travel insurance, which will cover transportation to Western Europe in the event of an emergency.

SECURITY

Despite the poor economic situation, petty crime in Bosnia and Herzegovina is not common. If you take the usual precautions, such as not leaving obviously valuable items in a parked car, you will be safe in Bosnia and Herzegovina. Nevertheless, it is preferable to leave your car in a secure car park or garage at night, if you can.

Also, as everywhere else in the world, take care to secure your valuables and wallet from pickpockets in crowded, touristy areas. Also, when travelling, make sure you keep an eye on your luggage.

Female travellers travelling alone should have no problems. Bosnia and Herzegovina is not an overly conservative society and so couples travelling should also have no problems with public displays of affection. The exception is perhaps with gay and lesbian visitors, public displays of affection by same sex couples are still regarded as awkward even in the larger towns.

Events

FEBRUARY

Sarajevo Winter, Sarajevo
An annual arts festival covering a range of themes and held since the 1984 Winter Olympics.

JUNE

NAFF Neum Animated Film Festival, Neum
International festival of animated film, including workshops, competitions and much more.

JULY

Mostar Bridge Divers, Mostar
The annual tradition of diving from the heights of the Old Bridge in Mostar. Young men from the region compete by diving into the green waters of the Neretva, 21 metres below the ancient bridge.

Vrbas Summer Festival, Banja Luka
The "Ljeto na Vrbasu" festival involves kayaking, a raft race, diving competitions and a boat parade.

A dance performance during the Sarajevo Winter festival

A diver leaps from the Old Bridge in Mostar (see p. 135)

Mostar Blues Festival, Mostar
An international blues and rock festival held below the Old Bridge since 2003.

AUGUST

Sarajevo Film Festival, Sarajevo
Probably the largest and most important film festival in the region attracting international stars and artists but also focusing on local film. Includes a varied programme of events and a colourful party scene.

Banja Luka Summer Festival, Banja Luka
A rock and pop festival lasting several days is held every year in the Kastel in Banja Luka and also includes theatrical performances and poetry readings.

A rock and pop festival lasting several days is held every year in the Kastel in Banja Luka and also includes theatrical performances and poetry readings

A boat race is just part of the Vrbas Summer Festival

OCTOBER

**MESS Theatre Festival,
Sarajevo**
International theatre festival held
annually in Sarajevo since the 1960s
showcases the best theatrical troupes
from the region and beyond.

DECEMBER

**Jahorina Ski Season Opening,
Jahorina**
The grand opening of the ski season
on Jahorina spans several days and
includes both a colourful programme
of events and cut-price skiing!

Jahorina

Welcome to Bosnia and Herzegovina
Experience Diversity

www.bhtourism.ba

CIP - Каталогизација у публикацији
Народна библиотека Србије, Београд

338.48(497.6)

HEESKENS, Jörg
  Bosnia and Herzegovina in your hands /
[Jörg Heeskens ; photographs Luka Esenko ...
[et al.]. - Beograd : Komshe, 2014 (Beograd :
Publikum). - 260 str. : fotogr. ; 22 cm

Tiraž 1.500. - About the author: str. 2. -
Registar.

ISBN 978-86-86245-18-2

а) Босна и Херцеговина - Водичи
COBISS.SR-ID 204753676

silvatur

European Travel

Forests

Travel for nature lovers and culture connoisseurs with forest expert, Georg von Graefe

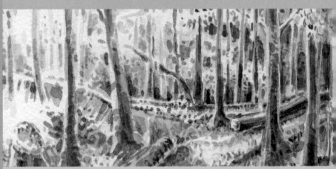

Dinaric Forests and pearls of the Adriatic

Round trip Bosnia-Herzegovina – Croatia – Slovenia

From the silvatur program:

- *Northeastern Poland – Lithuania* including a sleigh ride through the royal winter forest of Rominten
- *Lithuania – Poland* Curonian Spit and fabulous Poland

- *Serbia – Romania* Transylvania and Moldavian Monasteries
- *Slovakia – Ukraine* The Carpathian forests and the lost world of Galicia

silvatur gmbh, Zürich
reisen@silvatur.ch, www.silvatur.ch